PUTTING THE PIECES TOGETHER

THE GRAFFITI MODEL FOR INDIE FILMMAKING

BY BENJAMIN MORGAN AND THE QUALITY OF LIFE TEAM

A BEHIND-THE-SCENES
LOOK AT THE MAKING OF

QUALITY OF LIFE

Dedicated to
LUCAS ROBERT DAELLENBACH
March 27, 1981 – June 09, 2005

You live in my heart forever.
-Ben

RELENTLESS CO. PRESENTS A

QUALITY OF LIFE STARRI

BURNAM LUIS SAGUAR MA

FROM SOULS OF MISCHIE

BENJAMIN MORGAN BRANT

MULLOWNEY CLAY BUTLE

BRIAN BURNAM BENJAMIN

SMITH BENJAMIN MORGA

PRODUCERS STEVE POPPER B

DIRECTOR OF MUSIC COUNT EDIT

DIRECTOR BELINDA GARDEA

ROBERTSON DIRECTE

SUMMERSHINES PRODUCTION
LANE GARRISON BRIAN
KENZIE FIRGENS AND TAJAI
HIEROGLYPHICS STORY BY
SMITH BRIAN BURNAM TOM
ARON COLEITE WRITTEN BY
MORGAN PRODUCED BY BRANT
MEIKA ROUDA EXECUTIVE
ANT SMITH JOHN DOFFING
SHARON FRANKLIN CASTING
DIRECTOR OF PHOTOGRAPHY KEV
BENJAMIN MORGAN

DAN OGAWA   (C) 415-341-3752

SET DESCRIPTION	SCENE	CAST	D/N	PAGES	LOCA
LL ADVERTISING AGENCY- visit Lisa @ work	14	1,2,3,11	D2	2	589 Howard
LL ADVERTISING AGENCY- Heir gives photos to Lisa.	66	1,3,11	D5	27/8	
OFFICE – Lisa trys to talk with Robert and intro. Heir ...	67	1,3	D5	7/8	
LL ADVERTISING AGENCY- gives mock-up.	79	1,11	D6	1/8	
LL ADVERTISING AGENCY- Makes scene.	103	2,3,11,20	D7	2	
LL ADVERTISING AGENCY- Designer hiding.	105	20	D7	1/8	
LL ADVERTISING AGENCY- in office.	100	3,11	D7	2/8	
LL ADVERTISING AGENCY- Hears police.	107	2,3,11	D7	1/8	

refer to today's shot list for updated shooting

Please refer to today's shot list for updated shooting Order.

CAST	W	#. CHARACTER	PICKUP	MAKEUP	SET CALL
Lane Garrison	W	1. HEIR		7:30AM	7:00AM
Mackenzie Firgens	W			7:30AM	7:00AM
Gerald Black	H	4. DEVIN		7:30AM	7:00AM
Mackenzie Firgens	H W	5. LISA		8:00AM	8:30AM
Frederick Pitts	SWF	11. ROBERT		8:30AM	9:00AM
Davis Duffield	SWF	20. DESIGNER		1:00pm	1:30PM
Daniel Chacon		8. DES		7:30AM	7:00AM
Frederick Pitts		11. ROBERT		7:30AM	7:00AM
Count	SH	12. HUFFINGTON		7:30AM	7:00AM
Andrew Rolfes	SW	13. CHARLES		7:30AM	7:00AM

#	ATMOSPHERE	CALL	ON SET	ADDITIONAL NOTES
4	Designers			
	Spectators	7:00AM		

ADVANCE SCHEDULE

DATE	SET DESCRIPTION	SCENE	CAST	D/N	PAGES
8/4	EXT. CEMETERY- Vain's funeral	111	1,4,5,6,8,9,12,15	D8	5/8
	EXT. CEMETERY	112	1,3,4,5,7,9	D8	2/8
	INT. HEIR'S ROOM- Heir pulls shoe boxes out of closet.	65	1	D5	1/8
	INT. HEIR'S ROOM- Heir goes through old photos.	114	1,9	D8	1/8
8/5	EXT. HEIR'S HOUSE- Pops pulls up with truck.	119	1,5	N8	1/8
	INT. POPS' RIG- Heir and Pops exit job site.	36	1,5	D8	1/8
	EXT. MARKET STREET- Heir is sitting at bus stop.	37	1	D8	3/8
	EXT. VAIN'S APARTMENT- Heir and Pops sit in rig.	87A	1,4,5	D7	2/8
	EXT. VAIN'S HOUSE- Vain doesn't show up.	101	1,2,5	D7	4/8
	EXT. VAIN'S APARTMENT- Heir and Pops leave.	73	1	N3	1/8
	EXT. PAINT SITE #2- Heir and Pops are working.	64	1,5	D5	3/8
	EXT. PAINT SITE #2- Heir and Pops work on a job.	92	1,5	D7	1/8
	EXT. PAINT SITE #2- Heir and Pops take a lunch.	93	1,5	D7	3/8

1ST AD: James Duisenberg   UPM: Dan Ogawa

CONTENTS

FOREWORD

The so-called "American Dream" surely doesn't guarantee happiness. But young people, as they are growing up, are constantly searching for acceptance and a lifestyle that often seems well beyond their reach. They are assaulted daily with thousands of billboard and advertising images urging them to buy or do something that they cannot afford. Their ears are filled with sounds of the rich and famous telling them how to make millions or what to do about who knows what. Society has disenfranchised and alienated large segments of the youth population by its inattention, financial cutback of programs and lack of opportunity. It is not just the growing gap between rich and poor, but actually a sort of low intensity war between authority and youth. Living in a very fragile and combative world, there is no optimism for a brighter future among many of its young inhabitants. So, what to do?

It is no wonder that some thirty-five years ago a response to these feelings began to develop in NYC and spread around the globe in the ensuing years. It was called HIP-HOP and graffiti writing was a major component. For some it developed into a highly skilled art-form, for others it was a compulsive desire to be continuously "getting up" on all visible surfaces both high and low and in-between. It became a rewarding way of life and in many cases, all consuming. It included elements of excitement not found in everyday living. There was fame and recognition for some, but as important was a street friendship within the culture. Crews of two and more writers were formed and became the "Fraternities of the Streets." The law mistakenly or purposely branded these crews as gangs so they could lump them in with so-called "Quality of Life" crimes (prostitution, drug running, etc.) and therefore exact heavy penal penalties against the perpetrators. Corporate wheat pasters and advertisers using many of the same spaces went unchallenged.

Set against this backdrop, *Quality of Life* examines in the larger sense the challenges and frustrations of finding one's place within the society, issues that a viewing audience of all ages can relate to. The emotion generated by seeing the completion of the unfinished rooftop graffiti piece at the end of the film and then the compelling Buddhist resolution, reaches our core as a sense of completion and fulfillment, yet at the same time a challenge for new creation and vision.

Benjamin Morgan, the director, brings to the film thirteen years of experience in working as a social worker with at-risk youth. To be skillful in those relationships takes inexhaustible patience and the ability to build trust. One might not suspect that those particular skills would make for such sensitive direction, but the balance and insightful touch that Ben employs in developing the characters' roles combined with his own "street" background makes the counterpoints of joy, despair and even violence convincingly real.

Cool, bad, and real are the vernacular of street culture descriptions, and I would add "authentic" as a historical prerequisite in making a film using graffiti writers as the storyline. *Wild Style*, an early 80's film by Charlie Ahearn, became a seminal work because it was just that — authentic. Although *Quality of Life* should be seen in its larger contextual sense, its hardcore reality is very cool, bad and real.

Peace and Respect,

Jim Prigoff
Co-Author, *Spraycan Art*

"IF THIS ISN'T THE HARDEST THING WE'VE EVER DONE, WE'RE DOING SOMETHING WRONG."
Kev Robertson, Director of Photography

Introduction
by Benjamin Morgan

September 14, 2005

We are exactly four weeks out from our theatrical opening in SF. We currently have $209 in the bank (we need about $400K to release the film). We know what we have—a flawed, but entertaining independent film with a strong core niche audience. Basically, we know *QoL* can have a pretty strong little theatrical run and we have gone to great lengths to prove that this venture is profitable. The investors we talk to seem to be pretty amped on it. And yet, here we sit, $399,791 short of our budget. The story of our lives.

We actually faced this same exact challenge to get the damn film made. Fundraising is an incredibly frustrating process—a necessary evil. Yet, somehow we raised enough cash to get the movie made. I'm sure distribution will be the same. So we keep throwing the tracks ahead of the train like Wile E. Coyote chasing after that ruthless, spiteful little bird.

And, oh yeah, we're supposed to have this book (the one I'm still writing) ready in four weeks as well.

The funny thing is, this all seems doable somehow. I don't know how, but it will happen. Call it blind faith. But I believe. "Follow your bliss and doors will open where there were no doors before."[1]

We made this movie on fumes. And when the fumes ran out, we got out and pushed. So why should distribution be a walk in the park? In fact, as Kev said, if it's not the hardest thing we have ever done, we're probably doing something wrong.

[1] *The Artist's Way*, Julia Cameron (Tarcher Publishing)

13

Getting myself psyched up? Sure. What other choice do I have? Getting myself bummed out is way too easy. There are few options outside of success that don't involve a chair and a rope.

We made this movie on faith. People believe in this movie. The people who made it, the people who are going to see it, and the people who contributed to this book. Why stop believing now?

The truth is, faith is all we have. I honestly do believe that if you are passionate about something and pursue it with everything you have, doors will open. But this shit is incredibly discouraging. What if we aren't able to get the film completed and projected on that big screen on October 12 as planned (i.e., what if we can't raise the money)? What if this book never gets published? What if I have put ten years of my life into this film-making path only to end up broke and discouraged? That's some depressing shit right there.

We made this movie using the Graffiti Model. You'll hear about it a lot in this book. It was an extremely successful model for *Quality of Life*. And it will serve us well for distribution as well. Graffiti writers accomplish so much with so little. It's truly in-spirational. But theory only carries you so far. You gotta spend money to make money. (And if we don't make some money soon, there are going to be some long lines at the bankruptcy office.)

In case you can't tell, I'm a little distracted right now. The clock is ticking. Fast. The bills are piling up, and we are starting to miss deadlines. It is tempting to doubt. But we can't. We have to keep throwing down the tracks ahead of the train. We just have to hope that the black tunnel outline we paint on the side of the mountain opens up for us.

A few notes about what you are going to find in these pages: I interviewed as many *QoL* people as I could squeeze into my "free time." These interviews were all done via instant messenger, since I did not have time to transcribe interviews. We also put together a little Do-It-Yourself Film School section to give a glimpse into how a no-budget feature film is made. Nic Hill and Renos wrote a brief chapter on the history of the SF graff scene. And of course we included the feature script as well.

We have also included some photos for your viewing pleasure. Many are self-explanatory, others are not. Many of the people featured in the photos were directly involved with, or were around when we made the movie. Others contributed to the story simply by living the lifestyle. They are all part of the family, in one way or another.

Quality of Life has been one wild ride. I imagine we will look back on it fondly some day. And with luck, this book will inspire others to go out and create something of their own (poor bastards). The democratization of the filmmaking process is upon us. Much like graffiti writers have proven, resources don't mean anything. Heart means everything. True that.

Thanks to everyone who helped get this movie made (and seen). And thanks to everyone who contributed to this book. If you are reading these words, I guess we made it! Faith is some powerful shit, isn't it?

TWIST. THR

Paying Dues: A Brief History of San Francisco Graffiti
By Nic Hill and Renos 1

More important than the current pieces and the all-city King of the Month is the history buried beneath the walls of San Francisco. The layers of spray paint and buff collected over the last twenty plus years act as an impenetrable coffin of history. The way graffiti looks and the way we understand it are directly linked to the pioneers and the evolution of styles and attitude revolving around the graffiti culture.

I, along with the help of Renos and many of the most influential writers from the Bay, studied this dying history and documented the stories and passions of the culture here in SF. The following is a brief glance at the writing history of one of the smallest big graffiti cities in America.

The history of writing in SF is a long and unique tale (depending on who you ask). As far as we are able to tell, SF graffiti's roots were established during the late 1970s with the emergence of neighborhood writing among the local inner city youth in the predominantly Latino neighborhoods. These pieces were nicknames, usually followed by a street name or reference to the artist's gang affiliation. This particular writing style led the way for what was about to occur. Today, more than ninety percent of graffiti is not gang related. With the influx of the street culture known to-

day as "hip-hop," graffiti writing was introduced to the Bay Area. The youth were quick to pick up on the written word and embrace the craft. By 1982, SF was saturated with tags and pieces from kids of varied backgrounds. The racial divisions that existed outside of the art were no longer relevant; the kids were participating in a phenomenon that provided all the adventure and excitement an urban youth could desire. Along with break dancing and hip-hop music, the graffiti culture thrived and blossomed among the youth of SF, providing an alternative to the ready-made pitfalls of drugs and gangs that succeeded in swallowing up so many.

By 1985, the streets and the bus system were decorated with tags. The buses resembled moving notebooks and were covered in tags from all over the city. With tags covering the insides and the outsides, the underground subway system was just as colorful. Graffiti was starting to solidly entrench itself thanks to groups of writers that formed crews like TMF, TWS, TDK, FSC, KSUN, MPC, OTC, ICP, CTB, and the myriad others which decorated the city. There was also a place downtown called Psycho City, which served as an outdoor art gallery and gave a place for the writers to develop more elaborate and colorful murals. Psycho City served as a cultural hub for writers throughout the entire Bay Area (and the world). New coats of paint would be applied daily, and new pieces consisting of intricate letters and detailed backgrounds of comic book characters and palm trees would soon appear. By 1992, the city authorities were annoyed at the sharp increase in graffiti and made a serious effort to eradicate it. One of these steps included the closure of Psycho City and the promise that authorities would now fully prosecute anyone who attempted to paint there.

17

San Francisco's graffiti, previously confined to a certain area, now proliferated everywhere: the entire city became the new canvas for the masses of writers, and all surfaces were game. Walls once left untouched were now scarred with bright flashes of color and letters that only the writers could decipher. Painting on the streets, alleys, and rooftops was now the focus of the persistent writers. By shutting down designated and contained areas like Psycho City, San Francisco had unknowingly increased the amount of graffiti that its citizens would be exposed to. The look of graffiti changed too, as writers focused on quicker styles and faster ways of getting their art up on the city's walls. By the mid 1990s, writing was fully entrenched among the youth of SF and became a tradition handed down from generation to generation, a craft with its own credos and rules that thrived not only in SF but now around the world.

Writers from all over the planet would visit the iconic city and attempt to leave their mark, bringing with them their own interpretations and styles of writing. As a result, SF has become something of a melting pot in terms of writing style and innovation—so much so that it is often rare to meet a writer in SF who is actually from here. Cycle, Giant, KR, Bless, and many other writers from other cities all moved to San Francisco, bringing with them styles native to their cities of origin. SF has served as a beacon for many other writers throughout the world as well.

As of today (late 2005), SF has maintained its strong writing culture, which continues to evolve. The city's Herculean effort to eradicate writing is ongoing, and the endless battle plays itself out in the public eye. Crews like KUK, who recently faced prison time for their exploits, have first-hand experience with how seri-ously SF takes graffiti. Writers continue to write and preserve the tradition for the generations to come. The City buffs the wall a dull gray, and a kid with a can of paint changes it at night, only to come back the next day to see it a dull gray again.

I am not one to decide the merits of writing or to justify the application of a different color of paint on a wall—to decide whether it is right or wrong. I do know that writing is not going away anytime soon despite the draconian laws meant to prosecute the artists. When one can get in more legal trouble for writing on a wall than for selling crack cocaine or even for rape, something is dreadfully wrong with our social priorities.

As long as there are walls, there will be graffiti. There seems to be an innate desire among humans to communicate through markings on a wall. From the markings in the caves of Lascaux, France to the hieroglyphics of the pyramids to the tags and pieces of today, writing a message for the world to see will continue as long as someone is there to see it.

Graffiti will continue here in SF regardless of the opposition against it. Rebellion and creation are inherent to all, and people will always go against the grain, especially here in one of the most liberal cities in the world. I encourage you to search for and enjoy the impressive work going up on the walls of SF today. Document it if you can. Chances are, it will be buried the next time you walk by it.

For more information about the history of San Francisco graffiti, check out the documentary film *Piece By Piece*.
www.piecebypiecemovie.com

SMOG
CHECK
YO'SELF

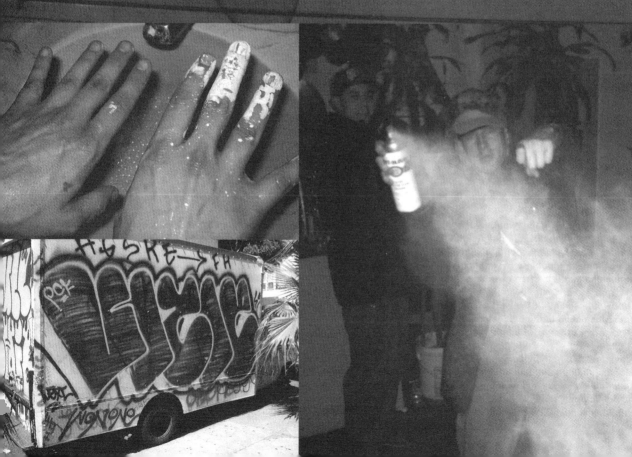

INTERVIEWS

Benjamin Morgan

DIRECTOR
INTERVIEWED BY BRANT SMITH, PRODUCER

SEPTEMBER 17–21, 2005

This interview between director Benjamin Morgan (shown below and throughout the interviews as **QoL**) and Producer Brant Smith tells the behind-the-scenes story from the perspective of the duo who led the team.

Morgan and Smith are the filmmaking partners behind *Quality of Life*, having worked at this point more than four years together on the film. Before *Quality of Life*, they worked together on some of Morgan's "student" projects at the local community TV station. As this interview is taking place, they are preparing to self-distribute the film, starting in a single rented theater in San Francisco.

Except during production and for occasional weekend visits, Morgan lived 800 miles away from Smith and the rest of the San Francisco *Quality of Life* home base. The Internet (and copious cellphone minutes with free long distance included) enabled the team to work together closely on a daily—often hourly—basis, so it seemed fitting to conduct all the interviews for the book as online chats.

QoL: yo!

Brant: Hello there Mr. Director Benjamin Morgan.

QoL: Sorry to do this to you, but I have to take a piss . . .

Brant: Typical.

Brant: I'm supposed to hold the bucket right? Indie filmmaking you know.

QoL: Don't forget the shake!

Brant: The shake isn't in my contract. Talk to my agent.

QoL: My ass!

QoL: The shake IS your contract!

Brant: Deferred though.

Brant: Okay, let's get started. The fine people reading don't want to waste their precious time on our potty humor.

Brant: Even though that's what got us through some of the darkest days . . .

QoL: OK. Let's dive in.

QoL: SO, we're about four weeks away from the promised land (theatrical). How you feeling?

Brant: Denial has got me this far . . .

Brant: It's actually both exciting and very scary.

Brant: We haven't cleared the film yet . . . still need to pay for the music rights and the SAG rights.

QoL: I feel you.

QoL: Why haven't we paid for them?

Brant: Well, we don't have the money, obviously. We've been running on fumes since day one pretty much and even now . . . with awards and distribution upcoming, it's tough for a small ultra-indie film to get investment.

QoL: Ah, right. The money thing.

Brant: Yeah. Filmmaking is all sunshine and puppy dogs except for the money part.

Brant: But we'll be fine.

QoL: So, we're a month out from theatrical (almost to the day), and we don't have two dimes to rub together.

QoL: Sounds perfect!

Brant: "Never tell me the odds" - Han Solo

QoL: We were basically in this same position two years ago.

QoL: Before the Punch event, we had nothing (aside from my dad's initial share).

Brant: Yeah, we flew the lead actor in from LA and he basically looked at us and was like, "What have I got myself into?"

QoL: "Ghetto ass production" was what I overheard him call us.

QoL: And he was right!

Brant: That's what we should have called our new production company.

Brant: I prefer "Two Louts Productions" after the lame *Variety* review that said the film was basically just "two louts running around town."

QoL: WTF is a "lout" anyway? Did he make that up?

Brant: I think a lout is what someone's grandpa calls the kids next store who play their Rock And Roll music too loud: "You louts get off my lawn!"

Brant: Anyway, speaking of kids, why don't we talk about your childhood . . .

Brant: (Nice transition eh?)

QoL: That was a life lesson right there: You better know WHO is reviewing your movie. Better not be some geezer who calls kids louts.

QoL: Sure.

QoL: Turning the tables on me, huh?

Brant: So you did some graffiti back in the day, right? Has the statute of limitations run out . . . can you speak freely...

QoL: I'm sure I'm fine.

QoL: My initial introduction to graffiti was cholo writing in LA. I grew up in SF and Berkeley. But I moved to LA with my mom in the early 80s and saw cholo writing everywhere. This gang-banger kid SLEEPY (RIP) used to show us hand-styles in class. We were pretty hooked on it. Thought we were hard, you know? Writing our names everywhere like we were some real gang. Until the REAL gang-bangers started coming after us. Then we switched it up a little.

QoL: Then *Wild Style* came out.

Brant: That's interesting that you bring up gangbangers, since a lot of people think that graffiti is all about gangs. Very often, I have to start out explaining that most graffiti has nothing to do with gangs.

Brant: So how did *Wild Style* change everything?

QoL: We were all bugging when we saw what these people were doing. My friend had a cousin from New York who sent him the album and gave him all the new terminology and stuff. When breaking came out, we just went apeshit. We had our cardboard on the corner every night. It was an incredible outlet for us. That's all we did, day and night. And it was embraced by the culture at large. We got sponsorships from the hip shops at the malls. We were recognized when we went to parties. People cleared the floors. We had FAME. And we had something that made us feel good about ourselves. And, most importantly for teenage boys, we had an outlet for our testosterone. *Wild Style* was really the first thing that leaked what was going on in NYC to the world.

Brant: So you were mostly a b-boy (break dancer)?

Brant: I feel like Ted Koppel.

Brant: I know the answer, but I pretend not to.

QoL: Yeah. I loved graffiti, but honestly I was never very good at it. I did my thing and I loved every aspect of it (the fame, the challenge, the excitement). But breaking was just so much more tangible for me. There was nothing like going into battle.

Brant: Yeah, that's an attitude that you've really carried with you into filmmaking. You are so intense. On the set, your gaze is like laser beams, which can be annoying since you are so focused it's tough to get your attention sometimes . . .

QoL: Yeah, it's funny because I can really be a klutz and a space cadet. But when I'm in battle (whether it's breaking, surfing, filmmaking, whatever), I am so hyper-focused nothing else exists. It was that distraction that was so appealing to me and my friends. In our little world, we were Kings.

Brant: Right, your b-boy crew in the Bay Area (Fantastic Fource, right?) was the top in the mid-80's. Of course, at the same time, I was barely figuring out how to dress (I think that was my Hawaiian shirt stage . . .).

Brant: But you got busted for graffiti didn't you?

QoL: Ouch. Love to see those pics.

QoL: Yeah, Fantastic Fource held down the Bay, especially around 1985. There were other very strong crews, don't get me wrong. But none that were really dominating in the mainstream contests, as well as on the streets. It was a really fun time.

QoL: But yeah, I got busted for graffiti around that time, too.

Brant: What happened?

QoL: It was some stupid shit. Seems like I always get hurt (or busted) doing stupid shit. I was catching a tag in a pretty prominent place in broad daylight in the Mission. And my friend Henry said he had my back. Then I heard the police "chirp" and I looked over at Henry catching a tag at the same time. I just looked at him like "you idiot." They cuffed us up and drove us around the city for hours, patrolling and making racist comments. Then I was held all day. Had to see a probation officer, etc. It never really went too far.

Brant: Things have certainly changed since then. Seems like the cops are pretty hot to lock up writers and throw away the key. You were pretty paranoid the local fuzz would shut us down. Talk about that.

QoL: Well the city was really hot when we shot *QoL*. Rumor had it that someone had snitched on a bunch of writers. A bunch of our friends received very serious warrants ("gang crimes" etc). The City was really cracking down on graffiti like never before. One of the supporting actors in our film, Dave Lieberman, was facing 18-21 months! So yes, we were totally paranoid that they would come through and rip the film out of

JENKELINGTON

24

NEKST&DEBT

25

the camera or something. We definitely approached the production with security in mind.

Brant: Yeah, I heard from a lot of people that they didn't even know a thing about us, since we kept such a low public and publicity profile before and during production. I wanted to blow it up big, but you kept telling me horror stories, like that documentary filmmaker who was doing a piece on graffiti writers and the cops impounded all his footage . . . even though he wasn't a writer himself . . .

QoL: He actually went to jail and faced charges himself! I believe he had a show called GraffTV or something and they claimed he was aiding and abetting.

Brant: Of course, if we did get arrested (not that we had ANY REASON to worry about that, ahem), it would have made a great press story. I can see the t-shirts: "Free Ben Morgan!"

QoL: Yay. My family would have been so proud of you.

Brant: Everyone loves seeing kids asking when daddy can come home from the pokey . . .

QoL: Oh yeah. It's a full on Disney moment!

Brant: Okay, so you had this background in breaking and graffiti, having grown up around it and doing a bit of it. Why make a movie about it? Tell us why where the first idea for *Quality of Life* came from.

QoL: I had this fuzzy weird dream that Picasso was a writer and he was chilling with us. I really didn't know much about Pablo Picasso and have no idea where the dream came from, but it stuck with me. I kept thinking about it. So I started researching his life and trying to find something I could write a screenplay about and I came across the incident with Casagemas. Picasso had a good friend named Carlos Casagemas who blew his brains out in front of everyone b/c his girl had left him (he took a shot at her, grazed the back of her neck). This tragic incident inspired Picasso to create "The Burial of Casagemas." which was really his first noteworthy piece, and subsequently inspired his blue period. So it was this basic concept of inspiration borne of tragedy that influenced the birth of *Quality of Life*.

Brant: Heir (played by Lane Garrison), in the early versions of the story, wrote "Picasso" and that was the working title of the film. Until we asked the Picasso estate for permission . . .

QoL: Right. They weren't really feeling it.

Brant: Of course, being our usually pushy selves (excuse, me RELENTLESS selves), we didn't just ask for permission to use the name in our wacked-out graffiti film, we also asked to use images of some of his artwork and instead of paying them anything, we wanted them to PAY US and invest in the film.

Brant: I don't see what their problem was.

QoL: Yeah. WTF?

QoL: In retrospect, it was the best thing that could have happened. When a script is in that embryonic stage, you're so protective of it. But sometimes you have to slaughter your darlings.

Brant: Right. And we ended up with possibly the worst working title ever (and some people think *Quality of Life* is bad): *Art Terror*!

QoL: Wasn't that your idea?

Brant: That was never my darling, so I'm glad it went to a quick death.

Brant: Oh, I take the fall, right.

QoL: If you insist.

25

Brant: Well, we were both outraged at the Bush administration's reaction to 9/11, that it seemed like a semi-good idea to tie the outrageous War on Graffiti to the outrageous War on Terror.

QoL: Yeah. Made sense at the time. Kind of like my pink Izod shirt in 1983.

QoL: Wait, that's back in style, huh?

Brant: Tell John Doffing that 1983 wants its shirt back. But when we ended up with *Quality of Life*, it was a good fit. It allowed us to have a title with multiple levels of meaning, which always makes the filmmakers look clever and smart.

QoL: Yeah. It's my hope that we can educate people who aren't "in the know" through the marketing and distribution of the film and shed light on quality of life crimes and offenses.

Brant: The whole idea of "quality of life" crimes is so offensive. It's like the suburbanization of the urban space. Literally a white-wash over the real problems.

QoL: It's offensive, and yet so typical.

Brant: It reminds me of the University President at a big mid-western university, whose idea of how to deal with problems with the campus climate toward students of color, was that white people should smile and say nice things more often to them.

Brant: Kind of reminds me of Grandma's joke (which got cut from the movie, but should be on the DVD extras): "That's nice."

Brant: So let's talk about writing the script.

Brant: Or are you taking a crap break?

QoL: I'm here.

Brant: Okay, so what was the writing process like? Talk about how you approached taking your idea from your dream, your research and your journal notes and turn it into a coherent story?

QoL: The undermining flaw with the "quality of life" theory is that it fails to recognize the root causes of these "crimes." If you want to rid the city of homeless people, great. Find them homes and start working with them on occupational training and mental health therapy. To think you can just "sweep the streets" and actually address the issue is so f'ing ignorant, it makes my blood boil. The War on Graffiti (and quality of life movement in general) has failed miserably because of this failure to address root causes and hyper focus literally on the surface.

Brant: Same with the War on Drugs. And the War on Terror. Hmm. Seems like all these "wars" create MORE of the "prob-lem" through repression and retribution . . . A nice way to keep alive these little quasi-military industries that pop up around them. Of course, I look at it also from the aesthetic perspective: what type of life do we want to live, if all our walls are blank?

QoL: There are two discussions here.

Brant: Want to tackle the writing process?

Brant: Up to you.

QoL: Declaring War on a noun fails to address the root causes and, thus, is doomed to fail. What we want our environment to look like is a much more subjective discussion. I know I'd rather see a nice tag than another Coke ad. But that's my opinion. The facts, however, don't lie. The War on Graffiti has not worked. The US spends $15-18 BILLION a year cleaning up graffiti. And yet we're cutting art and prevention programs every year and under-funding schools more and more. If the tax payers had the facts, this would be a more open debate. But it is so easy to paint this as a black-and-white debate.

Brant: Well, and our property-obsessed culture takes a dim view of anyone messing with anyone else's stuff. Money and property

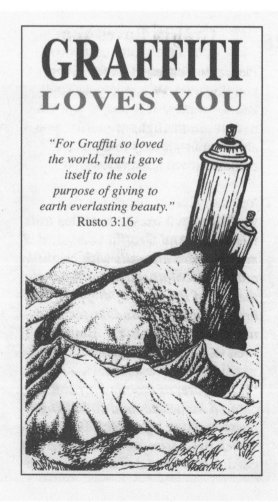

GRAFFITI
LOVES YOU

"For Graffiti so loved the world, that it gave itself to the sole purpose of giving to earth everlasting beauty."
Rusto 3:16

Ben, Kev, & Brian block a shot of Lane in his bedroom.

have been given almost religious reverence. So if you DARE trespass by writing on something that isn't yours, it's a big fucking deal. The same meme is active in the anti-piracy battles by the major music labels and movie studios. But that's the flip side of the coin, from what people call "remix culture" where artists/musicians/filmmakers take bits from other works and recombine into new art/music/films. In a way, that's what graffiti artists do, but not with digital media properties, but with REAL, tangible property: WALLS.

QoL: You're absolutely right. But I don't like my space being invaded either by telemarketers, or spam, or billboards.

Brant: Of course, we thought this was just an American problem, since so much of the Cowboy Lone-Idiot Philosophy is part of our US legal framework. We thought Europe was more enlightened . . . Then we went to Berlin, for our world premier at the big film festival there, and we heard stories of 5am busts by cops. It could have been the Mission District of San Francisco.

QoL: And the point is, let's say you want to eradicate graffiti. I personally don't. I like it. But if you DID, the way they have been going about it is just completely ass-backwards. And the results have proven this.

Brant: Graffiti is global. And so is the War on Graffiti.

QoL: That WAS surprising.

QoL: Really did think that quality of life laws were an American thing. Seemed to suit our culture better than Europe's. But Europe is cracking down HARD on graff, especially in Berlin and London.

Brant: Okay, let's talk screenwriting. How did this all translate into a story? Talk about the process, since you were the lead creative force behind it, leading the story, script and directing of the movie.

Brant: You could have made a movie about the cops vs. writers, with lots of action, etc.

QoL: Truth be told, I had no idea about process when I started this. I'm a very disciplined person, so I write every day and I have a thick skin so I can accept feedback. But I was really winging it when I started writing. I just started writing a story with Tom Mullowney. He and I kicked stuff back and forth. Then you and I started doing the same. But you were more strict about process. You really schooled me down about knowing where you're going before you leave the house. So, for months, we were kicking the story around. I'd do a re-write and then ask you guys for feedback.

Brant: I have to say, I feel like I constantly tore you a new one with nearly every draft. You DO have a thick skin. I don't think I could take some of the blistering feedback I gave you.

QoL: I'm all about feedback. Scripts aren't written, they are re-written. The one thing I learned was WHEN to bring in outside eyes. I think I had too many cooks in the kitchen early on with *QoL*. It's fine to have feedback (and in your case, you were basically teaching me how to plot out a story, develop theme, etc.), but if you invite it too soon, you risk losing your vision.

Brant: That's a good point. You have to have some substance there to work with, or too much is up in the air and there's no compass points to work with. To be honest, I'm still a bit amazed that I turned into the "process expert" for writing the story. Here's how it happened: I took a three day class at the Film Arts Foundation in San Francisco called "The 48 Hour Treatment." You spend two intensive days over one weekend (i.e. "48 hours") learning the bare bones three act screenplay structure, and then you have a week to write the treatment. You return for the third day, a week later, to read and get feedback. I think I was the only one that actually ended up going through the whole process, with a final complete treatment (it wasn't for our *Quality of Life*, but another project). People kept dropping out or just doing incomplete work. I think process is tough and people fight it, but it really took our script to the next level.

Brant: I seriously don't think we would be where we are today without that screenwriting rigor. We thought we'd spend a year on the screenplay and we decided on TWO years, in order to get it right.

Brant: And that really made the difference. With a solid screenplay, we were able to sign on some key staff (such as DP Kev Robertson and Producer Meika Rouda), who then helped bring on other key team members . . . and it snowballed from there. But it all started with a solid script.

QoL: Yup. It all starts with the script.

Brant: And that's why so many Hollywood movies suck: they don't focus on the script.

QoL: You can see it clear as day sometimes. Like, "If they would have spent three more months on the script, this movie could have been really good."

QoL: Story is King.

Brant: Yup. But in our case, the structure was only part of the story (so to speak).

Brant: Authenticity of the subculture was the other key element.

Brant: You originally brought in Brian Burnam to help with that. Tell us about how that happened. How did you know Brian, what was his background in graffiti and screenwriting?

Brant: What did he contribute and how did his role change?

QoL: Brian was my neighbor in Santa Cruz. He was twelve and I was eighteen when we first met. He was just this neighborhood skater kid and we kind of brought him up. We stayed really close over the years (he actually lived with me for a minute when his dad kicked him out of the house). But then he left SC and we kind of lost touch. I knew he had gone to SF and was involved with graffiti on some level, but I had no idea how deep he was. So, as part of my open gate policy, I called him out of the blue one day (tracked down his number from his dad) and asked him if he wanted to look at the script. At first, he was just providing feedback. But it was very surface level. I kept telling him to bring it, that he couldn't hurt my feelings. And he ended up going deeper and deeper to where he started writing some dialogue. Then I encouraged him to take on entire scenes. Then his involvement grew from there, to the point where the script was more him than me.

QoL: hello?

Brant: Sorry

Brant: When you started the writing process, what did you expect to come out with? How did it compare with what you ended up with?

QoL: The funny thing is, I never really expect specific things. I just start on a journey that feels right and pursue it with all I've got night and day until I get there. So my expectation with *Quality of Life* was to produce something strong and authentic and that would ideally start a career for myself in film. I had no idea that we'd work with Kev or Meika or Belinda or Sharon or that Brian would become as involved as he did. I just knew I had to do this thing and that, if it was going to lead somewhere for me, I was going to have to give it everything I had.

Brant: Turned out pretty good in the end, I think.

QoL: We'll see (-;

QoL: Not home yet.

This was our first photo op, for Screen International in Berlin. Ben made a crazy face at the end of the shoot and, of course, that's the one they used. Lesson learned.

28

S chauplatz des Films sind die Suburbs von San Francisco. Zwei Freunde, Michael „Hair" Rose, gespielt von Lane Garrison, und Curtis „Vain" Smith, dargestellt von Brian Burnam, leben ihr Leben und zelen ihr Hobby - Graffiti. Sie sind das perfekte Team. Neben ihrer illegalen Freizeitbeschäftigung müssen sich die beiden täglich mit den Problemen des Alltags herumschlagen: Streitereien mit Eltern, Freundin und anderen Widern - außerdem müssen sie Geld für das Lebensunterhalt und die schönen Seiten des Lebens heranschaffen.

Bei einem ihrer nächtlichen Streifzüge werden die beiden erwischt, wo da sich ändern sich die Verhältnisse: Michael versucht, sich auf legale Weise Gebie zu verschaffen, und Curtis schlägt einen selbstzerstörerischen Weg ein. Trotzdem bleiben sie Freunde. Eine Mischung, die gefährlicher ist als Dynamit und sich mit einem großen Knall endet.

Der Regisseur des Films, Benjamin Morgan, Anfang 30, hat in seiner Jugend selbst mit der Szene zu tun gehabt, wenn auch hauptsächlich als Breakdancer. Er wollte eine Geschichte drehelen, wie sie das Leben spielt, und das ist ihm mit diesem Film gelungen. Im Gespräch wurde deutlich, was die Beweggründe für dieses Leinwandspektakel waren. Und nebenbei gesagt, wird eine Seite der USA beleuchten, die man eigentlich lieber schnell wieder vergessen möchte.

BACKSPIN: Wie wichtig war dir für deinen Film der Hip-Hop-Kontext?
MORGAN: Meine persönliche Beziehung zu Graffiti kam durch Hip-Hop. Anfang der Achtziger war ich ein Breaker. Schaut euch den Videoclip auf der Website zum Film auf www.qualityoflife-themovie.com!! Heute jedoch ist Graffiti viel weiter gefächert. Die Großzahl der Writer heutzutage hat wenig mit Hip-Hop zu tun. Ich denke, dass die Öffentlichkeit dazu tendiert, Graffiti nur mit Hip-Hop zu verbinden. Doch das verwirrt den Blick auf die eigentliche Größe dieses Phänomens. Die Wahrheit ist, dass Writer in den USA kleine weiße Kids sind, die aus der Mittelklasse stammen und in Vororten wohnen. Dies ist eine wesentlich rebellischere Macht, eine, die sich schwer in Stereotypen festigen lässt: Die Hauptfiguren in „Quality Of Life" repräsentieren diesen neuen Typus von Writern in San Francisco. So sind Leute wie du und ich. Diese Typen hören Hip-Hop, Punk, Indie, Rock und so weiter. Es ist wesentlich komplizierter als die zweidimensionale Kategorisierung, die normalerweise durch den Bezug auf Hip-Hop stattfindet.

BACKSPIN: Wusstest du während der Dreharbeiten schon, dass du eine Geschichte aus dem Alltag von fast jedem Writer der Welt erzählst?
MORGAN: In dem Film geht es hauptsächlich um Alltag. Das Ziel war nie, den Leuten etwas über Graffiti zu erzählen. Viele der Leute, die das Skript gelesen haben, sagten uns, dass wir mehr über die Szene erzählen sollten. Natürlich ist das auch interessant, aber wir wollten keine Dokumentation machen. Wir produzierten ein dramatisches Stück über Menschen. Beziehungen und Entscheidungen, die Menschen fällen. Alles, was ich mit Filmen erreichen möchte, ist, Authentizität darzustellen. Wenn es glaubhaft und unwiderstehlich ist, dann habe ich mein Ziel erreicht.

BACKSPIN: Der Film hat seinen Namen durch die so genannten „Quality Of Life Offenses" bekommen. Dies sind Straftaten, die die Qualität des Lebens in den USA beschneiden. Graffiti fällt darunter. Wie hoch sind die Strafen für solche Vergehen, und ist ein solches Vergehen mit diesem speziellen Namen typisch für die USA?
MORGAN: Dank unserer zurückgebliebenen Politiker sind die Gefängnisse in den Staaten mit Häftlingen überfüllt, die wegen gewaltloser Straftaten verurteilt wurden. Wir verdanken diesen Lebensqualitätsstraftaten eine unglaubliche Hysterie gegenüber denen, die sie ausführen. In San Francisco kann man bis zu drei Jahren Haft und 21 Monaten für Graffiti absitzen. Dies ist doch absurd. Ich versuche nicht zu sagen, dass es o.k. ist, auf anderer Leute Besitz zu sprühen, auch wenn man in der heutigen Gesellschaft das Argument hervorbringen kann, dass man bei all der Werbung und Umweltverschmutzung das Recht haben sollte, sich so zu äußern, wie man möchte. Allerdings

sollte man hier vernünftiger vorgehen. Es ist keine Problem, wenn man Leute, die keine wirklichen Verbrechen begangen haben, ins Gefängnis steckt.

BACKSPIN: Du hast zwei Wege dargestellt, die ein Writer gehen kann. Den legalen und den selbstzerstörerischen. Siehst du noch andere?
MORGAN: Es ist für jeden, der ernsthaft bei der Sache ist, eine Vollensucht. Ein wahrer King kann nicht einfach aufhören und sich auf seinen Lorbeeren ausruhen. Es muss irgendein Übergangsstadium geben. Viele Writer finden ein Ventil in Grafikdesign, andere in Kunstgalerien, und wiederum andere malen, bis sie tot umfallen. Dies war nie mein Weg. Also, wie kann ich beurteilen, welches der richtige Weg ist? Das Wichtigste ist doch, dass du am Ende eines Tages zufrieden bist mit deinem Lebensstil.

BACKSPIN: Wie war es, das Resultat auf der großen Leinwand zu betrachten? Welche Reaktionen hast du erwartet, und warst du zufrieden?
MORGAN: In Berlin, das war praktisch eine Weltpremiere. Und es war das erste Mal, dass wir den Film auf einer großen Leinwand zu sehen bekamen. Es war eine unglaubliche Erfahrung. Ein wirklich sehr emotionales Erlebnis. Die Reaktionen des Publikums waren echt Klasse. Wir wissen, wo wir stehen, und demnach sind wir auch davon ausgegangen, dass das Publikum dies erkennt. Dieser Film wurde mit sehr geringen finanziellen Mitteln gemacht. Das Resultat ist kein strahlendes Hollywood-Epos. Trotzdem haben die Leute über die „Indie-Qualität" des Films hinweggesehen und die Authentizität auf der Leinwand erkannt. Wir waren wie die Punk-Band in einer Talentshow. Wir können zwar keinen Mozart spielen, aber wir glauben an uns, unsere Story und unsere Charaktere. Das haben die Zuschauer respektiert. Sowohl Writer als auch normale Filmbesucher waren fasziniert von unserem Ergebnis. Wir wurden auf der Berlinale sogar lobend hervorgehoben, was ich als phänomenal empfinde, wenn ich mir die anderen Filme auf diesem Festival im Vergleich anschaue. Das Verblüffendste jedoch war die äußerst positive Reaktion der Übervierzigjährigen. Wir hatten niemals mit einem solch gemischten Publikum gerechnet. Zusammenfassend lässt sich sagen, dass die Reaktionen unsere Erwartungen bei weitem übertrafen. Angesichts der Reaktion der Leute, die wir ursprünglich ansprechen wollten, Writer und Jugendliche im Allgemeinen, rechnen wir mit einer recht hohen Zuschauerzahl in den Kinos. Ich hoffe, euch alle dort zu sehen.

Abschließend lässt sich sagen: Checkt www.qualityoflife-themovie.com, um euch noch weiter zu informieren, und haltet die Augen auf, denn früher oder später werden die lokalen Programmkinos diesen Film bestimmt spielen ... ☺

Brant: So how did Brian become a hot star actor in the film? After all, he's ugly as shit and mumbles every line.

QoL: True dat!

QoL: Brian wanted the lead so badly, but he and I are like brothers. And we fight like brothers. So I told him that it would be totally unhealthy to have that dysfunctional family thing going on on set all the time. And I didn't want the screenwriter on set either. Just something you don't do. The visions will clash and it will drive everyone nuts. Fate overruled (when our lead actor dropped out a week before production) and the rest is history. Brian and I DID fight like cats and dogs on the set every day and it WAS unhealthy for the crew. But the end result made it all worthwhile . . . sort of . . .

Brant: Yeah, you were more like an old married couple that loves each other, but knows how to push each other's buttons. My favorite moment was when he (always the in-charge guy) yelled "action" when *he* wanted to end a debate with you about how a scene should go. Everyone on the crew just looked at him. But he really brought such deepness and honesty to the role. He really reached inside somewhere vulnerable and brought that out on screen. He stepped up in a way that genuinely surprised me and I think a lot of the people on the crew.

Brant: I think the best complement for him is when people ask us who the "real" actor is and who the non-actor is. He was that good.

Brant: And he and Lane (who played Mikey) really had a great rapport.

QoL: I started calling him Miss Director. He definitely was a little clueless about his role and how to get ideas to me. But his heart was in the right place. And he had a lot on the line. If this thing went south, his reputation was on the line. That's huge. I respected that and knew I needed to hear him. And he is an incredibly talented guy. Just a complete nightmare to live and work with.

QoL: I need to wrap up here fyi

Brant: Hell no. We're just getting started. We haven't even talked about the starlets throwing their thongs on the stage at Berlin!

Brant: They say casting is 90% of directing . . . and to be honest, casting was 95% of pre-production, since we spent so much time writing the script, searching for money and having day jobs. Talk about casting the film, how you found Lane Garrison and what it was like to work with him.

QoL: That really is true. (And the same goes for crew.) We hired an incredible casting director, Belinda Gardea. I spent MONTHS calling all of the hottest casting agents in LA. (I watched my favorite movies and looked to see who had done the casting.) I asked them if they had any assistants who might be interested in casting an indie feature. It took forever, but I believe Mary Vernieu finally led me to Belinda. Belinda came in guns blaring. My friend Troy was able to get us some free office space at the post-facility he was working at for the casting office, and Belinda went off. She sent out the breakdowns to every agent in LA and had hundreds of head shots within the first few days. She was a maniac. Belinda eventually narrowed it down to the strongest actors and had them read for me.

QoL: Lane and one other guy (our long-forgotten friend who abandoned us at the altar) were head and shoulders above everyone else.

Brant: Lane had long hair in the audition shots I saw. Looked totally different too.

QoL: Yeah we changed his look a little, but his heart sold me from the first read.

Brant: Lane is an amazing guy. Both as a professional and as a person. He had the best attitude, totally down for the cause. He too had a hard time growing up and he was able to use that, I think, in his performance. These guys weren't that far from where he could have been . . .

QoL: Yeah, I could see the struggle in his eyes. I knew he had something. What I didn't know is what an incredible team player he was. His attitude was everything we needed it to be. He was open to learning new things, open to direction, and willing to do whatever it took to make this movie. I have met people with that kind of attitude before, but have never met someone as talented as Lane who had the "can do" attitude to boot. A rare breed, that lad.

Brant: He is truly a great actor. He's nothing like Mikey, in real life. Unlike Mikey, Lane is a total smiling sweetheart. Mikey was so brooding and mopey, which is not how I experienced Lane at all. Brian, on the other hand, well, I think Curtis was closer to him in some ways. Not too close, luckily.

QoL: Pretty close, though. Brian was really living that lifestyle at the time, especially during production. He got into that character.

Brant: So talk about how you directed the film. How did you work with the actors and the DP to craft the scenes that we see in the movie.

QoL: Well honestly, from my perspective, I hardly directed this film at all. I managed chaos. I have never had the opportunity to "direct." I spent so much time running around getting props and putting out fires, I truly was not able to focus on directing. With that said, I do like to give my actors a lot of freedom to be who they are. I think a lot of actors want the director to come in and solve everything for them and I like to flip it on them and say, "I trust your take on it." I always make my actors write bios/personal histories of the characters. And we have some mandatory bonding time before production where we talk about who we are as people and what our take on the script is. But I am really not a very invasive director. The actors know I am going to protect them, the environment

QoL: is safe. And they are going to have one or two takes to do their thing. I don't do a ton of coverage, so that allows them to stay in the scene (i.e. they aren't distracted by close-ups, different angles, etc.). It's a really relaxed, almost documentary environment. I'm still typing.

Brant: K.

QoL: As far as Kev goes, the same applies. Kev did not really have many opportunities to shine either. He was in doc mode. I prepared him as best I could, as I did with the actors. I gave him graff books, mags, and videos and had writer friends take him on tours. But, since we didn't have our locations scouted, he was really winging it too. So neither of us really had that creative freedom that comes with a more organized (read "funded") production.

QoL: Alo?

Brant: Ah yes, the "drama verite" approach. Talk about that. Also, who are some of your influences as a filmmaker and why?

QoL: I love what Woody Allen does. He just sets the camera there and lets the world unfold in front of you. Mike Leigh.

QoL: Mike Leigh's process is fascinating. I studied him a lot and have borrowed from him, in terms of allowing actors to be a part of the development process. Marc Levin was a huge influence as well. Danny Boyle blew me away with *Trainspotting*. So funny and so hardcore at the same time.

QoL: I have a pretty diverse group of people I draw from. I can learn from anyone. I try to keep an open mind. It's the same with music.

Official Invitation

Internationale Filmfestspiele Berlin · Potsdamer Straße 5 · D –

Mr. Benjamin Morgan
Quality Of Life Film

54. Internationale Filmfestspiele Berlin

It is a great pleasure to invite you to attend
Filmfestival, due to take place from Februa

The festival is pleased to offer you hotel ac
during the festival.

To arrange your visit, we ask you to kindly
your earliest convenience.

Looking forward to welcome you soon in
experience with us.

Yours sincerely

Dieter Kosslick

Dieter Kosslick
Festival Director

This invitation is personal and not transferable.
Please return the attached hotel reservation form toge

26.11.2003
G46 - 64207 J

ernational

5 days

d form at

exciting

Internationale
Filmfestspiele
Berlin

Guest Management

Potsdamer Str. 5
D - 10785 Berlin

Tel. +49·30·25920·500
Fax +49·30·25920·599

welcome@berlinale.de
www.berlinale.de

Ein Geschäftsbereich der
Kulturveranstaltungen des
Bundes in Berlin GmbH (KBB)

's Film Festival

photo.

Brant: We talked a lot about Marc Levin's movie *Slam* during pre-production. The film is about Slam Poetry and also very low-budget and authentic. It was a great model, in terms of what it was trying to do. Finding the right Director of Photography was key. I'm still blown away by the look of the film. How did you pick Kev Robertson? Talk about working with him and what he brought, both in terms of camera and beyond.

QoL: FYI, by pushing this back so late, it's cutting into time I promised to Amy. Need to go soon.

Brant: We need to finish though. not sure how much time it will take, but we gotta get through some of this stuff. Great stuff. Need to document it.

Brant: When can we finish?

QoL: We interviewd a bunch of DPs. And I was impressed with the work of several of them. But Kev & I bonded from the first phone call. He understood the punk rock ethic that drives graffiti and would ultimately drive the production. He is an incredibly talented DP. But our relationship was the deciding factor. I knew he could (a) understand why someone would write their name on someone else's property and (b) be able capture beautiful images under extreme conditions.

QoL: I can finish later tonight?

Brant: I'm down. When?

QoL: 9?

Brant: Perfect.

QoL: ttyl

Brant: We'll start from Kev. Great stuff.

Brant: You oughta be in pictures . . .

QoL: I'm here.

Brant: Welcome back to "My Time in Hell," a serialized dramatization of the process called "indie filmmaking" which is also banned under certain Geneva Conventions . . .

Brant: But then again I was out until 2am last night getting flyers into clubs . . .

QoL: Won't someone please put us out of our misery!

QoL: You're a madman.

QoL: Was anyone helping you?

Brant: Actually yes, we have a pal named Adam who puts on the amazing Opel Production events—mostly very from-the-heart electronic music events. He gave me some pointers and we swapped cards, so he's distributing ours and we're distributing his.

Brant: And Alicia (shout-out!) is out there doing her thing too.

QoL: Perfect. How many people do you think you reached? How many butts in seats did you cultivate last night?

Brant: Plus a bunch of random people have asked for flyers since they know lots of people. Mackenzie also took a box: she's a freakin' machine.

Brant: Time will tell. It's all about impressions: getting as many people as possible to see the name of the film and become interested . . .

QoL: We're pretty fortunate to have her on the team. We've got a strong core group of people. Pretty amazing, when you think we shot this thing over 2 yrs ago.

Brant: Yup.

Brant: Let's go back to those days of yore . . .

Brant: We were talking about Kev Robertson . . .

QoL: btw we never talked about the Graffiti Model . . .

Brant: Okay, we'll get to that next.

Brant: Since it fits in with Kev's style for shooting.

Brant: So . . .

Brant: How did the graffiti culture (the setting of the film) influence how you made the film (i.e. what's the relationship of the medium to the message)?

Brant: Uh oh, foresee a long response.

QoL: bite me!

Brant: It's the learning moment.

QoL: We originally set out to raise a million dollars to make this movie. This is a lot of dough for a first-time filmmaking team with no stars and no organizational or studio backing. So, needless to say, we came up short. WAY short. In the process of strategizing for production, we came up with the Graffiti Model. Graffiti writers create these powerful, compelling images with little or no resources. We adopted that as our production model in place of a larger budget. So the concept was to plan and prep as much as possible (like writers do, scoping out spots, practicing handstyles), but be prepared to get down and dirty, hit it, and get out. And that's how we shot the movie. We infected the cast & crew with this philosophy from day one and it really caught on. We couldn't have made the movie any other way.

Brant: Okay, so let's talk specifics.

QoL: Let's!

Brant: How did that influence any given location or set-up?

Brant: <looking at watch>

QoL: On a traditional shoot, you scout the location, maybe do shoot some test footage. Then, when you shoot, you light it, do some set design, and shoot lots of coverage (wide shot, two shot, close-ups, etc.). With the Graffiti Model, we'd show up (often at locations we had never seen before), whip out the camera, usually no lights or very minimal lights, shoot the scene once or twice, and get the hell out of dodge. That allowed us to stay within our timeframe and budget, and also gave the film a very raw, spontaneous feel. It was the perfect production model for this film.

Brant: Do you think this model could work for other films? When is it appropriate?

Brant: Honestly, it sounds damn risky.

QoL: Totally. If you're shooting *The Aviator*, it's obviously not going to work. But for films that are supposed to be raw and REAL, the Graffiti Model is the shit.

QoL: It IS risky. But safe sucks.

Brant: We didn't see what we had on film (our "dailies") until production was over.

Brant: We had scheduled a weekend of pick-up shots, but we couldn't reshoot the whole thing . . .

Brant: I have to say, the Graffiti Model sounds like old skool indie filmmaking (before "real" movie stars started slumming in the art house films . . .).

QoL: What's the question?

Brant: Right, that's one of those statements to incite a thoughtful response, like as though you're an intelligent, easy-going kind of guy.

Brant: My mistake.

Brant: Moving on.

QoL: dailies? pick-ups? graff model?

Brant: So what was your reaction when you first saw the footage?

QoL: It's funny. Everyone else was so shocked. But we got pretty much what I thought we got. I really wasn't very surprised. What was your reaction? Was Sharon's place the first time you saw footage?

QoL: <looking at watch>

Brant: I had seen some raw telecine files (unedited) on DVD prior to our second art show. Remember, we were going to project them on the wall or something . . . ? But I couldn't figure out how to get them to work right on the computer. That was my first sight of the actual "film" and what we were working with.

Brant: WHATEVER, Dr. Hunt-And-Peck

QoL: What did you think?

Brant: My reaction was: "We have a film."

Brant: It looked like a movie.

Brant: Oh, an investor is requiring me to chat. I gotta go for a bit.

QoL: Money talks.

Brant: Sorry. Money talks and Brant walks . . .

Brant: hey.

QoL: What's up, Dr. Ledorhosen?

QoL: OK. We're back. How'd it go with the investor?

Brant: Pretty well: we closed the deal. We have a lead investor to fund the start of our theatrical release!

QoL: Wow!

Brant: And also to fund the clearances for our home video.

QoL: So we can show the movie now?

Brant: As soon as the wire transfer clears and the checks go out . . .

QoL: Don't celebrate til the check clears.

Brant: Now if we can just get the MPAA to stop rejecting our trailer, we can actually be in business . . .

QoL: If only that was the end of our worries.

QoL: We're three weeks out and we have a dozen MPAA-type issues to deal with.

Brant: They don't want kids to see the five frames of fake blood or they might go out and start smoking weed or something . . .

Brant: Indie filmmaking is more about technical bullshit and sweet-talking than anything else . . .

Brant: That and whores.

QoL: Ah, the whores.

QoL: So, we're three weeks out, we've got three months of work to do, and we have day jobs. What's your prognosis?

Brant: We're going to get to the finish line, just as the fucker falls apart on us, same as usual.

Brant: But we're gonna cross the line.

Brant: And then it's all in the hands of the audience.

QoL: The *Quality of Life* way.

Brant: It's either gonna be buffed in a couple weeks or it will run for years and we'll be kings (that's me talking like a graffiti guy).

QoL: That's you. The big "graffiti guy."

Brant: Heh. Well, I really came to this from the outside: you (and Brian, even more so), were the insiders. I feel like I got adopted.

QoL: You are the step-child.

Brant: The red-haired stepkid with the cool older siblings . . .

Brant: So I get laid before all the other kids in class since Brian's my older bro . . .

Brant: That's funny, since he's not THAT much younger than me though he acts like he's about 17.

QoL: That's the theory.

QoL: So let's get on track.

Brant: Right. Okay, before I got called away, I was giving my impression of my first view of the film.

QoL: This is the 1st thing a lot of people are going to read. We want them to keep reading.

Brant: Right. As long as there aren't any pictures of you, we'll be fine.

Brant: Anyway. Basically, I looked at the raw footage and the shots looked like a movie.

Brant: I just said to myself: this looks great—thank god we shot on film instead of video!

Brant: On video it would have looked like the 6 o'clock news or out-takes from COPS (the TV show). Instead, it looked like Cinema.

QoL: Remember when I made that call. I was like, "No major decisions right now, but we're shooting on film, not video."

Brant: Yep.

QoL: That was a pretty major decision.

Brant: Now here's where we had a different experience: watching the completed film. You were living with the various edits, working with Sharon. I hadn't seen anything before the rough cut was assembled.

QoL: Hardly anyone had, since we didn't have dailies.

Brant: I remember watching it for the first time in my apartment alone—and I starting running around the room, shouting and crying. I was so fucking impressed. All our hard work. And it showed up on the screen.

QoL: Crying, really?

Brant: Hell yes.

Brant: I cried the first dozen or so times I saw the film—at the end of course.

Brant: It still gives me goosebumps.

QoL: Wow. Thanks for sharing your sensitive side with us.

Brant: My inner hippy is never far beneath the skin. Thank you UC Santa Cruz.

Brant: The investor is asking for my time again. Um. Gotta go.

QoL: Jesus Christ. Are you kidding me?

34

QoL: Money can't ALWAYS talk.

QoL: TTYL

QoL: Hi.

Brant: Okay, back again.

Brant: Damn investors.

Brant: Can't live with 'em . . .

Brant: etc.

QoL: Oh NOW you want to talk.

QoL: You realize I don't have any money, right?

Brant: Um . . . gotta go.

Brant: J/K

QoL: F'ing producers . . .

Brant: So as I was saying: the film looked great and the story really played well. I was jazzed.

Brant: Let's talk about the festivals.

QoL: Let's!

Brant: What did you expect from the festival process? Where did you want to play?

QoL: Originally, I had the same dreams as everyone else: Sundance, Berlin, Toronto.

QoL: And of course get picked up by a distributor right away. Bidding wars, etc.

QoL: Not exactly our story.

Brant: What happened?

QoL: We were way too late for Sundance. Got a huge extension, but had to send them a VERY rough cut. (We ended up re-shooting like half of the 1st 10 min, the most important section for screeners.) And we had no "in" there really. But we got into Berlin. What a stoker that was, huh?

Brant: That was amazing to get into Berlin. But let's stay with Sundance for a minute. They saw the same cut as Berlin. In Berlin, two people on the programming committee were in tears watching it. At Sundance, no love. What's up with Sundance? Many (most?) of their films seem to be by star "indie" directors and/or have actual real movie stars in them. Is that the "indie spirit" we hear about: Hollywood lite?

Brant: I read the Sundance mission statement and marketing fluff and I gotta say: there's a credibility gap.

QoL: Bagging on Sundance has become a little passe. But you're right: there is a lot of nepotism going on at Sundance. They don't seem to have room for the very films their mission statement claims to support. I know several people who went to Sundance that year and said *QoL* would have been one of the stronger films in the American Spectrum section. Part of the problem with Sundance and all festivals, really, is that they develop these huge relationship webs that unfairly impact their selection process. They still discover people. And they still show good films. But they have definitely struggled with the growth process.

Brant: I think nepotism is part of it. Maybe part of it is also that the general quality of indie films may not be so high and only the "indiewood" style films (i.e. indie films with stars and multi-million dollar budgets) are worth sitting through (except for the occasional gem like *QoL* of course).

Brant: Bagging on Sundance (and some of the rest of the fest world) may be passe, but there's a reason. And I suppose I am bitter (and not too proud to say it). Simply getting into Sundance is a HUGE step up for a film: it's the difference between making it and making it really hard. They're the king-maker of the indie scene—and yet I read their line-up and I can't help wondering how these Hollywood stars keep showing up in supposedly independent films.

Brant: The real indies are left outside, waiting at the velvet rope . . .

QoL: It's incredibly complicated. But yeah, if you can get a star attached to a small indie, you get organizational and fiscal support, credibility, and strong performances. So it's tough to compete.

QoL: It's totally true. Deals get made at Sundance. Period. Just being there increases your chances of success exponentially.

QoL: Hard not to be bitter (-;

QoL: Next time.

Brant: Let's talk about the industry in general a bit more for a sec. Stars are a big issue. The biggest. They say for a small business, the three most important things are location, location, location. With films, it's stars, stars, stars.

Brant: What could we have done if we had "a single recognizable face?"

QoL: Yup. Stars open doors. Theoretically, fundraising would have been a lot easier. Sales would have been easier. (That's always the first question a distributor asks: "Who's in it?") But stars also bring problems. Your budget instantly increases, due to accomodations, salaries, expectations, etc. And then you lose the Birthday Cake angle. It's a double-edged sword, for sure.

QoL: yo

QoL: I hope you have been saving this. I just got cut off.

Brant: I am.

Brant: Hey, just talked to Max on the phone (he's designing this book). He says he's basically overwhelmed and can't put all the extra stuff in (non-scanned photos, scrapbook stuff, etc.). And he needs the rest of our content (includng this interview and your acknowledgements) ASAP. I told him by EOD.

Brant: (End Of Day)

Brant: So we gotta keep going.

Brant: Back to the topic . . .

Brant: Yes, movie stars are the magic pixie dust that makes a film marketable.

Brant: From a business perspective . . .

Brant: Since there's no way to really say whether a film will do well or not—statistical analysis has proven this—people in the industry gravitate to risk-aversion . . . And stars pretty much guarantee SOMEONE will watch it.

QoL: Yup. And, creatively, you can usually bank on a good performance. That's huge.

Brant: So we got into Berlin. Talk about that.

QoL: That was HUGE. Gave us so much momentum. Berlin is one of the top 5 festivals in the world. Many rank it #1 in terms of film selection, organization (they are Germans, after all), and filmmaker treatment. We were all so psyched. We rallied a posse of like 20 people. Producers, DP, editors, actors, artists (Sam Flores, Bryan Dawson), spouses. We took over!

Brant: Berlin was truly one of the highlights of my short life. I'll never forget it. Seeing the film so BIG on their screen. I think my mouth was in my lap the whole time. And the Berlinale staff was amazing. Big shout-outs to Maryanne and Thomas and the rest of the Kinderfilmfest crew!

Brant: I can honestly say that if they didn't believe in us, we wouldn't be where we are today: writing a book and starting our theatrical run.

QoL: It was carzy b/c no one had seen the print. Due to some post-production madness, I had to carry the print on the plane over there. Such a rush seeing it on that HUGE screen for the first time in a foreign country. Truly a World Premiere.

Brant: So being in Berlin was one thing: already we had hit the big time for an indie film: a major festival "official selection" and all the credibility that brought. But then we went on to win the Special Mention award (basically that means we got second place—still an award though). Did you expect to win an award? What was that like?

QoL: Oh, for sure. Turns out like two people on the selection committee had kids that had been arrested for graffiti.

QoL: I did NOT expect to win an award.

QoL: We were definitely the punk band at the talent show.

Brant: We were in the new 14-plus section of the festival. What was that all about? What types of films were we up against? Do you remember?

QoL: It's funny, you go to these festivals and you're so busy pro- moting your own film, you don't get to see any of the other films. But I did manage to catch a couple. They were really good. We were the only American film in the section. 14-plus was all about reaching an audience that is usually neglected by film festivals. Really brilliant concept, actually. Perfect place for us to be.

Brant: What audience was tht?

QoL: Doye. The 14-plus audience. Teenagers.

Brant: Hey, I know it, but our readers don't, doofus.

Brant: I think that's the primary reason why we didn't get into most film fests and didn't get picked up by a larger distributor: they don't understand the youth market.

Brant: The older people were, the less likely they were to "get" the film. I was reading a review yesterday of the new *Outsiders* DVD and the critics HATED that film, but kids ate it up. The en- trenched critical film world really does take a snobbish view of youth-focused films . . . And our film was about the people they cross the street to avoid when they go from the festival gala to their parking garage . . .

QoL: So true. It's a very difficult audience to reach. But, after working with youth for 13 years, I have a pretty good idea of what they like and don't like. I used to work at a residential treatment center and we'd watch movies every Friday night. That was great market research. I really started to get a feel for exactly what turned them on. It wasn't always what I thought it would be. But after a few of these little fuckers bitch you out for bringing in a wack movie and blame you for runing their Friday night, you start to develop some instincts.

QoL: Look at *Napoloen Dynamite*. I LOVED that movie. And it was obviously very successful with the youth audience. But a lot of adults I talked to HATED it. They just didn't get it. They'd SAY that. "I don't get what all the hype is." My kids & I own the movie and have watched it like 10 times. It's a classic. And yet, in the wrong hands, a film like that could get shelved.

Brant: Yeah, it's like you've had 13 years of non-stop focus groups with kids. I don't think the gatekeepers of the indie film world (producer reps, fest programmers, acquisitions execs) understand kids. So few indie films actually target a younger crowd (I don't mean 5-year olds, I mean 17- or even 20- year olds). Man, it sounds like I'm slamming people left and right here, but I was just amazed at the closed doors, when so many (younger) people were red hot for the film.

Brant: There's a generational bias against films targeting anyone younger than about 25 or 30 (and who might not be college educated . . .).

Brant: Youth doesn't go to art house theaters. Anyone in the industry will tell you that.

Brant: But when they do (*Napoleon Dynamite*, *Open Water*, etc.) it can really blow up big. The industry just doesn't know how to reach youth. But that's a problem with marketing people in general and kids are so savvy. They can smell fake a mile away. That's why authenticity was so important for *QoL*.

QoL: That's why we're playing primarily cineplexes.

Brant: Trying to.

Brant: So what was the rest of the festival experience like?

QoL: Honestly, I burned out early. Berlin was one of the best experiences of my life. And Seattle is a great festival, too. But I am so result-oriented, I quickly realized that I needed to focus my energy on bringing this shit home. Brian, who is single and a lot less tied down than I, gladly took my place and went to Stockholm and Spain. He had a blast. Ended up staying in Europe for months.

Brant: Yeah, how the hell did Mr. Mumbles end up on the European Vacation Plan while we were stuck home schlepping?

QoL: The beauty of being young, single, and irresponsible.

Brant: Is it true they needed to change his bedsheets every day at the hotel in Berlin and he drank the entire minibar?

QoL: Dude, I told that fucker: "Hands off the minibar. It's a trap!" Yeah right. Who drinks from the f'ing mini-bar? It's like $10 a drink. Go to the store and buy a case of beer for the cost of one little sampler of JD. But it brings up the age old question: WWBD (What Would Brian Do)? So he ended up with this huge tab. He bailed on it and the festival had a cow. It was pretty burnt.

Brant: So here we are, writing this three weeks to the day before we have our theatrical opening in San Francisco. One theater. One shot at hitting it out of the park and going big. How do you feel?

QoL: I'm a wreck. I'd be fine if this was all we were doing. I can handle 12 hr days. But the day job is pushing me over the top. I'm so distracted. I wake up in the middle of the night and work cuz I can't sleep. But I'm confident, just as I was in pre-production. Things are just as messy now, but I know what we have, just as I did then. How you feeling?

Brant: I feel like I'm drinking from two fire hydrants at the same time. The day job is tough, since my boss is now an investor (yes, I'm that dumb). But more than anything, I'm upset that we spent months—years really—planning out this detailed guerilla, grassroots, viral marketing and outreach plan, and we haven't been able to spend the time do it right. It's killing me. You and I have this image that we use: we're looking down on a theater and it's filled with people. And every time we miss an opportunity to outreach or spread the word, a few people go away, just pop like bubbles and turn into empty seats. We have a great film and the success of our theatrical run—and ALL our distribution (DVD, TV, international, etc.) will rely mostly on word of mouth.

Brant: We've carried the film this far, now the film will need to carry itself from here.

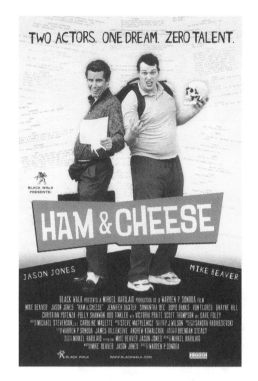

Anläßlich der 54. Internationalen Filmfestspiele Berlin

Der Botschafter der Vereinigten Staaten von Amerika und Frau Marsha Ann Coats

sowie der Vorsitzende und CEO der Motion Picture Association
Jack Valenti

laden Sie herzlich ein zu einem Empfang zu Ehren der amerikanischen Gäste und Teilnehmer der Internationalen Filmfestspiele Berlin

am Mittwoch, dem 11. Februar 2004, 17.00 - 19.00 Uhr im SONY Europe Gebäude, Sky Garden Kemperplatz 1 (am Potsdamer Platz)

Aus Sicherheitsgründen bestätigen Sie bitte Ihre Teilnahme
U.A.w.g. Tel.: (030) 31107-437/424; Fax: (030) 31107-433
e-mail: meadhs@state.gov

Diese Einladung gilt für zwei Personen - Bitte bringen Sie diese Karte zum Einlaß mit

On the Occasion of the 54th Berlin International Film Festival

The Ambassador of the United States of America and Mrs. Daniel R. Coats

and the Chairman and CEO of the Motion Picture Association
Jack Valenti

request the pleasure of your company at a reception in honor of the American guests and participants attending the Berlin International Film Festival

on Wednesday, February 11, 2004, 5 - 7 p.m. at SONY Europe Building, Sky Garden Kemperplatz 1 (at Potsdamer Platz)

For security reasons please confirm your attendance
Tel.: (030) 31107-437/424 Fax: (030) 31107-433
e-mail: meadhs@state.gov

This invitation admits two persons — This card is required for admission

54 ■ Internationale Filmfestspiele Berlin 5.–15.02.04

Benjamin Morgan

K

35 Kinderfilm 17

CINEMA SEATTLE PRESENTS

SEATTLE INTERNATIONAL FILM FESTIVAL

MAY 20 - JUNE 13 30TH ANNIVERSARY

ADMIT ONE

K1 GUEST

Brant: We spent three weeks in production, but more than two years since then working on distribution. That's the REAL story of indie filmmaking . . .

QoL: It's all about money. If you have the backing, you can focus on your job (same with directing, which I was completely distracted from). If you don't you triage your way through it. We're like the bulls in the china shop right now.

QoL: I gotta go. Back in 45 min or so.

QoL: No investor, unfortunately . . .

Brant: Okay, talk to you then. We'll wrap it up and send this fucker off to Max to add into the book (one of the last pieces, though one of the first that people will read . . .).

Brant: Good evening. Feeling profound?

Brant: Hello . . . earth to Ben . . .

Brant: Ahem.

QoL: Ahem this, motherfucker!

QoL: All right dude. Enough interruptions already.

QoL: If an investor calls this time . . .

QoL: I'll have to let you got talk to them.

Brant: And say, "Thank you sir, may I have another?"

Brant: Okay, I think we're winding this up. Thanks to everyone who's still reading. Believe it or not, in between all the gaps and breaks, we actually secured financing to release the film theatrically and got our soundtrack nailed. Plus fought a bunch of other fires.

QoL: That's an interesting little arc, huh?

Brant: Not the least of which is the amazing people at Chen Design (hi Max) are designing the book and we're still not done writing it.

QoL: We always used the "throwing down the tracks ahead of the train" analogy (like Wile E Coyote). Writing this book while it's being laid out is the epitome of throwing down the tracks.

Brant: Sounds like the *Quality of Life* way.

QoL: Word.

QoL: Alright, let's wrap this shit up.

QoL: BTW—I just watched Sharon's first cut of the *PtPT* DVD.

Brant: Oh, you mean the *Putting the Pieces Together* "behind-the-scenes of *Quality of Life*" DVD available soon on the *QoL* website at http://www.qualityoflife-themovie.com/—does that count as product placement if we talk about it?

QoL: You are such a producer, homey.

Brant: Someone's gotta keep food on the table around here . . .

QoL: You ain't lying!

QoL: Sharon FedEx'd me the rough cut today. It's pretty dope. She worked miracles once again.

Brant: Sharon is great. Have we talked about her yet? This thing is so long I forgot what we've covered already . . .

QoL: We've been going on so long, I doubt anyone's still reading at this point. Way to start off the book!

QoL: Sharon has her own chapter. She's a goddess. Best damn FCP editor on the planet . . . now let's wrap this goddamn thing up already. We're putting folks to sleep.

Brant: Zzzzz

Brant: Sorry. BUZZ!

Brant: So let's go back to the big picture.

QoL: Shall we?

Brant: Looking back . . . what did you expect out of this project four (!!) years ago?

QoL: Really almost ten years ago. I set the plan in motion with *Coming Down* (my 1st "student film"). I wanted to produce 3 no-budget features on video, spend no money, learn as much as I could, put them on the shelf and then move on to a "real film intended for theatrical release.

QoL: So I expected to start a career with *Quality of Life*. Start a company, actually. One with complete autonomy.

QoL: We're almost there, right?

Brant: If the audience shows up, we have a shot.

QoL: Are we there yet? Are we there yet? Are we there yet?

QoL: That's what it all comes down to.

QoL: But it's on US to reach them.

QoL: (With no advertising budget.)

Brant: True that. Self-distribution is right next to self-immolation in the dictionary . . .

QoL: Uh, forgive my ignorance (along with half our readers). What is self-immolation?

Brant: We're running late, bro. It's a Google moment for later. Anyway, that's not true: we have $5,000 for advertising.

QoL: How many tv spots will that buy?

Brant: Barely zero.

Brant: After legal fees.

QoL: Admit it, you don't even know what it means. You just wanted to throw some intellectual sounding shit out there. Probably made it up. Simp . . .

Brant: You're gonna look real dumb after that Google search.

QoL: What search?

Brant: Ignorance is bliss.

QoL: What's goggle?

Brant: Ahem. Back to the big picture: so how was this *QoL* trip different from what you expected?

QoL: It met my expectations in many ways. But I really did believe in the purest dream: go to Sundance, sell to a distributor, roll naked in cash.

Brant: I'll never use cash again after that image.

QoL: Don't lie. You know you're pushing down a chubby right now.

QoL: But this path has taught us SO much more. It has enabled to establish independence for the future.

QoL: It's like when my dad used to say, "You need to earn it" when I'd ask for handouts.

Brant: I heard John Madden on the radio today say: "You gotta go through the dumps to get to Easy Street."

QoL: Success is measured by the sacrifices you make.

40

It Takes a Village to Make a Movie

Be part of the community bringing *Quality of Life* to the screen and be immortalized in film history!

Level	What you get	Examples of screen credit
Supporter $125	- On-screen "thank you" in the credits (name only) - DVD of the film, upon home video release	Mary Fremont
Producer's Circle $300	- A message of your choice of up to 40 characters* plus your name in the on-screen credits - DVD of the film, upon home video release	John C. Fremont: Congrats Ben, I knew you could do it!
Director's Circle $500	- A message of your choice of up to 80 characters* plus your name in the on-screen credits - DVD of the film, upon home video release - Two tix to the Bay Area premier of *Quality of Life*	Fremont's Flowers: Always the freshest flowers in the Mission District. We support the community.
Angel $1000+	- A message of your choice of up to 140 characters* plus your name in the on-screen credits - DVD of the film, upon home video release - Eight tix to the Bay Area premier of *Quality of Life*	Mary and John Fremont: It's an honor to be part of a project such as this and we want to encourage everyone to tell their friends about *Quality of Life*.

Includes spaces and within reasonable limits of taste

This is how small independent films get funded: by friends, family and community-members. In order to complete this project, we need your support. Thank you for being part of our team and for your consideration of making a contribution. Without you, this project would not exist.

Please print clearly:

Name: _____ Phone: _____

Email: _____ @ _____

Mailing address: _____

Contribution level (circle one):

Supporter - $125	Producer's Circle - $300	Director's Circle - $500	Angel - $1000+

Or you can select a contribution level of your own. Whatever you do is deeply appreciated: $ _____

Check here to pay later (we'll bill you): O

Checks are payable to: Quality of Life Film, LLC

If you contribute $300 or more, you have the ability to include a note in the credits. Please write your draft note now (you will have the chance later to edit it, so if inspiration doesn't strike, you'll have plenty of time):

_____

_____

Note: This is NOT a tax-deductible contribution. You are essentially buying space in the credits of the film as a sponsor. If you use this space to promote your business, it may be deductible as a business expense; please consult your tax accountant. We appreciate your support!

Send to:
Quality of Life Film, LLC
525 Mandana Blvd. #310, Oakland, CA 94610
Questions: 415-543-5504 or email us: team@qualityoflife-themovie.com

---

Brant: I'm glad—at least—that Google has NO idea what "pushing down a chubby" means either.

QoL: Did you just do a goggle search?

Brant: So what else was different from what you expected?

QoL: Fundraising. Honestly I thought more people would be down for it. But that has been one of the most valuable learning experiences for me. I have a tendency to assume that people understand my vision without me having to go to great lengths explaining. Almost like they just trust that I know what I'm doing. But that kind of respect is EARNED not given. So *QoL* has taught me to work harder to explain the vision, in the script, business plan, pitch, etc. It's a skill, one that really doesn't come naturally to me.

Brant: Well, even though you often say I'm the business guy on the team, the reality is that you're the best "salesperson" for the film, to press, investors, whomever. Your passion and authenticity and clarity is obvious. You're a powerful guy. Anyone who steps into their truth is.

Brant: How was it living 800 miles from your production office?

QoL: It was absolute hell. But the internet saved me. It's funny, the very thing that chased me out of the Bay—the dot.com boom—is what enabled me to run a business from 800 miles away.

QoL: Co-run, that is (-;

QoL: Suffice it to say, the commute has been brutal.

QoL: And without question, the project has suffered.

Brant: Yeah, the net saved us. But it was really tough on me having you so far away. I think we could have raised all the money months ago if you were here . . . to say nothing of the publicity and outreach/speaking opportunities . . .

Brant: Not trying to harp on you, just saying it like it is, for those who will follow . . .

QoL: Yeah, it is definitely a huge obstacle.

QoL: But like so much of this project, we made the best of it. "It is what it is" was a *QoL* mantra.

Brant: Yup. We said that all during production (and before) . . . and then Lane ad libs it in that one scene with Lisa. It was perfect. The behind-the-scenes mantra makes it onto the screen.

QoL: Kind of like this interview. We'd like readers to be interested. But it is what it is.

Brant: So why do you think people didn't believe in this project more? Investors, distributors, (more) festivals?

Brant: (FU, BTW)

QoL: Art is subjective. It's very difficult to evaluate. The only objective measures are talent and budget. Names and cash. We had neither. Nor did we have experience, quite frankly. As far as festivals go, we didn't look like the other films. We were gritty and raw. But so was *Blair Witch*. I don't really know. So many factors went into our festival rejections: lack of connections, misunderstood youth audience, extremely competitive marketplace. I have no regrets, though. We took the best path. We have learned so much. Can you imagine if someone else had been at the wheel this whole time, telling us what to do?

Brant: Basically, by the numbers, we should have folded up the tent and gone home a LONG time ago.

Brant: I think that's what really defines the independent artist (filmmaker, musician, etc.): we don't ask permission. We just find a way to do it.

QoL: No shit. There were a lot of good films at the festivals that didn't get picked up. And the filmmakers get so discouraged. No one wants to put in the same level of labor and love all over again for the same piece of work.

QoL: We're freaking masochists.

Brant: Yes, that's what's different with us. Maybe it's a congenital flaw: we've been hurt, bruised and beaten. And now we're back for more: distribution.

Brant: I will say this though . . .

QoL: I love the pace. I'm excited to learn more about all aspects of filmmaking.

Brant: I was working on the end credits today. Typing in the final "thank yous" and so on.

Brant: And you look through the list of people who worked on this project over the past few years—and you think of the many more who will help with distribution—all for basically no money (or damn close).

QoL: Pretty inspirational.

Brant: It really is amazing to me the hundreds of people who stepped up.

Brant: It's like we're marching up this mountain, heads down, working our asses off and then we look back and we see both how high we've gotten (what a view) and jesus, there's a fucking army following us!

QoL: Are they shooting at us?

Brant: Quick, let's duck into this theater . . .

Brant: So what's your advice for filmmakers who want to do what we did?

QoL: Don't do it.

Brant: Word.

Break dancing exhibition

Boys do break dancing at corner of Woodman Avenue and Burbank Boulevard Friday night. Break dancing is a new style of dance done by young people in which they spin like tops. Above Anthony Jones, 16, dances into the night and below Ben Morgan, 14, tries his variation. Both boys are members of Cold Crush Crew, a break dancing group.

42

Lane Garrison
ACTOR (MIKEY "HEIR" ROSARIO)

JULY 26, 2005

QoL: Waddup, homey? BUZZ!!!

Lane: ok--let's DO IT.

QoL: Word.

QoL: Alright, let's dive in.

QoL: So how did you first hear about the film?

QoL: Hello? Are you typing one-handed or what?

Lane: My roommate and best friend who has known me my whole life was working as an assistant to a manager and saw a breakdown from casting. He immediately called me and said there is a gritty indie film that you are perfect for.

Lane: FU

QoL: So it wasn't directly via your agent?

Lane: No. At the time I didn't even have an agent. So when I got the job, my best friend suddenly became my manager. It was really a great moment for both of us.

QoL: That's great.

QoL: So how did you get the sides for the audition?

Lane: He called Belinda, the casting director, and pitched who I was. She then set up an audition and faxed him over the sides to fax to me.

QoL: What did you think when you saw the sides (or script)?

Lane: I thought it was, no bullshit, the freshest piece of material I had read all year. I was so used to reading WB crap that just never fit my personality and when I got the whole script I said, "I'm doing this movie!"

QoL: Not to pump myself (or Brian) up, but we got that comment a lot. That it felt real, unlike the bullshit all these actors were so used to reading.

QoL: Why is it that Hollywood can't seem to produce authentic material?

QoL: It doesn't seem like rocket science.

Lane: Because the studios are now controlled by larger corporations and have to answer to shareholders. So if they can't have an action figure that can be placed in McDonald's and marketed to the world they're not going to make the movie. Sadly, it's all about cash and not the story.

QoL: Two hands on the typing, bro. Seriously. Let go of the shaft for a few minutes. I'm on the clock here.

Lane: I had to run to the bathroom dick

QoL: Of course the bottom line is going to drive the creative process to some extent. If they don't see returns on their investments, no more movies. But I just can't figure out why authenticity is not valued as an asset. Authenticity = butts in seats (when combined with drama, performances, and execution, of course).

Lane: I agree. And in actuality that's why the studios are beefing up their specialty divisions like Fox Searchlight.

QoL: True. Anyway, back to you. We were instantly moved by your read. I was looking for someone who could read REAL, not perform, which was an incredible challenge. How was it that you felt so natural in this role?

Lane: Well I grew up like these kids, I knew these kids and immediately related to every word that they were saying in the script. Because I myself grew up feeling hopeless, like you're not going to make it out of this environment so you might as well cause as much harm and do as much damage as possible because you're not going to make it out anyway.

QoL: That's heavy. That's def what drove Brian and I as well.

QoL: So, we had grandiose visions of raising a bunch of money and doing this movie right.

QoL: And when we released the breakdown, we really envisioned it as a $1M picture.

QoL: But, since we refused to yield creative control, we ended up with a much scaled budget.

QoL: What was your perspective of the project as an outsider reading that first breakdown and how did that evolve as you were drafted into the trenches?

Lane: It wouldn't have been the same movie with a bunch of cash. That was part of the authenticity of guerilla film making and not knowing if we could even complete the film.

Lane: Well when I first read the breakdown I was reading for the role of Vain. And that is actually the part that I booked. So I had prepared that role all the way up until I got to San Fran. Then you told me I was going to play Heir. I had to do a 180 and throw everything, out which I think was the best thing to do.

Lane: I have more . . .

Lane: As for getting in the trenches, we were there. We moved into a shitty flat in the Mission District, shaved my head and lived just like my character would have—it wasn't a pretty existence.

QoL: What about your financial expectations?

QoL: At what point did you realize that this was going to be a ghetto ass indie with no money?

Lane: You always think when you're going on location that it's going to be the most lavish thing. Hotels, town cars, groupies etc. But this was completely ghetto and I knew there was going to be no money when I saw where we were staying.

QoL: I tried to be as clear about this as possible.

QoL: But still, actors have expectations.

QoL: You were such a trooper. We put you in the grimmest conditions. Most actors would have bailed (or bitched) long ago. How did living the way you did during production (in the Mission, no money, partying with Brian, etc.) affect your performance?

Lane: Shit . . . I'm glad it wasn't like that. It would have felt fake. The whole key to the film was making it feel real and everything we did accomplished that. And I think that ties in for the second part of your question. Living in a dirty flat with Brian and meeting the real characters changed everything for me and my performance. You actually have tangible people that you can watch and take words and movements from.

QoL: We knew we couldn't turn you into a writer overnight. But we did want you to have a genuine understanding of that world.

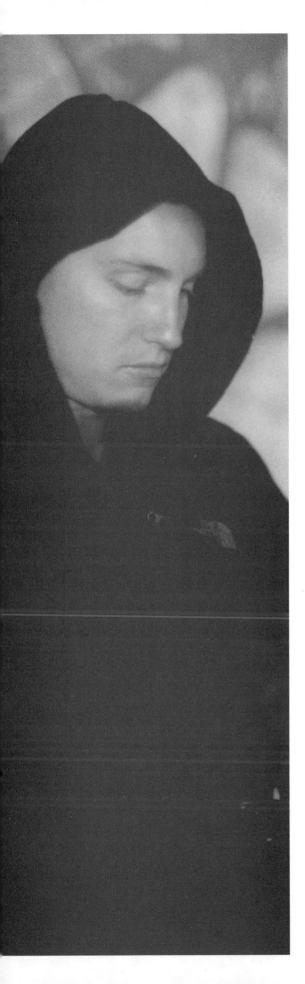

How was it hanging with Brian?

Lane: CRAZY!!! Writers live in the night and sleep during the day. They are modern day vampires. At first it was hard for me to hang but I quickly went back to my roots where I didn't give a damn and would go all night right into shooting.

QoL: That HAD TO have an impact on your performance.

Lane: To give you an example, in the opening of the film, Heir has been out all night painting and then has overslept for work. I really fell asleep in that bed because I was out all night with Brian.

QoL: I remember that. I actually asked you to go ahead and try and sleep while we set up. I think you actually caught some Zs.

QoL: are you typing?

Lane: No I'm waiting on you.

QoL: All the homies were down for this project since day one. Although writers are really skeptical of outsiders, they totally took you in. Everyone was really supportive. That was a huge asset to the project: to have the community let you in and observe and abosrb.

Lane: I was skeptical of how they would perceive me when I first got there. A long-haired sunshine actor from Hollywood. But when they got to know me and all that I had been through in life and where I was from they let me right in.

QoL: Speaking of hanging with the homies. Brian is a tough act to follow. He's a full-throttle kind of guy. You guys must have had some wild times together.

QoL: you typing?

Lane: Yeah you could say that. Our first night out, he hooks me up with this girl and sends me away with her. Little did I know that was his version of initiation.

QoL: Tell me about the infamous tranny bar incident.

Lane: I just told this story yesterday and had people crying from laughter. We wrapped shooting and Brian tells me that everyone is headed over to a bar down the street. I forget the name of it. But I said cool, I'm just going to change and I'll meet you guys over there. So I head over and throw open the doors and walk right into this bar. It was like a scene out of a movie because the music literally stopped as I found myself in the middle of a Mexican tranny bar! Needless to say, I hightailed it out of there where Brian was standing across the street laughing his ass off.

QoL: Classic. What a douchebag. You gotta love Brian.

Lane: I laughed about it because that was the sort of relationship Heir and Vain had. We were best friends while we were shooting.

QoL: You guys totally became those characters.

Lane: That's why I think it worked that our roles were switched. Our personalities fit with our characters.

QoL: See? Never question the mastermind.

QoL: I'm always curious how my directing style affects actors. I try to be clear in pre-production that I don't want to over-rehearse or over-shoot and that I want performances to be natural. But does it piss you off to only be able to do one or two takes? Or does it help performances somehow?

Lane: Well the whole motto for graffiti is get in, paint, get out. And that style of shooting I thinked worked really well. We knew we would be lucky with two takes. I think it helped our performance because we stayed on our toes.

QoL: So, jump forward: what did you think when you saw the first cut of the film? Was it what you were expecting?

Lane: No. Honestly because we had shot the film so quickly I wasn't expecting anything to be good. And then I saw the first cut of the film and couldn't believe what we had pulled off in 18 days!!

QoL: It's funny. I think I was the only one who was disappointed. Everyone seemed really surprised.

Lane: Why?

QoL: Your performance, mostly.

Lane: You dick!

QoL: No, there were just so many things that I wish we could have done differently.

QoL: It wasn't really about money, but manpower.

Lane: I get that. (Like Dino says . . . You can't change the past.)

QoL: Having my entire production staff working day jobs resulted in me being really torn and distracted.

QoL: Yup.

QoL: "It is what it is" was our motto on set.

QoL: And you actually improv'd that into your scene with Lisa (when you tell her Curtis had been fired).

Lane: I think we were discussing the location right before we shot the scene. And you said, "It is what it is." I thought that was a perfect way to look at the scene.

QoL: That's funny. There was definitely a contagious sense of spontanaeity. I was really glad that you were flexible and adept enough to incorporate that into your performance.

Lane: I was glad that you were a director who would allow that freedom. It really helped the trust I had for you in helping me get to dark places.

QoL: Thanks, man. The respect was mutual.

QoL: What was the worst thing about working on this movie?

QoL: Maybe start with . . .

QoL: What was the best thing about working on this movie?

Lane: The best thing about working on this film was losing myself and going back to my roots and dealing with issues that I never fully dealt with. It helped me mend a relationship with my father before he passed away. He was just like Pops and everytime I did a scene with Luis I thought of my real dad and all of his pain and struggles.

QoL: Wow. That's heavy. Your father passed away last year?

Lane: Yeah last July. He was a painter and an artist as well.

QoL: Wow. It's amazing how connected you were to this material. That really came through in the auditions.

QoL: That should be a lesson to aspiring actors: Always bring who you are to your read.

Lane: It was one of those things that you just feel in your gut . . . you have to feel it!

QoL: So, as we've discussed, we clearly put you through hell on this project. But we agreed that it helped in some way. But what stood out as the bunkest moment? Was there something at any time that made you feel like,

QoL: "Fuck this. I'm over this thing"?

Lane: Not to sound like a Zen master but . . . I don't look at things like that. The only time I was ever frustrated was when we shot the scene in the tunnels. I know when something is forced and not working and want to make sure, for the good of the film, that it works.

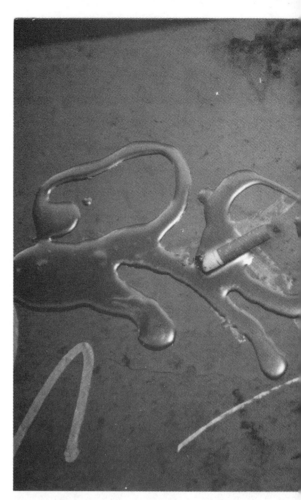

Above. TOP.R. Smoke em' if you got em!

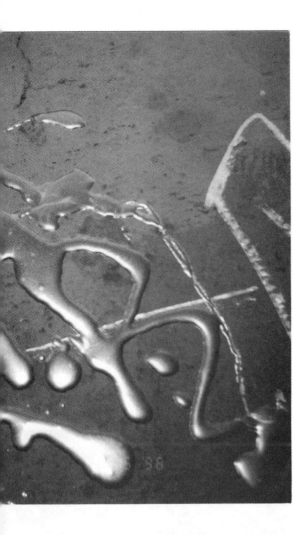

QoL: sorry. my computer just froze up.

QoL: That was the first (and only) time I remember you snapping. We had backloaded the schedule with all of these locations that we couldn't secure during production. So we have like 3 days of shooting to do in one night. And many of them were the toughest shoots. I was totally rushing that scene. And you snapped. I knew you were onto something, or else you wouldn't have lost it.

QoL: And we ended up re-shooting the scene later.

QoL: So what's on your agenda these days?

Lane: Well I just completed another film called *Crazy* with Ali Larter. It's based on the true story of Hank Garland, he was a famous guitar player from the 50's, and now I'm writing another screenplay.

QoL: You sold a screenplay to Maverick Films (Madonna's company) when you were what, 22? What's the new one about?

Lane: Yeah, I was 22 and then I wrote another movie called *Succubus* for MGM which was recently bought by Sony. The new script is actually a turn from my darker side. It's an action comedy in the vein of *True Lies*. I could tell you the title but then I'd have to kill you.

QoL: You're a badass.

Lane: No my friend, you are!

QoL: We can say we knew you when . . .

Lane: I hope that's never the case. I hope you can say I know that actor and he's a good guy, no ego.

QoL: Yeah, right. Save the bullshit, Hollywood guy.

QoL: I'll have to arrange lunches through your manager.

Lane: Ok fine. I'm actually at the Skybar right now sipping a martini.

QoL: Well, it was an absolute pleasure working with you, Lane. Aside from the phenomenal performance on the screen that everyone can see (and raves about), your attitude behind the scenes kept this train moving every day. We absolutely would not have been able to make this movie without you.

QoL: Thanks for slumming it with us.

QoL: Now get back to your martini.

Lane: Wouldn't have changed it for the world. Keep it REAL!!

QoL: I'll tell your boys at the tranny bar you said what's up!

Lane: Speak to a guy named Raul, he wears the pink tutu. He'll take care of you.

QoL: I'll bet he will.

QoL: "Give me the Lane special."

Brian Burnam

SCREENWRITER AND ACTOR (CURTIS "VAIN" SMITH)

SEPTEMBER 1, 2005

QoL: So, Mr. Jetsetter, you're finally back from your trek around the globe. We were starting to wonder if we'd ever see you again.

QoL: Where were you?

Brian: Yeah, it's been nice. I've been living in London and traveling to film festivals. Sweden, Spain, Germany, England . . .

QoL: How did you end up in London?

Brian: Well initially Bryan Dawson and I went to Stockholm for a festival in Nov. After 12 days in Stockholm, Bryan returned to the States and I went on to Gijon, Spain for another festival. I had a round trip ticket flying to and from Stockholm. A good friend of mine was living in Barcelona, so I went to see him. To make it short, I missed my return and decided to go to London. I knew if I went home I wouldn't make it back for some time. It worked out though; it was convenient when we were invited to other European festivals. I wouldn't have been able to attend had I come back to the States.

QoL: A lot of us felt that the film could actually perform stronger overseas (esp. in Europe). What was the response in Stockholm?

Brian: It was great. Everyone who worked for the festival was really nice. Theaters were full. We had so much fun. People really anticipated seeing the film. A group of local artists held an event at the club below our hotel. There were a few live acts, and a packed house.

QoL: How about Gijon? How was Spain?

Brian: Gijon was nice. Plenty of cidreria and tapas. It's a beautiful city with really nice people. The screenings went great there as well. A local youth group held a graff event in the park following one of them. Being solo wasn't a problem at all. There were plenty of events the promoters planned and I was well busy.

QoL: I heard they sold out that first Gijon screening a month in advance. How did the graff event go? And what about screenings? Any notable celebs come to our screenings?

Brian: Yeah Traci Lords was there. She was jocking though. As for the theatres . . . they did sell out. Standing room only. The event was cool. Spanish kids are a trip.

QoL: Shut up. Tracy Lords, forrilla?

Brian: Well she looked like her—I only saw her from behind though.

QoL: Gotcha. Let's back up a bit, shall we? How did you get involved with the project?

Brian: It's funny. I had been living in S.F. for close to ten years when I decided it was time for a change. I had bought a ticket to N.Y. and was planning on giving it a shot. I went to visit my family up in Northern California for a few weeks to save some bread before I bounced. 2 weeks before my departure you called me with a script you had been working on. I hadn't heard from you in like ten years. You harassed me up until I was about to split and convinced me to stay. I cancelled my trip and decided to work with you. That's when I started writing.

QoL: It was crazy. I knew you had been involved with graffiti a little bit, but so had I, to a much lesser extent. Honestly I had no idea how deep you were. I was just calling a friend who I respected to ask for feedback. I remember you were a little cautious at first with your feedback.

Brian: Yeah, it was your shit man, and I was out of here. I remember being nice to you. Those were the days weren't they?

QoL: Ah, I remember it well.

Brian: The deciding factor for me to stay was when you told me, "Brian there's no such thing as too much feedback, break my heart." That's when I let you have it, and you invited me to work.

QoL: Yeah, I wasn't interested in being nice. I remember telling you that you couldn't hurt my feelings. And that's when it started raining notes.

Brian: That's when I felt I could make a contribution to the film, and realized I needed to return to SF.

QoL: And your insight wasn't just into the graffiti world. Obviously that was key. (And when you & I went to the city together, I understood how deep you were in the culture.) But you had a natural sense of character, pacing, and drama.

QoL: Had you ever written anything before?

Brian: I bought a journal December 2000. I thought it would be a good idea to have one beginning with the millennium. There are only 3 entries in it today—so no. not much writing under my belt. *Quality of Life* gave me the opportunity to try my hand at it.

QoL: Just a natural huh? Kind of like with your square dancing!

Brian: I don't dance, and I only wrote what I knew.

QoL: So, you and I cranked away on the script for months. And you started writing scenes. You definitely made it a more contemporary story, in terms of graffiti. My script was very dated in terms of language and culture. But the main thing that you brought to the script was the human element. I remember you slamming me because every scene was about graffiti. You were like, "We go to the movies. We do other things." I totally attribute the depth of the story and characters to you. I can't imagine what this movie would have been like if I hadn't made that call.

Brian: Yeah thank God they went to the cinema in the film. What would it have been like if they didn't do that?

QoL: That was pretty much the sum of your contribution. The Roxie/poop scene. Deep.

Brian: It's deep man.

QoL: I'm done kissing your ass. But it's true that you made these characters REAL and focused the story on human relationships, as opposed to just graffiti, which, interestingly enough, is what the average reader kept demanding.

Brian: I couldn't tell you what the average reader kept demanding. All I know is the script was written for my peers and my city. This film is a conglomeration of true stories that come from San Francisco and that are still being played out to this day. It's not an easy place to come up in.

QoL: All along, you wanted to play one of the leads. I was opposed to it for a few reasons: 1) You and I bicker too much. Can't have that dysfunctional family thing on set. 2) Screenwriters are never allowed on set. It becomes the director's vision at that point. Having the screenwriter around will cloud the vision of the

film. 3) You had never acted before. But then fate took over and you were hurled into the lead role at the last minute.

Brian: True, and the opposite role I desired to play. It worked out for the best though. I don't really identify with the role of Mikey as much as I do Curtis. I guess I just wanted to play the protag, since the attitude of Curtis hits so close to home. I kind of hoped to grow out of some shit as I played that role. But I feel now in retrospect that I achieved the same goal. I guess in a sense I killed the negative part of myself when I killed Curtis. Can we turn this fucking interview into a self-help book now or what?

QoL: You had begged for this role. But when you finally got it, you seemed a little scared. Was it the short notice? Or did you suddenly go, "Oh shit. This is is a huge f'ing commitment!"

Brian: You're a motherfucker for this! For months I told you I wanted to play a part, you said no every time, told me I could have a cameo. Thanks friend. Then a week before production you tell me your man backed out and I was in. Shit, you didn't even want me on the set, then you're giving me a lead—so yeah there was some pressure. First of all I'm writing about my sub-culture (for someone else to direct); that's a tight fucking rope. If it gets screwed up that's bad. Then all of a sudden I'm playing the part. If it doesn't come off, that's devastating! A lot was on the line. I have never done anything like this before so naturally I was concerned.

QoL: It was one of those things. In my heart, I knew you could do it. But my mind was playing tricks on me. When the other guy dropped out (he allegedly got some 6-figure tv deal), I was re-lieved. A big smile broke out across my face. The producers were tripping, but my response put everyone at ease. I knew it was meant to be. Can't fight fate, you know?

Brian: Yeah, I was destined to die.

QoL: It was funny because all of the stuff I worried about was absolutely true. You and I DID fight on set every day. And it WAS unhealthy for morale. But it was always in the best interest of the film. I understood what was on the line for you and why you were tripping so hard. I knew that the pressure was on you to make sure the shit came off, so, although it was brutal for everyone, I heard you out.

Brian: Yeah except for that time you ran out of Q-tips.

QoL: It's called selective listening.

QoL: Seriously though. Brawling or not, the movie was better off for it. Our actor friend would not have brought that.

Brian: Not even if Shaq was with him.

QoL: Oops. That's the closest we have ever come to revealing his identity. Classic. I remember at one point in one of our many on-set battles, you said, "I don't want to make 420." I was blown away that you actually thought even for a second that we were still in student film mode. You obviously respected Kev and Lane a great deal. What did you think you were getting yourself into?

Brian: Yeah. I read your original script, and had seen your mov-ies. (Since we're done kissing ass) you've come a long way. No disrespect. I wouldn't be here if it weren't for you and Brant. But like I said, there was a lot on the line. A lot of high hopes and a lot of worries. I think it's safe to say we broke even with our ex-pectations. Kev is great. Really easy to work with and supportive. He helped me get through to you on plenty of ideas. Lane's cool too; the fact that his role was switched a week prior to production gave us both the same pressure when on the set. He handled it well.

QoL: Yeah, he did. It was definitely the right call. Lane is obvi-ously a "traditional" actor and you're a natural first-timer. But you guys both had an incredible ability to stay in the moment.

What was it like working with him?

Brian: It was fun. He knew the script well and we mostly just ad-libbed each scene. We lived together for the shoot and had a good time.

QoL: What was your first response when you saw some scenes at Sharon's house?

Brian: I was pumped. I remember watching the first rough cut and thinking, "Damn, we actually got a movie."

QoL: Not 420 huh?

Brian: Not exactly.

QoL: Then we got into Berlin and shit started rolling. How was the Berlin experience? Had you ever been overseas?

Brian: No I hadn't. That was the shit. The festival was huge. We spent 9 days there and were about to come home when we were told we had won an award. We extended our tickets and stayed for the ceremonies. That was pretty big.

QoL: And all the other films had budgets. We were definitely the punk band at the talent show. Felt pretty validating to walk away with an award.

Brian: Yeah I remember inviting other actors to watch our film but they just never made any of the screenings. At he awards ceremony they shit their pants when *Quality of Life* was called onstage.

QoL: We pushed you really hard to let us use "former graffiti writer" in our press materials. But you were really opposed to it. But at the first Q&A in Berlin, you caved. There was obviously some heavy shit going down in SF with warrants and everything. But what was the resistance about and why the change of heart?

Brian: Well I wasn't in SF. At the time I wasn't looking to be spot-lit by the vandal squad back home.

QoL: How has the reaction been from your friends (esp writers)?

Brian: As for my friends, they're feeling it. Those who have seen it. I'm sure there will be some haters but screw them. This wasn't for them.

QoL: I think ultimately your motivation to not wack out in front of your friends was one of the hardest driving factors in making this movie come off. Was it a huge incentive for you?

Brian: Yeah it was. Definitely. Not just my friends but San Francisco as a whole. There were a lot of things in the city I wanted to incorporate. Some showed support while others did not. I just hoped to represent S.F. as much as I could. Some of that I achieved, while some I didn't.

QoL: Well, I think the tension between you and me and all the bickering paid off. It was hell, but the end result benefited.

QoL: What's next for Brian Burnam? You writing? Scripts, that is?

Brian: Yeah this whole experience has really got me going. I've learned a lot from it and am currently working on a project of my own. The shit ain't easy though.

QoL: You ain't lying! Look forward to seeing it. I'll give you some feedback. But only if I can star in it.

Brian: I'll give you a cameo.

QoL: You got a Dirk Diggler kind of character?

Brian: There's a part where this con tries to fuck his new inmate.

QoL: BLACK ACTING SCHOOOL!

Brian: You're the inmate.

QoL: Do I have to toss his salad?

QoL: I prefer syrup.

QoL: A lot of filmmakers cringe about distribution. But I'm actually really excited about it. How are you feeling? You ready for the plunge?

Brian: Ready? Shit, I gave up. That's why I stayed in Europe for a year. I didn't want to come home till this shit dropped. One thing I learned is this stuff takes time. I'm ready.

QoL: No kidding. We were ready to release this time last year. It's tough when you're working a day job and have no money or studio backing. But I'm looking forward to working with you again . . . Well, not really.

Brian Yeah man, fuck Hollywood . . . I mean fuck you.

QoL: No, no. Fuck YOU!

Brian came home from Europe after he saw this photo. According to Jase it was the only thing he missed.

Mackenzie Firgens
ACTOR (LISA)

AUGUST 29, 2005

QoL: yo!

Mackenzie: hello

QoL: what's up, big mac?

Mackenzie: nothin getting ready for Burning Man!

QoL: who isn't?

Mackenzie: yeah—i've never been.

Mackenzie: i'm also downloading some new music!

Mackenzie: how are you doing?

QoL: great!

QoL: but slammed.

QoL: theatrical is eating me alive.

QoL: well, the day job is eating me alive.

Mackenzie: yeah?

Mackenzie: how so?

Mackenzie: ah

QoL: movie is KEEPING me alive.

Mackenzie: as it should.

QoL: just not enough hours in the goddamn day, you know?

Mackenzie: YES I hear ya for sure.

QoL: so you ready to do this?

Mackenzie: I can only imagine how it will be for me the day I make my own films . . .

Mackenzie: sure

QoL: Let's dive in . . .

Mackenzie: Sounds good.

QoL: So how did you get involved with *QoL*?

Mackenzie: I first saw an ad for *QoL* on the Film Arts board and they were looking for crew. Since I was such a huge fan of graffiti art I contacted the production team and just sent in an email letting them know that I loved the art form and was very interested in being a part of the film.

QoL: It was funny beacuse Greg Harrison was a mentor of ours, so I obviously was familiar with your work (from *Groove*). Def some synchronicity working there.

Mackenzie: There was a lot of crazy synchronicity in this film—especially in casting.

QoL: And you had a late-night audition, no?

Mackenzie: That's right, I came down to the office really late. I remember I wanted to be Lisa so bad. I had my first audition a month before and I literally had every person I knew trying to find out how casting was going. Then I got the call to come in late one night to read with Lane and Brian.

QoL: I think you came in at midnight or something, right?

Mackenzie: Yes it was very very late. Really fun though to meet everyone and Lane and Brian. I was so nervous and tried very hard to keep all my emotions under control. I really wanted *QoL* to be the second movie I did, it really meant a lot to me.

Mackenzie: I remember the decision was to made the next day, and I was on another job the next day at Cisco handing out compasses, dressed in a safari outfit. I kept checking my messages every minute.

QoL: And we were psyched to bring you on board.

QoL: Did you have any idea what you were getting yourself into (in terms of LOW/NO budget)?

Mackenzie: I had worked on *Groove* and some other films before, but I had never done any guerilla kind of films. It was really thrilling and a great learning experience. I really like this style of filming because you get to really create a team and unit and there is a sense of family that can come from it.

QoL: I remember feeling like such a sap the first day you showed up on set. You were like, "Where do I go for make-up?" I tried to be clear about expectation, but, due to time constraints, I dropped the ball sometimes. Were you kind of shocked day one?

Mackenzie: I was a little, but that is what filmmaking is all about—adapting, going with the flow. All films to me seem like a little obstacle course and we all just see how few we get through each day.

Mackenzie: It was also a great opportunity to really become a character and get to take more care about the look than you normally get on some films.

QoL: Totally. Filmmaking is just one big problem-solving expedition, at the end of the day.

Mackenzie: Yes.

QoL: Do you think we would have been better off with a bigger budget?

Mackenzie: Of course it's always wonderful to have a huge budget but it didn't seem necessary for this film. We didn't have any big special effects or any kind of action sequence, so I don't really think a huge budget would have made a difference. Ok, maybe a big luxurious trailer for the crew would have been nice, because of those super-long 12+ hour days.

QoL: I agree. Having more money would have made certain things a lot more bearable (i.e., it would have freed me up creatively b/c I wouldn't have to stress about props, locations, travel, accommodations). But, as you said, being small really contributed to the family atmosphere. Everyone was part of the team b/c we **NEEDED** everyone's help. There were very few buffers. You have done both big and small. What are the benefits to each?

Mackenzie: It's funny because when you come down to it, big-budget and small-budget films still end up having the same kind of challenges. Big-budget ones just seem to have more people to go through to solve a problem. There are some great pluses to the bigger budgets because you do have things like assistants and lots of P.A.s and transpo, and the list goes on and on. There is a lot of help on the big-budget ones. They also though, can lack a sense of community, and can really have a higher stress level. The smaller ones can be crazy and stressful, but somehow it's all a little easier cause it just comes with the territory. Call sheets

"One of the most moving pieces I've seen all year."
- John Petrakis, Chicago Tribune

Robot Stories

WINNER
OVER 23 AWARDS
including

SPECIAL JURY AWARD
FOR EMOTIONAL TRUTH,
Florida Film Festival

BEST SCREENPLAY
Hamptons Int'l
Film Festival

GRAND PRIZE
Rhode Island Int'l
Film Festival

BEST DIRECTOR
BEST ACTRESS
Puchon Fantastic
Film Festival

BEST SCREENPLAY
BEST ACTRESS
St. Louis
Film Festival

AUDIENCE AWARD
Boston Fantastic
Film Festival

BEST FEATURE FILM
Sci Fi London
Film Festival

Everything is changing...

... except the human heart

 PAK FILM SHOTWELL www.robotstories.net

---

are rare, times change at the last minute, scenes are added or deleted, but being a small team can make this all a lot easier. Communication can be more direct and things get solved easier.

QoL: Interesting.

QoL: Given what you/we went through on set, were you surprised by what you saw at the first cast & crew screening at the Roxie?

Mackenzie: I was very surprised, because for me every time I do a film I never know what it will look like in the end. I have my side of the camera and it's pretty rare I ever see a shot. For *QoL* I was blown away at the camera work Kev did and the whole look of it. It had these rich blacks and colors that as an actor you don't really get to see when you are doing a scene. I was very excited and I actually cried during the film! The story really has a lot of heart.

QoL: I always ask that question because I'm curious about what people's expectations were, especially during the chaos we all endured on set. Did the film exceed your expectaions? If so, what were you expecting? If not, what was it that you saw on set that let you to believe we were onto something?

Mackenzie: Well I have to say I went into the film without seeing any of your work yet, so I wasn't sure what to expect. I think I was so surprised because when you are on set and everyone is running around and grabbing shots when you can—its just so hard to tell if that will turn out. I remember the first scene I shot was with Lane sitting on the sidewalk and I remember we had some sound issues and when I saw the scene there was no issue at all. Then when I saw it, there was the shot that was so great with this pole in between us, creating an interesting mood.

QoL: i'm on a quick phone call (with lane). be right back

Mackenzie: As for being onto something, that is in the chemistry I think of the crew and actors. It's hard to put a finger on, but I could just tell from the performances and the people involved that there was something "good" here.

Mackenzie: Ok.

QoL: i'm back. sorry about that. needy actors, you know . . .

Mackenzie: LOL

QoL: So what are you up to these days?

Mackenzie: I just finished some ADR for *RENT*, which I was so blessed to be a part of. I am originating the role of April in the movie. The second trailer just came out and none of my friends recognize me because I have this short red hair for the film. Getting ready for the premiere on Nov 11 05. It's going to be a busy fall.

QoL: It took me a second to recognize you, too (in the trailer). I was surprised to hear it's coming out already. That was incredibly fast!

Mackenzie: I love looking different in every film I do, I get so excited when people don't recognize me. Talk about a fast turnaround! Another advantage of the big-budget films. They were editing while we were shooting, and also Chris works so fast too. We were picking up shots on many days that were scheduled later.

QoL: That's amazing.

Mackenzie: But you worked really fast too, didn't we shoot in just a few weeks?

QoL: Three weeks, yeah.

QoL: We could have been on that pace, too. But we were stalled by lack of funds.

Mackenzie: I did a film recently that stopped and then restarted when funds came through again.

QoL: Money's a bitch, I tell you.

Mackenzie: I think this can happen often in the indie scene. The journey is always so interesting because of it.

QoL: Word.

QoL: Even when we do have bigger budgets, I still want to maintain the indie structure. It breeds creativity and ingenuity.

QoL: Well, Big Mac, it has been a pleasure interviewing you. I'm really excited about distributing *Quality of Life*. I look forward to pounding the pavement with you (-;

Mackenzie: I agree. I have been eagerly awaiting this time. The heart and soul of this film is really strong and I think a lot of people are going to be surprised when they see the film. All the feedback I have gotten has been so positive. I look forward to the rest of the journey with you.

QoL: Ditto. You know how we always used the Mount Everest analogy during production?

QoL: Well the real journey is COMING DOWN. That's when most of the accidents occur.

Mackenzie: LOL

QoL: As Brant would say, we've achieved the impossible. Now comes the hard part.

Mackenzie: That's great!

QoL: Saddle up, little doggie!

QoL: Thanks again for the interview. You rock.

Mackenzie: I'm ready for the bump and grind!

Mackenzie: You too. See you soon.

QoL: Talk to you soon, Mac. Very soon.

QoL: OCT 12 BABY. MARK OUR CALENDAR!!!

Mackenzie: WHOO HOOO!

QoL: ciao . . .

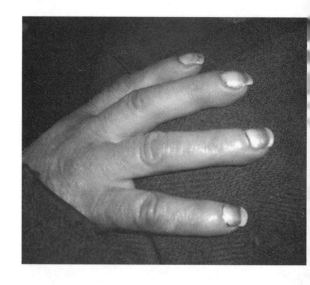

56

Tajai
ACTOR (DINO)

DECEMBER 23, 2005

QoL: What's up Tajai? What's the latest in the Hiero Imperium Universe?

Tajai: Chilling, getting ready for the new year and some new releases. About to do a European Tour.

QoL: That's hot. How many cities?

Tajai: 15 cities. It's Souls of Mischief and Zion I.

QoL: That's a hot ticket!

QoL: How long has Souls been together? Seems like forever.

Tajai: I have been making music with A Plus for about 22 years, and we have been the Souls of Mischief for about 16.

QoL: That's unheard of in the music business, or any entertainment field. How do you maintain a relationship for that long? What's the secret?

Tajai: We are friends first. Music is just one of the things we do together. Plus we are in control of our own careers, so there are no side-liners/execs, etc. who can pry us apart.

QoL: The relationship issue is huge, obviously. But talk about how being independent effects the flow of the business. How would it be different if you guys didn't control the creative and financial process from beginning to end?

Tajai: We would not have any music out. Our careers would have ended after our second album on JIVE, "No Man's Land." If you look at the music landscape, very few (read: zero) acts bounce back after being dropped from their label. Being Independent just makes it harder to compete with artists who have multi-billion dollar conglomerates backing them. However, we can at least show up to the game because we have a business and family that believes in our output.

QoL: It's the same with film. We can't get into the "right" theaters b/c distributors (which we don't have) bring multiple films (every MONTH!) and P&A budgets. We have neither. But we do have an audience that is writing us every day asking when/how they can see the movie. You guys have managed to successfully reach your core audience (you obviously have a rabid fan base-- without them the concept is dead in the water) without the backing of these powerful conglomerates. Do you see this as the wave of the future (esp with the internet)? Or are successful indie bands, filmmakers, etc. the aberration and the majors will rule forever?

Tajai: Touring is our "secret." Fortunately for us, music is still performance art, so we can go out and perform on any given night in any given locale and reach our fans. At that time we can promote our products. I think it may be a little harder with film, but perhaps a film "tour" where it is showed in different venues nightly would be helpful? I'll make the t-shirts! Seriously, the majors will always control most of the market share because "Cash Rules." But I think that the internet is helping to disseminate stuff. Plus, a lot of independent music and film is good, thought-provoking and inspiring. The major distributors/labels/film houses are churning out b.s. So maybe quality will prevail in the end.

QoL: Yeah, that's the trick. But the key element is the same for music and film: the venue. Somehow you have to be able secure a venue that can draw on its own, or else you end up doing all the work. As far as the mainstream coming around goes, I wish you were right about quality prevailing. But, if you take a look at where Gangsta rap has gone over the past 20 years. Artists are encouraged to "give the people what they want". Or at least give them what they think they want. Likewise, Hollywood will always churn out crap. But what I am hearing you say, as many independent artists from all walks of life are starting to say, is that there are alternative means to reach an audience. And, the most important thing is, there isn't an insurmountable point of entry anymore.

Tajai: Well, I believe that we have to look at the global market rather than just domestically. That is the wonder of the internet, fedex, etc. we can deliver product to the whole world. But as far as domestically...we are the highest ignorance to wealth ratio, so I don't really know how bright the future looks here with regard to products that make you think.

QoL: Sad, but true.

QoL: We have kind of taken it upon ourselves to disseminate this information. So many artists are afraid to show anyone their cards. We need to share knowledge and join together in this battle. Hold hands and sing "Kumbaya!"

QoL: OK. Maybe not the singing part, but we seriously do need to work together, esp now that communication is so immediate.

Tajai: Yeah, everyone wants the benefits of community without sharing. Still have the mainstream mindstate. The kids here are starting to wise up, though. I think the future is bright even at home.

QoL: Yeah, we've getting so much love from a handful of smart, savvy, and community-oriented companies (you guys, Quannum, etc.). There are enough of us to collectively make some shit happen. Maybe I'm still young and naive, but I really do believe the revolution is upon us. And the internet is a key component of this. How has the internet affected how Hiero does business?

Tajai: We use it as one of our main resources for promotion, and we sell a bunch of shirts and specialty items from the Hiero Emporium online. Still, the majority of our sales are from brick-and-mortar stores.

QoL: So your bread-and-butter still comes from traditional outlets? Do you foresee that changing at all?

Tajai: I don't know. I buy my music at the store. But I release my artists' (on Clear Label Records) singles digitally (mainly because singles are not flying off the shelves in any genre). I also go try on clothes at the store and then look on the internet to see if I can find them cheaper. I think in the Bay Area we are immersed in tech so we get a warped view of how much of a role computers play in people's consumer activity.

QoL: True. There is a lot of uncertainty about how far the internet will go. I'm the same way about clothes. And it's nice to go to a music store and listen, touch, and feel. But it's also really convenient to do it from your living room. That's why I love dvds so much. You can pause it, eat good, healthy, cheap food, watch in your draws, etc. But the point is, there is this "new" medium that allows artists to reach their audience directly, establish and maintain a relationship with them, and even do business with them. That's some powerful shit right there.

Tajai: Definitely. But I like the social aspect of going to the movies,

going to a concert, even going to the mall. I don't think that that will ever change for me.

QoL: I agree. I hope that aspect never changes. Folks need to get out and interract with other humans.

QoL: Let's talk about the movie for a minute. (Why not?) How did you get involved with the film? I didn't know you directly, but of course knew of you as a fan of your work. How did Belinda (our casting director) get a hold of you? And what was your first reaction to the script?

Tajai: Daria from the Hiero Imperium told me to come out, and when I did, I was thoroughly impressed with the premise, script, cast, director, etc. It is refreshing to do a "Hip Hop" film that isn't necessarily a "Hip Hop Film." Graf doesn't get the respect it deserves, and this film humanizes it while still being interesting.

QoL: You're an extremely intelligent (Stanford grad, no?) and spiritual cat. How did Dino's character resonate with you? How much of him is in you?

Tajai: I am not really as reflective, meditative or calm as Dino, but I am into spiritual progression/growth and maturity with regard to one's actions. I also have made a business out of my art so I do have some similarities.

QoL: The role definitely came natural to you. I think part of it was that Lane and Brian looked up to you in real life, respected who you were as an artist, businessman, and human being. You are someone who has done what both of them want to do for a living in real life (i.e. make a living from their art). So the respect was genuine. That def came off on screen.

Tajai: I am glad that you are happy with the performance, I was very nervous.

QoL: I sensed that when we first met. You had kind of a "what am I getting myself into?" distance in the 1st read. But I never had a doubt. Anyone who can grab a mic and do what you do can do anything on any stage. You were a rock, man. Totally tied the whole movie together. You get a lot of strong praise at screenings. People can't believe that you and Brian had never acted before.

Tajai: I hope a lot of people get the opportunity to see the movie, I really enjoyed it, and I want feedback from a variety of perspectives. Thanks for the opportunity!

QoL: It was my pleasure. We know what your performance has done (and will do) for us. I hope your involvement w/QoL helps keep your creative momentum moving in that steady forward progression you've been on for so many years.

Tajai: Hell yeah. When it finally does come out on DVD, please make a PSP version. I think a lot of the younger heads would pick that up and benefit from the lessons in the movie. The movie has a classic quality, so it's not tied to a specific timeframe. For real though, a tour with some of the acts from the soundtrack and showings would be dope. Maybe show the movie at 8 and then have cats rock afterwards...

QoL: That would be the shit. Really hard to coordinate (esp locking venues and artists, etc.). But we need to make that happen. Esp for NYC and LA (March-April). You down?

Tajai: Fa Sho! Even like, Souls and Lyrics Born, or something like that.

QoL: There's a billing!

QoL: Where do I sign up?!

Tajai: We will be back after January, probably do a snow tour in February and then we are free.

Tajai: I might be able to get someone to book the tour as well. At least in the major cities.

QoL: Seriously, a big part of what we want to do represent for the Bay. For filmmaking, art, and music. So much talent in this little densely-packed region of ours.

QoL: Let's take that discussion off-line and make it happen! That would be a beautiful thing!!!

Tajai: Definitely.

QoL: OK. I don't want to take any more of your time. Thanks for helping us get this thing off the ground, and now out to the world. Really enjoyed working with you and look forward to future synergy.

Tajai: One Love. You have my full support, feel free to call me whenever.

Tajai: I also can get at Mr. Lif for touring opportunities.

QoL: Oh shit! Now you're talking.

Tajai: Just let me know!

QoL: I love Mr Lif. There's an underrated artist if I've ever seen one.

Tajai: Yeah, but once again, you have to think when you listen to him.

QoL: Exactly.

QoL: That doesn't fly with everyone, for film and music alike.

Tajai: Sad state of affairs, but these younger kids I think are going to pick up the slack. They seem interested in learning, esp. with regard to entertainment and tech and how they intersect.

Tajai: Kids have pro tools and email in the classroom now.

QoL: I sure hope so. I'm not ready to dumb down my message for anyone.

Tajai: Hey, Jay Z made millions like that! lol

QoL: Oh right?

QoL: I'm going about this all wrong!

QoL: Dammit!

Tajai: haha

Tajai: I think he regrets it a little, even.

QoL: How can you not?

QoL: But then again, being able to feed your family for generations is pretty nice.

Tajai: Well, in the Hamptons they have this regret management system that seems to work pretty well.

QoL: Huh?

Tajai: Just kidding

QoL: Funny man.

QoL: Alright, man. Better wrap this up. To be continued in the next book (-;

Tajai: One love!

QoL: Thanks, Tajai. Keep fighting the good fight.

Tajai: You too.

QoL: Have a great holiday. Peace.

Tajai: Peace

QoL: See you at the movies!

Dave Lieberman
ACTOR (STICK-UP KID)

AUGUST 3, 2005

QoL: are you there?

Dave: yeah

QoL: There's my boy!

QoL: I may get pulled away, but let's see how far we can get.

Dave: alright i have never really done this so bear with me.

Dave: word

QoL: First, a couple ground rules.

Dave: sure

QoL: Please use proper punctuation (caps, etc.).

Dave: dude are you serious?

QoL: I know, very unchat-like, but I am going to cut and paste for the interview.

Dave: Alright.

QoL: Very nice.

QoL: 2nd, let's try not to type over each other whenever possible (so we can react to each other's msgs).

Dave: Like wait for each other to be done?

QoL: Yeah. It should say "Ben is typing" somewhere (down at the bottom?).

QoL: see, i'm typing. look at me. yay!

Dave: Yeah I understand.

QoL: Word.

QoL: Finally, I will give you an opportunity to review the interview before we publish.

Dave: Sounds good.

QoL: Let's dive in.

Dave: Handle it.

QoL: How did you become involved with *Quality of Life*?

Dave: I first got involved because I am friends with Brian. I went with him up to Portland for this hip-hop film festival where he was meeting up with you to talk about the script, I guess.

QoL: Yeah. That's when you & I first met as well.

QoL: Had you read the script before that trip?

Dave: Totally, and I didn't really know much or really think much of it at the time. It was more of just an excuse for a road trip. Soon I started seeing how serious everybody was, and I started getting pumped on the idea.

QoL: I think you actually saw a pretty raw version of the script, before Brian started re-writing. True?

Dave: Yeah it was there, but we were like driving and partying . . . I don't think I really read that much. Of course Brian would be ratteling on about it, but I mean that trip went in its own way . . . we could probably make a movie just about that.

QoL: I heard about that. What happened on the way home?

Dave: I went to jail overnight for speeding, driving with no license, and having a warrant for stealing spray paint. Then once I got out we continued back to Cali only to get snowed into a hick town where Brian tried to fight an off-duty cop, we got drunk, convinced the bar we were in a rock band, went home with the cute bartender . . . etc.

QoL: I had forgotten about the cute bartender part.

QoL: Brian called me from her house, I think.

QoL: You guys are pretty much rock stars.

QoL: Anywho, back to the movie.

QoL: Actually, some of the dialogue from the movie came from a conversation Brian had with his mom after that trip.

QoL: Some of the dialogue between Pops and Mikey in the van.

QoL: So, aside from being a creative consultant, we ended up casting you as the stick-up kid. You didn't really get much rehearsal or direction. But you pulled it off pretty well, considering you had never acted before.

QoL: The process was so chaotic for all of us. Throwing down the tracks ahead of the train, you know? How was the experience for you?

Dave: Well I would say crazy for sure. The dynamics between you and Brian were nuts . . . I think it was ultimately good, but at times it just seemed like arguing. It worked though.

QoL: That was my biggest reservation in casting Brian. We fight like brothers 24/7. And that shit is unhealthy on set. But I agree that it ended up working out because we were usually arguing about how to make the movie better.

QoL: How was that stick-up scene in the alleyway? We had no stunt coordinator or anything. And Brian had to plow you in the alleyway.

QoL: Wait that didn't come out right. You know what I mean.

Dave: Ha ha . . . well the nastiest thing I remember was having to lie in that alley and let Brian put his foot on my face . . . or maybe it was the mattress you guys found on the street for me to fall on. I mean that is hands down one of S.F.'s nastiest alleys, and this is a nasty city.

QoL: Where's Mr. Clean when you need him?!

QoL: You should have gotten hazard pay for that. I'll talk to your agent.

QoL: So you're headed to court on Monday. This has been a long ass battle for you. How long have you been in court over these charges?

Dave: I have been going to court for the same group of charges in S.F. and Oakland for the last 3 years.

QoL: Holy shit.

QoL: Who else was facing charges with you?

Dave: There were like 7 other people, members of my crew K.U.K.

QoL: And most of them had their own attorneys (i.e., not public defenders), right?

Barry McGee collection.

Dave: Yeah pretty much.

QoL: Did that help, having all of those attorneys against one DA?

Dave: Totally . . . I mean we have gotten a lot charges down . . . tired out a few D.A's and a lot of people have gotten off.

QoL: You were originally facing like 2 yrs in state prison. Was everyone looking at prison time?

Dave: Not everybody . . . me and like one other guy pretty much. He still is actually, I'm on like my 4th bail right now, but unfortunately the other guy can't get his together right now and has been in for like the last 4 months. They are trying to give him 16 months right now.

QoL: Crazy. And they came with some bullshit gang charges at one point, didn't they?

Dave: Yeah they still are. We got that charge dropped, but the D.A. took it to appeals and we lost. That is one of the more serious charges cause it is a felony and it adds an automatic year to your sentence.

QoL: WTF makes it a gang charge?!

Dave: A group of people all getting together to commit a crime. I mean it usually applies to violence or drug sales, or using violence to control drug sales I guess. On paper though it can translate to about anything. It's actually kind of a big deal . . . cause if we took it to trial and got convicted we would be the first in California and it would set a precedent and affect all cases in the future. So for that reason it has kind of gotten a lot of attention.

QoL: That's just madness. That's how quality of life laws started in the first place. They wanted to treat non-violent crimes (i.e. drugs, prostitution, and graffiti) as more serious offenses. It's such a misguided politically driven approach.

QoL: So these gang charges are still hanging out there. And you go to court on Monday. How are things looking?

63

Dave: I will most likely just take a deal Monday that doesn"t include the gang charge. The state doesn't really want to go to trial . . . but they will, and I don't want to go cause if I lose then I will go to prison, but I can plead guilty to a few of the graffiti charges and get county time . . . a few weeks ago they said a year, but my lawyer says on Monday it will be more like months. So I am just going to take it.

QoL: You obviously broke the law. Do you think jail time is appropriate for graffiti-related crimes?

Dave: No. And I meant to write 6 months, not just months.

QoL: Why not? What WOULD be appropriate?

Dave: I think that people put too much value on property. Putting someone in jail for something that can just be painted over seems excessive. My differences in opinion with the rest of the country run quite deep, so I understand if they don't agree with me.

QoL: Especially when you look at crimes that have ruined people's lives. Like what Enron, Citigroup, et al are doing. Stealing people's pension funds and shit.

QoL: Do you think there's any hope of turning this get tough on crime climate around? If so, how?

Dave: No, I don't think that the "get tough on crime climate" will ever change.

QoL: It's all about who has the money.

QoL: The crimes that are being committed by rich people are not considered "quality of life crimes." But they RUIN people's lives.

David Lieberman from a scene in Clarion Alley.

Dave: Definitely. That's the reality of the situation.

QoL: If you would have had Johnny Cochrane, you probably would have gotten off in the first week.

Dave: Of course.

QoL: Well, Braeden (my 2 month old) is yelling at me.

Dave: Okay.

QoL: Good luck on Monday. Our thoughts and prayers are with you.

Dave: Thanks.

QoL: Don't be surprised to see a gang of us with :"FREE DAVE" shirts on marching at City Hall.

Dave: Rad.

QoL: We'll start an ABHOR fan club. They'll bring in laundry bags full of mail for your ass.

QoL: Get out in time to tour with us, homey. Need to make up for missing Berlin and Stockholm!

Dave: Definitely.

QoL: Take care, man. Thanks for the interview. And thanks for working on the movie.

QoL: Peace.

Dave: Bye.

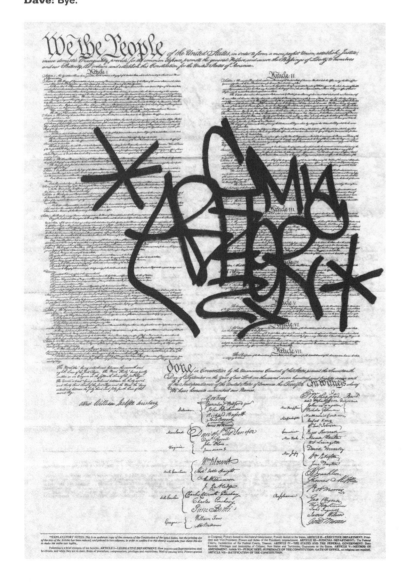

Meika Rouda
PRODUCER

JULY 7, 2005

QoL: Alo?

Meika: Hey.

QoL: Wow. Look at us.

Meika: So advanced!

QoL: And punctual!

Meika: Of course.

QoL: How did you find out about the film?

Meika: I found out about the film through craigslist.

Meika: There was a posting for a UPM and a Marketing Director job and I applied for both.

QoL: And ended up doing neither.

Meika: Right.

Meika: When I met Ben and Brant—we clicked.

QoL: You kind of came in and said, "Hmm. Those both suck."

Meika: Right. Actually, my husband had been a graffiti artist in the late 80's in SF so the script really resonated with me and I wanted to help however I could.

QoL: Back to the posting . . . What attracted you to it? There are shitloads of postings on craigslist. Was it this? The graffiti element, or what?

Meika: I think any feature work in SF attracts me since there isn't a ton of production going on.

Meika: When I read what the subject matter was, I was hooked.

QoL: And we were hooked on you (-;

Meika: And after I read the script I knew I wanted to be a part of the project.

Meika: Ben and Brant were very clear about their vision for the film

Meika: and the script was great.

QoL: Your experience was key, and you made a great impression in the interview. But the fact that your husband was a writer definitely made you stand out.

Meika: I loved the idea of exploring the world of graffiti though the eyes of these two kids trying to find their place in the world.

QoL: So what were you expecting when you signed on? Because I'm sure you didn't get what you signed on for.

Meika: I didn't really know what to expect.

Meika: There was a big push to raise cash and make the starting date of July 28 (I think), no matter what.

Meika: We had a lot of hurdles to jump to make it happen but we were all determined and that kept momentum flowing.

QoL: Did that give you the idea that the film was going to get made no matter what? Or did you think we were crazy?

Meika: I knew this was the first feature for both Ben and Brant and we had a big learning curve.

QoL: Yup.

Meika: I knew the film was going to get made.

Meika: Ben—wait a second. Should I refer to you as "Ben" or "you" in this interview?

Meika: I am confused!

QoL: Ben.

QoL: Were you expecting a typical indie? Or garage band?

QoL: Or "real feature"?

Meika: Okay. So Ben was very determined. He kept saying he didn't want to be another guy with a great story in his pocket who says he is going to make a movie and never does.

Meika: I was thinking garage band but with great musicians.

QoL: That's what I'm talking about!

QoL: What were your initial responsibilities and what did that evolve into?

Meika: My initial responsibilities were to find the crew.

Meika: We did a lot of posting on craightlist.

QoL: And how did that go?

Meika: And used UCSC, Ben and Brant's alma mater, to recruit.

Meika: We ended up with a great and slightly motley crew.

Meika: Eventually, I ended up doing whatever needed to get done from craft service to location scouting.

QoL: We were all so slammed, working day jobs and such. How was it trying to hodge-podge this film together in such a short time frame with no money?

QoL: Talking pre-prod.

Meika: It was hard. I think we all ended up putting our day jobs aside a bit (don't tell our bosses) but I remember juggling a lot.

QoL: You really did end up doing so many things, as all of us did. And one key place you got assigned to was locations. Talk about finding Jason and securing locations on your own as well (community support, etc.).

Meika: We were really rushing to get everything together for the start date.

QoL: We had a pretty ambitious location sched.

Meika: We had a hard time finding a location manager. Most of the people we interviewed wanted up-front cash.

QoL: Which we didn't have.

Meika: Everyone had to work on deferment, so paying a scout wasn't an option.

QoL: So how did you find Jason?

Meika: But I did end up meeting this guy Jason who came on board to do locations.

Meika: He was this eclectic photographer who was excited to work on a feature.

Meika: He knew of a lot of locations because of his photo experience.

Promotional flyer for the Gijon film festival by Spanish youth group Abierto Hasta el Amanecer.

Meika: Some of the locations, however, we found literally 15 minutes before shooting.

QoL: What about finding locations on your own? Was the community receptive to and supportive of us coming onto their property and shooting? Why?

Meika: There was a lot of on the fly scrambling to find places when our schedule ran over.

Meika: I found the community to be incredibly supportive of our project. I don't think there was a single place I approached that said "No" to us.

Meika: Everyone was excited to support an SF indie feature, especially one that took place in the Mission.

Meika: We couldn't have made this film without the support of the community.

Meika: I was amazed at what people agreed to and even went out of their way to help us.

Meika: A great example was Wayne from Therapy.

Meika: He let us shoot on his roof, the final mural scene.

QoL: He was amazing.

Meika: It was an all-night shoot, and he stayed downstairs in his shop and slept on a couch.

Meika: He didn't mind at all!

QoL: And he's got a family.

Meika: We were like 4 hours late showing up and he was still into helping us, even though it took all night.

QoL: Why would he do that?

QoL: Is he bonkers? Or did he see something in us that inspired him?

Meika: Remember we were not paying these people a cent, so I don't know what his motive was except good will.

Meika: I think there was an element of humanity that permeated this film and you can see that feeling of everyone pulling through in the film.

Meika: It was definitely a big group effort.

QoL: A big part of the scrambling, getting locations the same day, etc., was due to the lack of pre-production time (working day jobs, etc.). Do you think we should have backed off on locations and scaled the film down? Or, to take it a step further, should we have either waited until we DID have the cash or all quit our day jobs? Or did we do it right?

Meika: It is so hard to say, looking back, because everything worked out in the end.

QoL: A lot of synchronicity.

Meika: I think more prep would have been great but I also think we would have made changes and been scrambling anyways.

QoL: True.

QoL: Let's talk about some specific craziness.

QoL: How about the time the grip truck got hit by a car?

QoL: Hit and run!

Meika: It would have been great to not have day jobs and be able to really focus on the film right up to the shoot instead.

Meika: Yeah, we had rented this beat up grip truck.

Meika: It is actually featured in the film as Pop's rig.

QoL: A good one, though.

Meika: Wait, is it okay to mention that?

QoL: Good gear inside.

QoL: But looks like crap on the outside.

QoL: Perfect cover.

Meika: Anyways—we were shooting late one night at Lisa and Vain's apartment

Meika: and the back door of the truck got hit.

Meika: Of course the driver of the other vehicle fled.

Meika: And there was our poor truck with its door dangling on one hinge.

QoL: And we're thinking, "We're fucked!"

Meika: That night we had to park it with the back up against a wall so no one could take the stuff.

Meika: Since the door wouldn't shut.

QoL: Insurance wouldn't cover it either.

Meika: We were screwed.

QoL: (Deductible.)

Meika: Plus we had no cash for repairs.

QoL: Yup.

Meika: I took it to an auto body shop.

QoL: Cost?

Meika: And they pretty much laughed at the idea of fixing the door.

Meika: They said it would cost more than the truck was worth.

Meika: So I started to call some junkyards.

Meika: And actually found a door.

QoL: Of course.

QoL: Resorceful Meikie!

Meika: it was newer but still fit our truck, at a place near my house.

QoL: How was that junkyard?

Meika: I went over there and since this was my first junkyard experience, I wasn't really dressed properly.

QoL: Classic.

Meika: It was the summertime and I was wearing a tank top, skirt and flip-flops.

QoL: Perfect junkyard attire

Meika: Never go to a junkyark in flip flops.

QoL: I'll remember that.

QoL: Were they just tripping on you or what?

Meika: But I found the door. It cost $50, which I paid with petty cash and shoved the door in my car.

Meika: The guys didn't know what I was doing there.

QoL: How did you get it on the van?

Meika: I was like a mutant.

QoL: A filmmaker!

Meika: But they were very helpful.

Meika: Don't think they see too many girls at the yard.

QoL: With flip-flops.

68

Bryan Dawson works on Vain's memorial piece at 5 a.m.

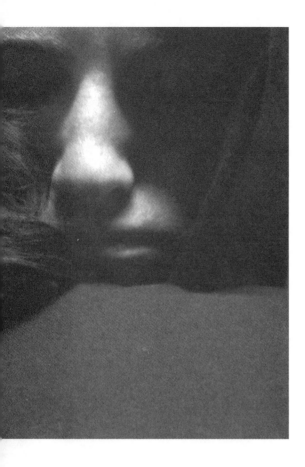

Meika: Right.

Meika: I think Brian ended up putting the door on the van and it fit perfectly.

QoL: Burnam?

Meika: It was a little newer and had one of those "Tell me how I am driving" stickers with a phone number, which was hilarious.

Meika: yeah—I think so.

Meika: Or maybe it was Darrell?

QoL: Better get that one right for the book.

QoL: Give credit where credit is due (-;

Meika: Right. I can't remember now, but it did fit and we weren't charged anything by the grip people.

QoL: Classic indie filmmaking story.

QoL: If we had a Hollywood budget, we would have spent thousands on that. Instead, $50 and a memorable trip to the junkyard.

Meika: Exactly.

Meika: It always felt like the film was sort of blessed.

Meika: Like we had a guardian angel or something.

Meika: Whenever we hit a major problem it got solved easier than expected.

Meika: And there were a lot of them.

QoL: A LOT!!!!

QoL: Daily. Hourly.

Meika: :-)

QoL: What were your thoughts when you saw the first rushes at Sharon's house?

Meika: I was amazed.

Meika: It looked so much better than I ever expected!

Meika: No offense Ben and Kev but I really wasn't prepared for how professional it was.

QoL: Was that gratifying?

Meika: We were always scrambling so much, I couldn't imagine that it would turn out so well.

QoL: After all the blood sweat and tears?

Meika: Totally gratifying.

Meika: Made it all worth it.

Meika: In fact I had totally forgotten the pain of production after I saw the rough cut.

QoL: Amazing how that happens, huh?

Meika: Yep.

QoL: Seems like everyone had that experience.

Meika: I think so.

QoL: At least for a minute (-;

Meika: I think it is so typical for no-budget films to look like it was a no-budget film.

QoL: Did you expect the film to get this far (major fests, distribution, etc.) when you first saw the craigslist posting?

Meika: But *QoL* really looked like we had CASH and we didn't.

Meika: But we pulled it off.

QoL: We had passion.

Meika: I knew the subject matter was a great one and knew that a good story about it had great potential in the market.

Meika: Nothing about graffiti had been made in years.

QoL: Right. 20 years.

Meika: And it is something that has evolved so much as an art form.

Meika: We see it in advertising, museums, magazines, even in store displays.

QoL: Looking back, what was the worst thing about working on this film?

Meika: But what was great about *QoL* is that it wasn't about exploiting graffiti, it was story about these 2 friends who just happened to be graff writers.

QoL: Sorry, I keep stepping on you . . .

Meika: No worries.

QoL: Looking back, what was the worst thing about working on this film?

Meika: Hum, that is a tricky one.

Meika: I think the worst thing about working on this film was asking people to work their asses off and not be able to compensate them at all.

QoL: Yes, that sucked.

Meika: I mean, we were all grateful to the many interns and others who came through for us.

QoL: Was it because you had no accountability? Or because you felt bad for them?

Meika: but I sometimes felt guilty asking people to work 6-day weeks, 14-hour days for free.

Meika: Even though it was the best learning experience ever.

Meika: We were really lucky that we ended up with a crew who was willing to stick with it.

QoL: Totally blessed.

Meika: Even when times got tough, no one ended up quitting (although many threatened to leave and I couldn't blame them!)

Meika: I had my days where I was wondering "What the hell am I doing? I am exhausted, haven't seen my husband in weeks

Meika: and for what?"

Meika: But obviously, I stuck it out and really feel it was worth it.

Meika: It is like you go to the brink of what you can take.

QoL: Exactly. I had the same feelings. And it was MY freaking idea to do this.

Meika: Sort of like *Survivor* in a way

QoL: In the Mission.

QoL: That would be a good show.

Meika: Yeah, reality indie feature show is a good idea.

Meika: Oh wait a minute—

QoL: *Film School.*

Meika: they did that with Project Greenlight.

QoL: on IFC, too.

Meika: yeah—film school.

QoL: But not in the Mission.

Meika: yeah—those guys have sets, we had the Mission.

QoL: On *Film School*, some of them were shooting 5 min shorts in 18 days.

QoL: We shot a 90-min feature in that time.

Meika: PLEASE!

QoL: With probably the same money.

QoL: phone call. Stand by . . .

Meika: FYI I have about 20 minutes left on my battery.

QoL: i'm back

QoL: What was the best part of production?

Meika: The best part of production was

Meika: hum

QoL: come on!

Meika: I think the times we totally gelled as a team.

QoL: there had to be something!

Meika: and we got amazing stuff.

QoL: Such as?

QoL: Come on, Meika. Dig deep.

QoL: There had to be something good.

Meika signed off at 10:45:46 AM

QoL: What happened?

Meika: Battery died.

QoL: Did you think of anything good?

QoL: Good timing for the battery to die ;-)

Meika: Classic.

Meika: I believe the good moments of production

Meika: Yes. A few scenes in particular stand out for me.

Meika: One is the Valencia Street sequence with Heir and Vain walking down the street, shoplifting the Converse and then getting pizza.

Meika: So much of it was improv

Meika: and we got the pizza location minutes before shooting.

QoL: Talk a little about that.

QoL: How do you get a location

Meika: what the location?

QoL: for no money

QoL: minutes before we shoot?!

Meika: We had another location lined up but were running late. Plus it was a pretty tight space.

Meika: Luckily there was another pizza joint a few doors down from Subterranean where we shot the Converse scene.

Meika: I just went in and asked.

QoL: How convenient.

Meika: It is amazing what you can get when you ask for something :-)

QoL: Why do you think they said yes?

Meika: I think we also bought the crew pizza there which helped.

Meika: All the patrons were great—

Meika: signed release forms, and were low-pro during the shoot.

QoL: That pizza place was open while we shot.

Meika: I also love the part outside—the tomatoes shtick.

Meika: Another good shooting moment was the party scene.

Meika: It was a really hard scene to coordinate.

QoL: Another last minute success story.

Meika: We had a lot of extras in a guy's loft who was out for the evening and gave us permission to use his place for the party.

QoL: John Doffing.

Meika: It was a really long night and tension was high.

Meika: John had been nice enough to loan us his place and we thought no one was going to show for the party.

Meika: But of course word got out and before we knew it we had 50 extras.

QoL: That was all Brian.

QoL: On his cellie all day.

Meika: we couldn't have cast a better set of extras.

Meika: The footage from the party is beautiful, the close ups Kev did and the whole freestyle bit outside.

Meika: I love all the impromptu moments that happened and were perfect.

Meika: Plus the fight was hard to choreograph but it came off without a flaw.

QoL: Talk a little about the man

QoL: oops

Meika: Scenes like that where we really relied on so many people and everyone pulled their weight.

Meika: Those were the great moments.

Meika: Oh—my man?

QoL: Talk a little about the mandala. We thought we could get some Monks to hook up a mandala.

Meika: Oh—Mandala!

QoL: And this was such a CRUCIAL part of the script.

QoL: Another ball that got dropped in your lap.

Meika: The whole Buddhist undercurrent was a theme that I really loved in the script.

QoL: A KEY component.

Meika: Ben and Brant had asked me to find someone to help us out with the mandala.

Meika: I didn't think it would be very hard since there are a lot of zen centers in the Bay Area.

Meika: But when I called around—they all thought I was insane.

Meika: Mandalas are not created by one person in a few hours.

Meika: It is a group of monks who spend weeks or months making one.

Meika: It is a long form of creation through meditation.

Meika: So the idea of having some monk come out to our location

and hook us up with a Mandala was out.

Meika: We decided to make one ourselves.

QoL: And then we all started shitting.

Meika: This proved more challenging than expected.

Meika: I think we were shooting the mandala in a few days and we had no idea how to pull this off.

Meika: Jason Goodman, our location scout, and I spent a few hours in my garage trying to create a stencil that we could filter the sand through.

Meika: It didn't work.

Meika: We tried gluing the sand and that looked really bad too.

QoL: Crazy Buddhists and their insanely difficult rituals.

Meika: I printed out some pictures of mandalas from a Tibetan site.

QoL: Why couldn't they make it easier?

Meika: One of which had a lotus flower in the center.

Meika: Jason and I realized the only way it would work is if we painted the design onto something like cardboard and then laid the sand on top.

Meika: That is when we turned to Bryan Dawson, our art consultant.

QoL: Jason is someone you hired as a location scout, mind you.

QoL: Bryan to the rescue once again.

Meika: Bascially I dropped off some ideas for designs, some paint and a whole lot of colored sand from the hobby shop . . .

QoL: And he ran with it?

Meika: Bryan designed this beautiful mandala and stayed up all night painting it.

Meika: I went over to his place to pick it up the day of the shoot.

QoL: With like sand and geso?

Meika: Again, he had been up all night working on this thing.

Meika: He wasn't quite done and I needed to be at the Temple in Japantown in an hour.

QoL: The *QoL* way.

Meika: We could only use the temple for a short while—

Meika: another miracle location, so time was of the essence.

QoL: Crazy Buddhists.

Meika: Anyways—I sat on Bryan's floor with his wife and the 3 of us painted as fast as we could.

Meika: It was barely finished when we tossed it in the car, still wet, and drove across town to the temple.

QoL: Thing turned out beautiful.

QoL: Looked real on screen.

Meika: There is when we applied the glue and sand to give it the texture.

Meika: The way Kev shot it made it totally look real.

Meika: That scene was another great production moment.

QoL: We had Val put real sand over it to give it depth and texture.

Meika: It looked amazing.

Meika: And the sand being swept away was perfect. You couldn't tell there was still a painted piece of cardboard underneath.

Meika: The tricks of the trade I guess.

Meika: That was our one sort of special effect.

Meika: ha ha

QoL: What does that do for crew morale when we keep pulling off last minute stuff like that: the mandala, shooting in a live restaurant, party scene, etc.

Meika: I think it was crucial for the film.

QoL: On the one hand, it's maddening. But on the other hand, it's gotta feel pretty magical.

Meika: When we pulled off the miracles it kept everyone believing we could do this thing.

Meika: We expected things to go wrong in a way.

Meika: The truth was, none of us had worked in the capacity that we were on a feature before.

Meika: But finding solutions to problems is really what producing is all about.

QoL: How do you think this film would have turned out with a $10M budget?

Meika: I think it would have lost the gritty feeling that makes it so real.

QoL: Why?

Meika: The renegade aspect, or the graffiti model as Ben and Brant say, is what gave the film its authenticity.

Meika: we were fast, low key, and effective.

QoL: Talk a little bit about the graffiti model: how effective it was and how it was passed down to cast & crew.

Meika: The graffiti model molded the feel of the production.

Meika: we knew we were going to do something sort of impossible.

Meika: But the idea of following in the theme of what the film represented set the tone for the production.

Meika: we all new we needed to be somewhat undercover since we didn't always have permits.

Meika: we knew we needed to be fast so we didn't draw too much attention.

Meika: many times we only took one or two takes.

Meika: mainly because we were trying to conserve film.

Meika: The leftover film we sold to pay for processing.

Meika: Forget what I was just going to say.

Meika: It was dumb.

QoL: What?!

Meika: I was trying to sum up the graff model and how it maybe helped the crew get what it might feel like to be a writer, always checking your back, creating something fast, in difficult conditions, always feelng like you might get busted.

Meika: Whatever.

QoL: It's true.

QoL: We were living the lifestyle in a way.

QoL: And in that sense, a Hollywood film would be more of a gallery take on a street phenomenon.

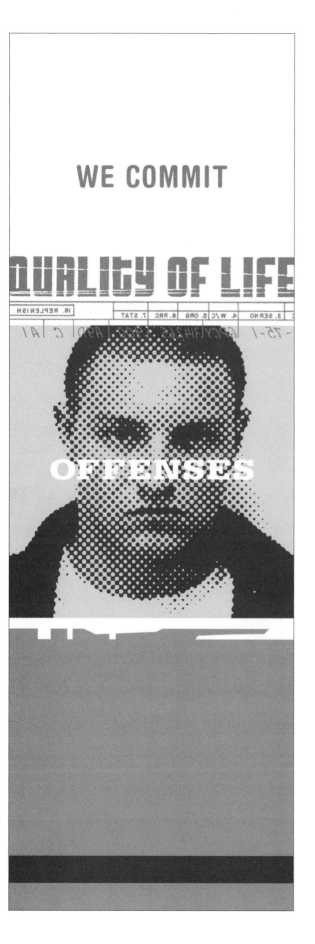

Meika: I think that helped keep the crew interested too.

QoL: Right.

QoL: Not as much standing around waiting.

QoL: More action.

Meika: I think the film would have felt like an exploitation of the scene instead of a real account.

Meika: The idea that the Thunderdome was real.

Meika: That the tunnels we used were the tunnels writers really use.

Meika: In a Hollywood—10 million dollar film all that would have been created by some fantastic art director who probably didn't know the first thing about graffiti.

QoL: What if they kept it real?

QoL: And hired real writers, etc?

Meika: I still think the reason the film came out so great

Meika: besides all our hard work, and a great director and script of course, is because it was real.

Meika: The idea of a set, with a huge lighting rig, tons of crew members, trailers, egg white omlettes for breakfast—it just would have lost that feeling that comes off so well in the film.

QoL: So what have you taken away from this experience, as a professional and as a human being?

Meika: Whoa.

Meika: Okay—

QoL: The sum-it-all-up questions.

Meika: Um—I feel really proud of the film and that it is something I contributed to.

Meika: I learned to keep your integrity no matter what.

Meika: What I mean by that is that everyone wanted the best for the film.

Meika: this wasn't just some job where you hire crew who may not have ever read the script.

Meika: It was a film that everyone who worked on it felt for and that is what movie-making is to me.

Meika: Sharing something with the world that is important to you.

QoL: Well it was an honor working with you. I look forward to doing it again.

QoL: Soon:-)

QoL: This is MY first interview.

QoL: Hope I didn't suck too hard.

QoL: OK

Meika: No way—you were great.

QoL: You're too kind.

QoL: OK. Back to the fricking day job. "Yes, master!"

Meika: See ya.

Darrell Lee
PRODUCTION ASSISTANT AND ASSOCIATE PRODUCER

JULY 31, 2005

Darrell: Hi.

QoL: Hey Darrell.

QoL: Thanks for joining us.

QoL: Ready to dive in?

Darrell: You bet.

QoL: So how did you hear about *QoL*?

Darrell: I had just finished up at UCSC, and was just killing time in Santa Cruz, but was still getting email from the Film & Digital Media department. One email was for an internship on a film in San Francisco—*QoL*.

QoL: What was the listing for? PA?

Darrell: Yeah, I remember not giving it much thought—didn't think I'd get it, but if anywhere, I thought a PA position was the place to get started.

QoL: You studied film at UCSC?

Darrell: Yes. "Film and Digital Media" was the official department title, but mostly Digital Media.

QoL: Had you worked on any (non-student) films before *QoL*?

Darrell: Nope, *QoL* was the first experience I had on a film set outside of a bunch of students running around campus with PD-150's or the like. Even IN school, the most we ever played with actual film was a day with some super 16.

QoL: A lot of people were surprised to hear that we were able to get anyone to even show up for an unpaid gig, let alone stick around for 3-4 weeks. What attracted you to the project? And, more importantly, why the hell stick it out for a month?

Darrell: Things just fell together—I got the internship, my old roommate offered me a place in his father's apartment (in SF), and I didn't really know how else to get started in the industry, so in I went. The family atmosphere helped motivate me and the professionalism of the crew members made me strive to learn quicker and work harder—show them I could do this. It was my first gig, and I wanted to make a good impression.

QoL: What do you mean by "family atmosphere"?

Darrell: As the first week rolled through, it felt like people had taken up cetain positions . . . Ben was the father, the head of the table who moved us forward with a goal. Brant was like the scolding mother, keeping us in line and on track. Ben R., Jeb, and I were the young PAs, the children, learning and growing under guidance. You spend over 12 hours a day around each other—it just gets very intimate.

QoL: Nice analogy.

QoL: What were you expecting when you showed up on set the first day? A "real" movie? Garage band?

QoL: Student film?

Darrell: I just remember being nervous. Like when you're about to head off to high school for the first day after leaving junior high. I was expecting some of the "real" movie things, like a huge camera with some old DP with a white beard, and a director that would never talk to me, big stars with huge egos. I guess I was just preparing myself for the pain of being a lowly PA. After the first day though, I just thought it was all very easy going and quite overwhelming.

QoL: And you just dove in hardcore. You stood out from day one as the guy who wasn't afraid to take on a new task. And you were always right there, asking how you could help and anticipating next moves.

QoL: Which is why we promoted you to Associate Producer after production.

Darrell: Well. You just can't hold back greatness . . .

QoL: Word

QoL: Aside from the core crew (Kev, Brian, Khamisi, Tom), we were really pretty clueless about the filmmaking process. I always wondered how that affected you guys (the PAs). To borrow your family analogy, if Dad has no idea wtf is going on (and mom is on the pipe, as Brant clearly was), how does that affect the kids? What was the chatter around the campfire?

Darrell: There were two worlds on the set: Creative and Technical. I saw both as equally important to the film, but there were different people working in each world. I learned the technical from people like Khamisi and Brian, followed their lead and studied their movements. The creative aspect, the harder to grasp soul of the process, I simply learned from paying attention. Listening to the interactions of the producers and AD team. As far as I was concerned, both worlds were professional—I was just learning.

Darrell: The PAs, we mostly talked about how hot certain women were and what we just saw happen on set.

QoL: Such as?

Darrell: It was all very light stuff, things college kids talk about. It never really got too far into the filmmaking process—we took it a lot like being in class. When a lecture's on and you're talking with classmates, it's about the subject at hand. When we got to gather, like during lunch or off to the side, off set, we were in between our classes—we talked about SF and hot chicks and that TV show we saw last night.

QoL: Did you have any idea what we were creating? What the end result would look like?

Darrell: Now that I think about it, it was kinda weird. We never really talked about the movie as a movie we were making—possibly because we didn't think our small roles were really a part of it. I think it was mostly because we just didn't know any better The movie didn't start coming together for me until probably halfway through principal photography. I just didn't know any better—had no previous experience to pull from and actually gauge how things were going or what to expect. The huge amount of growing and learning all about this new world blinded my perception of what we were really making till I had a couple weeks to soak it in and look back.

QoL: That's such a fascinating perspective. Part of it I'm sure is age-related. (You were what, 22?) But I wonder how universal it is for PAs, grips, etc. to have no concept of the big picture (so to speak). But you were pretty close to the action, given our small crew size and your ascent to the top of the PA ranks. You really had no idea what we were creating?

Darrell: I didn't know if this was just a step higher than a student film with a few bells and whistles, or if all film great and small were made in such small crews. Truthfully, I didn't even think about all that and the fact that I was part of a film crew—the 12+ hours, new gear to learn, locations differing every day, fifteen problems to deal with, watching Kev and anticipating Khamisi—it all drowned out other thoughts of the big picture. I just woke up each day and tried to keep up and show everyone I could kick ass.

QoL: And kick ass you did, my friend.

QoL: Your approach was so different from the other PAs. We had some outstanding PAs. And they all stayed on for the entire shoot (every day for 3 weeks), which is unheard of. But you just stood out from day one (which is why we refer you to other directors so frequently ;-). Is this just part of your DNA? Is it an Asian thing? j/k

QoL: What was your philosophy w/ this gig?

Darrell: I went in with the idea that, "This is where I want to go. This is the world I need to break into and move forward, or I'll just fall back." All go, no stop—two settings, "Badass" and "More Badass." I had heard the rumors, had an idea of my chances to make it in the industry—if you're going to go in with a low survival rate, you have to max things out and do what you can with what you got in every chance. The work ethic has still stayed with me today in the grip and electric world—and I've learned that it's not just me . . . If you plan on working in any department in filmmaking in the Bay Area, you have to have the work ethic. Work is so slow and small at times, we only keep the best—if you're not the best in what you do in Nor Cal filmmaking, you might as well move south and be another one of those know-nothing mooks in LA.

QoL: On the money, my man. A very mature prespective. That attitude served you (and us) well on *QoL* and will serve you well in the industrty in general.

QoL: Your rep is all you got.

Darrell: 50% hard work, 50% luck. So work what you can.

QoL: What was your reaction when you finally did see the rough cut? You were at the first cast & crew screening at the Roxie, right?

Darrell: I was, and it was just a huge mix of emotions. I felt proud. Prouder than any moment I've ever had in my short life thus far. I hugged everyone and was flooded with sentimental flashbacks at my time on the show with all the crewmembers around me. Scenes and shots I remembered being around I had actually seen on this screen—I saw the effects of the lights I placed and the camera moves that had been by Kev's or Tom's hands. The locations weren't just background, but fleshy, gritty moments captured in my mind—I lived part of that movie I had just watched, and it floored me. I don't really remember things that happened at the showing—just the feeling.

QoL: So you said that you weren't really thinking about the end result during production. But it sounds like it kind of surprised you, as it did for most people who were involved with the production. It was such a chaotic shoot, I think most people thought we'd be lucky to have anything to show. Where did it fit in your expectation scale?

Darrell: Again, with no idea of how things are supposed to be, I had little to go on as far as expectations—I was more just stoked to be a part of it and was excited to see what we had all done. I wanted to have a standard to compare from, and this was the start.

QoL: Talk a little bit about the last day/night of shooting.

QoL: [Feel free to hit enter every once in a while so we can riff about this one.]

Darrell: Oh god. I don't even remember how long it was, but at the experience level I was at, it seemed like forever. Working for over two years now on films, I've had my 16-hour and 18-hour days, but on *QoL*, the final day was a treck around the world.

QoL: You said it.

QoL: We had backloaded all of the hard stuff to the last day.

Darrell: There were lots of moments of delirious laughing and working like nothing mattered anymore. I lost track of time.

Darrell: I remember breaking into the abandoned warehouse near the docks with Brian, and when we pried the steel back, I thought, "We are so going to jail. Cool."

QoL: We had used this Mt. Everest analogy for the whole shoot.

QoL: That was definitely the climb to the peak.

Darrell: That night was a lot like the showing, I don't remember much, but I remember the feelings.

QoL: It was funny b/c we kept saying, "The air is getting thinner!"

QoL: And we had slimmed the crew down to like 3 or 4 of us.

Darrell: Yeah, it was a big push. Very hard. And then we had come down from the mountain.

QoL: I got this call from Kev about a week after we wrapped.

Darrell: Just when we had reached the top and wanted to do nothing but rest, it continued.

QoL: He had been listening to NPR in his car.

QoL: And he heard this show about climbing Mt. Everest.

QoL: Kev: "Ben, the guy said most of the deaths occur ON THE WAY DOWN!"

QoL: That was a real eye-opener.

QoL: After all of that hard work and finishing as strong as we did with that final crazy day.

QoL: To realize that the real work was just beginning.

QoL: Crazy.

Darrell: It's a process. I just wish it was a one-step process.

QoL: Not only did you stick with the film for the duration and perform above and beyond what everyone expected, you stayed on for the fest run as well. (And you better believe we're calling on your ass for distribution as well!) Did you ever hit a point where you wanted to quit and limp back down the mountain?

Darrell: Oh yeah. I found out quick that I needed to be out in the field. I'm a production guy, need to be around the action and on-set craziness. The two weeks I worked in the office after production to prep for the festivals and search for distribution, I was a horrible son of a bitch. Friends would call and ask what I was up to, and I'd just spit, "Going to the office. Bye."

Darrell: Office work doesn't sit well with me, it turns out.

QoL: Good to know (-;

QoL: What are you up to these days?

Darrell: I just finished a feature where I worked as the Best Boy Electric for the first time in my career. I need to keep moving and learning, and this step made sense. I'm loving the indie low-budget feature world of Bay Area filmmaking, and with my training from people like Khamisi and Kev, the grip and electric part of the process have done me well.

QoL: You're the man, Darrell.

QoL: Keep fighting the good fight.

Darrell: I'm like a shark—gotta keep moving forward.

QoL: We look forward to working with you again.

QoL: Thanks for the interview. I'll give you a chance to review before we publish.

Darrell: It'll happen sooner than you think—just wait.

Darrell: Cool.

QoL: And don't hesitate to write if you think of anything.

QoL: We're actually in development on another feature. Just made the final cut at the Sundance Institute. Fingers crossed. (Breath not held.)

QoL: But it's all about *QoL* right now.

QoL: Need to blow this shit up so we can do the next one right, feel me?

Darrell: fo sho

QoL: Thanks Darrell.

Darrell: Hell yeah man, always.

QoL: Don't be a stranger!

Darrell: keep me posted. I'll work you into my busy schedule ;-)

QoL: have your people call my people . . .

Darrell: cool, peace out homie

QoL: peas . . .

Bryan Dawson
CHIEF CREATIVE CONSULTANT

AUGUST 1, 2005

QoL: So how did you first hear about *QoL*?

Bryan: I became aware of *QoL* through Brian Burnam. He invited me to help with the project.

QoL: You had been writing (graffiti) for some time, no?

Bryan: I'd been writing before I moved to San Francisco and had done my fair share of bombing. I started getting down with it in Santa Cruz, where I grew up with Brian. He wanted to put me in charge of painting all of the graffiti in the film that Lane Garrison's character "Heir" puts up. I was happy to and painting was easy with that name since it was an alias I'd used before.

QoL: Can you talk about how you lost that name?

Bryan: Sure. I got popped one night doing an Heir piece in the Mission. I would've gotten away with it too if it hadn't been for those meddling kids.

QoL: From what I understand, that was supposed to be the christening of the new name. Was that the 1st and last time you wrote "HEIR"?

Bryan: It was the last time I'd written it until the movie came along. The name seemed appropriate for the character.

QoL: What was the first version of the script you saw? Was it called *Quality of Life*, or an earlier version?

Bryan: I remember Brian showing me a first draft after he began the rewrites with you. I was cracking up from the schemes and humor that were getting injected into the story. I also feel there's a lot of him and me in there, from our years of writing together. I don't remember the early titles.

QoL: Definitely a strong Brian voice in there. And shit that you guys went through together.

Bryan: Yeah, for sure.

QoL: So what did you think we were up to from a filmmaking perspective? Hollywood blockbuster? Indie? Community project?

Bryan: I was always behind the film—it was obviously coming from a grassroots level, not trying to sensationalize the world it was using as a vehicle for the drama of the characters.

QoL: That's what Brian brought to it. Honestly, my earlier drafts were much more ABOUT graffiti. More politically driven, you know? But Brian made it a human story. So you were brought on to double for Lane and provide some feedback on the script. But, like everyone else on this project, you ended up wearing many more hats.

Bryan: It's all based firmly in events that have happened to friends and the greater graffiti community lately. All that is spot on. I was surprised when we took the film to Berlin last year and found out writers there were getting their houses raided as well.

QoL: That was a real eye opener. I really thought it was a US phenomenon. But quality of life laws have been adopted around the globe.

Bryan: Apparently so. We learned a lot from talking to people who came to see the film there. The whole trip was—just getting that kind of recognition felt really inspiring.

QoL: You ended up wearing a lot of different hats like all of us. Talk about the mandala a little bit. How you got involved with it, how it went, etc.

Bryan: Well, Meika got ahold of me and said we needed a sand mandala for a key scene in two days, could I make one?

QoL: No biggie, right? Only takes monks weeks to create and a lifetime to learn.

Bryan: I realized if I designed something on a sandy textured surface, I could just paint with colors matching the colored sand we were using for the shoot. When Tajai Massey's character, Dino, is pouring the sand on there it looks legit, as well as when with a little camera trickery he sweeps it away. I got some mandala designs from Meika and freestyled something that would look authentic.

QoL: Did you try anything else first, or was that the first solution?

Bryan: That was my first idea, although I know there had been some panic after people tried pouring colored sand over a surface with adhesive on it. It didn't work.

QoL: There was plenty of panic to go around. So much was riding on that mandala coming off. The whole story revolves around it. No pressure.

Bryan: I was happy to help with that project. Kev's camerawork definitely helped pull off the scene smoothly.

QoL: I remember I was psyched on it when I first saw it, but knew it had to pass the Kev test. He took one look at it and said, "We can make that work." I was so relieved.

Bryan: That's one of my favorite scenes. Of course it ties into one of my others, when Heir paints a memorial for his fallen friend, Vain.

QoL: Another "no pressure" scene. The whole movie is riding on this piece coming off. You have three hours because we back-logged the schedule with three days of work in one night and the sun is coming up . . . GO!

Bryan: Totally. It was pretty hectic, but that's filmmaking, right? So I had a sketch for the memorial piece, we had the location, but the funny thing was every time a cop drove by and saw this hooded kid on a rooftop doing a burner with lights and shit I started cracking up—the look on their faces! The pressure was definitely on though. I even had you helping fill in! Which is kind of beautiful, you know? Everyone pitched in that night—a big shout out to my man QS for the helping hand.

QoL: For sure. QS definitely came in handy because we had to abandon you and go pick up some other shots.

Bryan: Then in the morning, I had just poured my guts out to do this piece and you were like, "Okay, Lane, start buffing." I was out of there—I couldn't watch my work get gone over after just finishing it.

QoL: My original vision was to film Lane starting to paint over the piece and then cut and fix the piece. And Brian hollered, "Bullshit. We can't be hypocrites, man. Paint over it." That was tough for me, but must have been 100 times harder for you.

Bryan: Yes, but in the context of the story it makes a lot of sense.

Bryan Dawson and Sam Flores at the Berlin Film Festival.

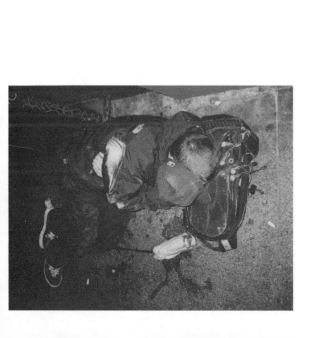

The Buddhist philosophy that Dino explains to Heir in the temple about the impermanence of everything is portrayed by Heir's actions. It also symbolizes the passing of the crown from one king to the next, the "Heir apparent."

QoL: This was something that I could not get old school cats (especially piecers) that I had grown up with to swallow. "Paint over your own piece? And a memorial?!" But it seems like the contemporary crowd has pretty much embraced it across the board.

Bryan: Sure, I can understand people questioning the realism, but it's a story and a fable based in reality but not stuck in it, right?

QoL: True. But we were living it, to some extent, by really painting over the piece. Is that something you can say you would live by? Have you accepted Dino's theory in real life?

Bryan: Good question. I think honestly that for me I would love to see that piece every time I walk up Valencia Street, but I don't have to because everybody sees it every time *QoL* plays! But seriously, I take that philosophy less literally and apply it to many aspects of my life. It really can be a weapon to think that way because you become stronger if you can embrace this way of thinking. Letting go can be hard to do.

QoL: So hard. If we were really living it, we would have dumped the film negative in the Bay.

Bryan: True that!

QoL: But it does put things into perspective. Every piece, every human, every tree, building, whatever, is going to get washed away at some point. Pretty heavy you can say that with a spray can.

Bryan: With any medium, really. I think film was the best one for this project and I'm glad to see it's done so well.

QoL: Word. Big ups to Kev Robertson! How did you come up with the concept for the memorial?

Bryan: That was a lot of your input there. I know the story is based on Picasso's painting the Death of Casagemas about his friend who killed himself. I based the shrouded figures in the memorial on the ones in the Picasso painting and altered the fallen figure of Casagemas to have a crown on his head, for Vain was a king. The piece is going into a Heavenly Gate with a peace symbol at the top of it.

QoL: Had you ever done a memorial piece before?

Bryan: Yes. Like I said there is a lot of truth in this story. Rest In Peace Sham and Josh Lear.

QoL: When we went to Berlin, we were definitely the punk band in the talent show. There were indie films, but they all had real budgets, etc. How was it seeing *QoL* on that HUGE f'ing screen that first night? And the warm reception we got from the incredible people at the Berlinale.

Bryan: It was truly unreal. My folks came down from England for the premiere and my Mom was like, " I know that was you!" every time a shot of me painting for Lane appeared.

QoL: That was kind of a life-altering experience for me. They just totally embraced us with open arms. They could tell we had heart, even though it was clear we didn't have money.

Bryan: But it was really a bug out when Brian and I got to rep the film in Stockholm last year. They really gave us the star treatment and threw a party in our honor at the hotel the last night. It was crazy! The best part was that we got to meet other filmmakers from around the world and every night they'd take us to a different restaurant or screening. I loved it.

QoL: Good festivals are the shit. (And bad festivals are shit.) I was so psyched when they offered to fly you to Stockholm as well. There's nothing like that creative synergy and recognition. I could do festivals for months if I had the time.

Bryan: I know—it was nutty because in Berlin we didn't really know what to expect, and there were a lot of us there to enjoy it. But in Sweden it was just Brian and myself, so some of the screenings had a Q & A session afterwards where we got to talk about the movie.

QoL: That's dope. So, word on the street is you're retired, true?

Bryan: Actually I came out of semi-retirement just recently. Don't you know writers only retire so they can make a comeback? But I shifted my focus from graffiti to studio work, probably a lot more after the movie came out. Last year a story about *QoL* came out in the *Chronicle* that got a lot of exposure. I painted a hotel room at the now world-famous Hotel des Arts, have continued showing, working in animation, and have begun a script for my movie. But it's summertime now so I've been hooking up walls around the mission, doing pieces with my friends, and enjoying life. An extra big shout-out to SMOKE, PCF, and CMA.

Left. Bryan Dawson's room at the Art Hotel in San Francisco (www.sfhoteldesarts.com).

Below. Bryan works on the memorial piece.

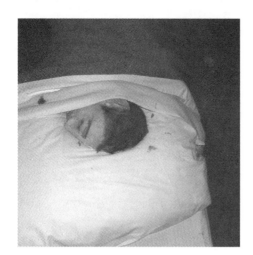

Kevin Heverin
ASSOCIATE PRODUCER

JULY 7, 2005

QoL: Waddup, Professor?

QoL: Well, let's dive in.

QoL: How did you get involved with *QoL*?

Professor: I responded to a Craigslist listing about a position for an associate producer for an indie film about "graffiti." That married a past life with present interests and work in small films I was doing.

QoL: Talk about this past life.

Professor: Let me take you back in time, the year is 1971 . . . I was born and raised in the Bronx, New York. My apartment building was adjacent to DeWitt Clinton High School, which in the early 70s was the epicenter for the birth of subway graffiti writing in NYC.

QoL: [For some reason, I can't tell when you're typing.]

Professor: Writing, or "hitting and piecing" as we mostly called it became infectious among my friends.

QoL: This is when graff was just getting started.

QoL: Who were some of the writers coming up in your neighborhood at the time?

Professor: The 2 writers who first influenced us most and made the biggest impression were Stay High 149 and Phase 2 (Lonnie). They were the equivalent of major rock stars in the 5 boroughs. After that, there's so many others . . . PNUT 2, BLADE, Billy 167, PEL were a few of my personal favorites who emerged shortly thereafter.

QoL: What an era to grow up in.

QoL: Did you have any sense that there was something special going on?

QoL: That over 30 years later

QoL: this hobby of yours would be adopted by every metro area on the globe?

Professor: The was a big fun component to the whole scene . . . the adventure of riding the lines to the last stop to hit-up . . . going into train yards or lay-ups at dawn or the middle of the night.

Professor: Sorry, typed over you. Yes, to live to see that this was something that would take on worldwide proportions has been absolutely remarkable and amazing.

QoL: When did quality of life laws start coming into play? At first, there really wasn't much crackdown, right?

Professor: We did not really see any "quality of life" tactics or legislation for graffiti in NYC in the 70s up to early 80s. I think that largely came into being with Rudy, and I had moved out of NY by his reign.

QoL: That's interesting. You hear a lot of contemporary writers talk about how the illegality of the sport has made it more appealing. Seems like there was a slightly different motivation back in the day. Although fame is always the key.

Professor: Fame and establishing individuality in a large city were huge drivers, or goals; everyone wanted to be a "king" not a "toy."

QoL: How is the contemporary scene different? And what about SF vs. NYC?

Professor: As far as the thrill aspect or being an outlaw, sure that was part of the appeal too, but I remember more how we all spent hours and hours drawing in black books and the like, to come up with something unique or stunning, or that topped somebody's work we had appreciated.

QoL: It was really the beginning of a new language.

Professor: To be considered in that same group or caliber of "artists."

QoL: For my peers, we cut our teeth on subway art.

QoL: We would sit in class and bite from SEEN and DONDI.

QoL: I always wondered what it would have been like BEFORE that language was developed. A pretty magical time.

Professor: I think you hit on it, that a lot of ideas about the "graffiti language" were circulating pretty quickly, fast and furious and if you had any sensitivity, as our circumstances did not often encourage, then it was a pretty exhilarating and "freeing" thing to be a part of. Magical is the way I remember it too, both the good and the bad.

Professor: And I've been chasing that feeling ever since!

QoL: At one point, after Giuliani starting going haywire with the quality of life laws,

QoL: a non-profit group (NOGA?) approached his office and said they would present proposals for pieces before doing them. They were thinking positive messages, like holiday themes and anti-drug stuff.

QoL: But, of course this proposal was rejected.

QoL: Do you think that, if Giuliani would have taken a more nurturing approach with graff, that we might not have a war on graffiti? Or would the "problem" have exploded beyond control?

Professor: Sure, how much can you expect the bureaucracy to think out of the box and embrace the street.

Professor: Well, graffiti spiked big-time in NYC in the years '73-'77, and why? Fad, only partly. I truly believe as the mayor at the time, Abe Beam, closed all the summer rec centers in his cost-cutting wisdom, the response to turning us all out onto the streets is that we did make our own fun and the greater 5 boroughs became one big rec center and canvas.

Professor: So, as we see elsewhere in the world, where there is a short-term gain you pay for it in the long-term, I think.

Professor: Or, think of it as the result of the disconnect between local government and the community. I don't care how earthy-crunchy that sounds.

QoL: It seems so obvious to me that this kind of overtly punitive approach does not work (as evidenced by the incredible global popularity of graff today). And yet cities all over the world are adopting quality of life laws. WTF?

QoL: are you typing? I can't figure out how to turn on my detector

Professor: Yes, going back-n-forth on my reply to your last comment . . .

Professor: The punitive course in and of itself has historically

proven never to be the answer or way to adapt.

QoL: Then why has it been so popular with local governments around the world?

Professor: But there you go, we're in a particularly punitive cycle in our society at the moment.

QoL: still typing?

Professor: no longer typing . . . FYI, I'm using a new beta of Yahoo IM

QoL: So, when we interviewed you, your professional skills and experience were key obviously. But your personal history with graff really put you over the top. (Bringing that photo album was a nice touch. That made my day. I hope you have that thing in a vault somewhere.) What did you think you were getting yourself into when you signed on with *QoL*?

Professor: I was impressed by the producer and director I met, and I thought they knew their shit! LOL. Then I separately interviewed with Meika later, and was further convinced of the validity of the project, and frankly that it was going to happen (as so many unfortunately don't).

QoL: That was definitely one thing we drove home: this film WILL get made. Did you think this was going to be a film that was a neat little local thing (considering we had no money), or did you think we had a shot at reaching the world?

Professor: I knew this was an independent film so prior experience prepared me to be ready for anything, to do anything, because that's the nature of the beast. But that's the fun, too.

Professor: I knew your *QoL* had global potential because of the worldwide graffiti passion and networks. All you had to do was execute it right!

QoL: Did you think we were being too ambitious in terms of the size of our cast, location schedule, and compact shooting schedule?

Professor: Ambitious definitely yes, which is good, but once you brought me on board, I saw a lot of pragmatism and daily adaptability which truly impressed me.

QoL: What was your role? Was it what you were originally hired to do?

Professor: That's funny, I guess my original role was perceived as soliciting "product placement" or corporate endorsements, but that quickly morphed into a more direct production-driven support and logistical role.

Professor: Whatever was needed that I had some connection or could fill in the blank!

QoL: Seemed like everyone had to wear multiple hats and do whatever needed to be done that day.

Professor: I helped with casting, didn't I?

Professor: You said it.

QoL: You were such a trooper and always came through. Why were you so inspired to work on this project?

Professor: It may look trite in print, but the team energy was absolutely infectious, and in some way, this is a document or legacy of what I did as a child that I can share with my children.

QoL: As a document or legacy, did the end result live up to your expectations? Despite the generation gap, did it capture some of the feeling and emotion behind writing your name on someone else's property?

Professor: The first time I saw a rough cut of the film with the soundtrack I really could've cried, because it was not academic, but it got me in a real sense memory way. I could honestly tell you what I saw characters on the screen, or another generation experience, was the same as I knew it.

QoL: That's heavy.

Professor: I really enjoyed the opportunity to work with so many young and talented people on the *QoL* team. I learned from you all!

QoL: A couple more quick questions.

QoL: How do you think this film would have turned out if we had a $10M budget?

Professor: If you had a $10M budget, the only way I think the movie would have been different—and it would have been majorly different—is that you would have been beholden to masters, who'd want to apply marketing demographics to tell the story. Of course, that's assuming you didn't fund a $10M film out—of your own pocket with lottery winnings and maintained complete artisitc control.

QoL: OK, so there are two avenues here.

Professor: The word I was searching for before to tell how the first screening affected me was "visceral." Because I'd been there!

QoL: One, how would the film have been different as $10M 100% indie film? And how would it have been different as a $10M Hollywood film?

Professor: Ok, I think a 100% $10M film would have allowed you access to a much greater pool of resources, talent, technical, what have you. But maybe in the final analysis is it good that with what you wound up with that you didn't have that access to resources? Nah, you can never say no to the $. Whereas, with a H-Wood backed production I just think it would have lost all its backbone by committee and it would be this kinda bland teen fare.

QoL: Aside from having no money (which did suck, esp. from a people-power perspective), it seems like, in so many ways, things just kept falling into place. Like synchronicity was on our side. What would you attribute this to?

Professor: Simply, good leadership, vision and luck.

QoL: What about the graffiti model?

QoL: How did our approach affect our luck?

QoL: What could we have done differently? What really sucked about working on *QoL*?

QoL: oops. wait on that last question . . . sorry

Professor: The story and subject mos def did matter and was key. Everyone on the film had what Norman Mailer called the "Faith of Graffiti."

QoL: What's that all about?

Professor: That it does matter. And that graffiti says something about who and where we are as a society. Not a passing fad.

QoL: You have seen quite an evolution in graffiti over the past 30 years. Where do you think it will be 30 years from now?

Professor: (hiccup) Pls let me re-phrase: that graffiti matters in a larger context. Not just an individual or ego trip.

QoL: Legalized? Taught at colleges? Totally outlawed? Punishable by death? Non-existenat?

Professor: The biggest thing I've seen in 30 years time is the movement of graffiti from strictly the fringe to find its way into the galleries and commerce. I just returned from Europe and I saw it everywhere! I have no doubt graffiti will wind up in more academic currents, or formalized instruction in art schools.

QoL: What could we have done differently in making this film? What really sucked about working on *QoL*?

Snow Monkey doing what he does best.

Professor: I had a very positive, actually what for me going forward to work on other indies, was a "reference" experience with *QoL*, so to evaluate the alternate choices that could've been made is a little hard to do off the top of my head. No suckiness.

QoL: Come on.

QoL: Give it to me.

QoL: Some suckiness, somewhere.

QoL: If we could go back in time, what should we have done differently?

Professor: Ugh, ok, hearing from my wife how Kev the DP shot her out of focus in her scene.

QoL: Oh man.

QoL: That sucked.

QoL: Talk about a rushed shoot.

Professor: Ok, ok, that makes me think of something: next time have a monitor on the set!

QoL: There are certain things I kick myself for every time I watch the movie. And that one gets me every time.

QoL: It was my fault, really. Wasn't conscious of coverage.

QoL: Monitor would have been nice (-;

Professor: I'm sure, but you can see now how critical such a piece of equipment is.

QoL: OK. Need to go back and ask ONE MORE Q . . .

Professor: go for it.

QoL: The art auction at Punch gallery really launched us into production. It gave us the momentum (and cash) we needed to go into production. You were instrumental in pushing this event. Talk about your involvement, the success of the event, and how the community rallied to support us (esp. with all the free stuff you brought to the table).

Professor: The Punch gallery event presented an anchor or presented a form of legitimacy for the film to engage a wide variety of converging groups and interests, introduce them to what we were trying to do, and get their support. I talked and received support from everyone from the Hotel Triton to the more upscale Crown Point Press, among so many others.

QoL: Why did these people support?

QoL: (local businesses)

Professor: Least of all, I'm very appreciative for personal moral and support for the film we received from Campo Santo-Intersection for the Arts.

Professor: These people or local businesses supported in part out of self-interest, knowing that the people and audience of the film were also their customers, but also in large part because key individuals at these businesses identified with the "underdog" story and indie nature of the project.

QoL: Word. It's great to recognize the symbiotic, recripocal nature of donations. We could not have made this film without their support.

Professor: That's right. It is an extended community effort.

QoL: OK. Gotta go. Day job is calling.

QoL: I really appreciate all you have done to bring this project to fruition. I look forward to finishing this amazing and hellish journey with you.

INTERVIEW: **Sam Flores**

CONTRIBUTING ARTIST
INTERVIEWED BY BRIAN BURNAM

SEPT 23, 2005

Brian: So how did you get hooked up with this project?

Sam: Well, Brian Burnam's my boy, we're in the same crew together. I know him from San Francisco. So he asked me to put my art up in the movie for Dino's art opening.

Brian: So you went out with us to the first film festival in Berlin. What were some stories that went down there?

Sam: Well, the premiere after party was kinda crazy. Staying up, no sleep for 2 days, tequila and orange juice, trying to keep Prince Paul away from my girl. Staying up drinkin absinthe til the girls took their clothes off and starting playing records, dancing around with only one sock on.

After the festival, the hotel sent the damage bill to the Berlin film festival director. But he wasn't even mad; all he said was, "Hey, you invite the Sex Pistols to a party, you expect a few things to get broken!"

I remember comin back to the hotel wasted, out on the corner buying K-bab sandwiches. You were running out in the street, stoppin traffic, cramming your falafel in your face, screamin at girls. Up until one of them yelled back, "Hey look, it's Frodo, from the Lord of the Rings!!"

We caught Mario Van Peebles sneaking out of one of the girl's hotel rooms in the morning from our movie.

Brian: What do you think about the movie?

Sam: I think it's a real film. Most of the shots were filmed illegal on the streets, pretty much everything was authentic. I remember when you shot the scene where "Vain" had to steal a taxi cab on the street, but you didn't block off anything, it was right in front of traffic on Mission street and "Vain" robbed it at gun point. A van saw it and chased you down the street trying to run your ass over. I like that it felt like it portrayed real situations that we all deal with and they rang true in the movie.

90

Opposite page. T-shirt artwork for *QoL* by Sam Flores.

Local artists Sam Flores (above left), Kelly Tunstall (above right) and
Andy Schoultz (below left) contributed greatly to the *QoL* cause.

DO-IT-YOURSELF
FILM SCHOOL

How do you produce a narrative feature film in the Mission District of San Francisco with dozens of actors and locations (including a fair share of night exteriors) in eighteen days for $30,000? A coherent strategy and vision is a good start. But the team you assemble to attack this mission is the key to success (or failure).

We were fortunate enough to work with a phenomenal group of professionals on this project. Their vision, expertise, and determination guided this shipwreck-waiting-to-happen safely to shore.

They say directing is ninety percent casting. The same can be said for crew. Which is why we diligently sought to bring together the best team possible and give them the same level of creative control and overall involvement in the process we were seeking for ourselves.

We are all for the democratization of the filmmaking process (which is why we're writing this section—doye!). But, as much as we all want to say "fuck Hollywood!" and hit the streets, camera in one hand, boom pole in the other, we need to first consider the ramifications of our approach and develop strategies that will enable us to produce something compelling. The old adage "if you fail to plan, you plan to fail" is as true for filmmaking as it is for any endeavor.

Our core crew members, who were largely responsible for developing these strategies, have taken the time to put together a brief overview of how we made this movie. Included are chapters on DIY producing, cinematography, sound, and editing. I will take a moment here to discuss the general philosophy and approach of the film before we delve into their specific and technical discussions.

THE GRAFFITI MODEL

We knew from the get-go that we did not want to approach this film in a traditional manner. *Quality of Life* is obviously set in the graffiti subculture, so the film had to be raw, authentic, and faithful to this world. In order to achieve this, we adopted The Graffiti Model.

Graffiti writers create powerful, compelling pieces with few or no resources. They accomplish this with passion, diligence, and teamwork. Our crew configuration (i.e. doc mode) was designed to approach the subject matter with this ethic in mind, and we infected everyone on the project with it.

The Graffiti Model allowed us to be relaxed and efficient under very stressful conditions. We didn't have to worry about hauling a huge crew and tons of equipment everywhere we went. Shooting doc mode gave us the flexibility to move quickly and effortlessly and capture things in real time. That isn't to say there weren't serious logistical issues. (There were.) Or even carefully staged scenes. But the Graffiti Model empowered us to work with the resources we had.

In many ways, *Quality of Life* may not have been as authentic with a real budget. Being broke was an advantage. Although The Graffiti Model was born out of necessity, this ethic actually became a *style*.

98

Nonetheless, we still needed enough cash for film stock, processing, and food.

SHOW ME THE MONEY

Based on initial discussions with industry folks, we knew this script would get raped by Hollywood. ("Make them tag-bangers." "I want to know *why* they write graffiti." "Couldn't Heir be a woman?" etc. etc.) Not an option. We knew we had to maintain creative control to ensure the film came off. And traditional financing can take forever. We didn't have forever. So we set out to raise a bare bones budget of $30K from friends and family.

As stated above, our budget dictated our production model. With the Graffiti Model as our guiding principle, we set out to produce *Quality of Life* with what many people told us was an unrealistic budget and time frame. Incredibly enough, raising even that small chunk of change was a huge challenge for us.

Films get green-lighted with stars attached. But we didn't want stars. Aside from the creative disconnect of seeing a recognizable face in what was supposed to be an anonymous setting, the logistical issues (trailers, per diems, accommodations, etc.) would have slowed us down considerably. So stars were not an option. Nor was relinquishing creative control. So we were forced to seek financing from private investors.

We were able to secure initial investment from close friends and family (my dad bought the first share). But, with the July 28 start date looming on the horizon, we did not have enough money to make the film. So we held a fundraiser to boost momentum.

The fundraiser (called "Putting the Pieces Together") was held at Punch Gallery in SF a month before production was set to start. We had *amazing* support from some of the city's hottest artists: Sam Flores, Andy Schoultz, BigFoot, Bryan Dawson, Trust, Snow Monkey, Renos, Dave Schubert, and Kelly Tunstall, among others. Although it drained significant resources from the production team (i.e. planning the event, delivering art, etc.), the art auction was a huge success and proved to be just the momentum we needed.

We raised $6,000 at this event and initiated conversations with potential investors. Other friends and family contributed an additional $5,000 through small donations of $50 and $100 in return for getting their names in the credits. With the Graffiti Model in place, we knew that we could make this film for $30K. But we were going to need the community to get behind us 100% to make it happen.

THE BIRTHDAY CAKE THEORY

When you go into a bakery and order a fancy Harry Potter birthday cake for your kid, you're looking at maybe twenty five. Go into that same bakery and ask for a wedding cake, you are looking at ten to twenty times the price. It's the same damn cake, right? Maybe a few more ingredients and some extra frill. But twenty times the price?! WTF?

The same holds true for indie vs. Hollywood films. When you walk into a location and start throwing your money around, people get what you're all about. And you get the wedding cake. But when you walk into that same location, plead poverty, and convey a sense of passion and community, you are going to get birthday cake treatment.

Sunup on the rooftop and the shoot isn't over yet. Three more scenes to can this day before the film is a wrap.

The Birthday Cake Theory explains why independent films have so much heart (and Hollywood films for the most part don't). Indie filmmaking is a hands-on approach to what can be a very mechanical medium. This is why you see so much innovation and creativity in independent films. Hollywood films use money to solve their problems. Indie films don't have this option.

BRASS TACKS

The Graffiti Model and Birthday Cake Theory are great principles. But they are concepts, not solutions. The crew we assembled developed and implemented practical approaches to guide us safely through this seemingly impossible and overwhelming journey. Let's pull back the curtain and take a look at how they did this.

THEN MAKE YOUR OWN DAMN MOVIE
PRODUCING AN ULTRA-INDEPENDENT FILM

BY BRANT SMITH, PRODUCER

INTRODUCTION: ALLOW ME TO GREENLIGHT YOUR MOVIE, RIGHT NOW

Ultimately, no one is going to make the movie if you don't.

Hollywood doesn't care about you, and this includes the art house and independent film organs of the movie industry (sometimes known as Indiewood). The entire industry is set up to push out a very specific type of movie: star-driven features (even star-driven "indie" features). If you're a filmmaker (lesson #1: start introducing yourself as a filmmaker right now), you're on your own as far as the movie industry is concerned.

101

They don't care about you or your movie.

They don't want to fund your movie or buy it.

They don't want to attach stars to it or invite you to Sundance or do lunch.

And they really don't want to hear your pitch.

If you get introduced through a mutual friend, stumble upon them at a party or find the right phone number, they may be polite to you, but behind the festival glad-handing and chipper-on-the-phone assistant is 100 percent pure we-don't-give-a-shit.

Basically, don't expect to get any help from Hollywood or Indiewood—or Ed Wood's second cousin, for that matter.

From the film industry's perspective, ultra-indie movies like *Quality of Life* aren't supposed to exist, or at least, aren't supposed to do anything other than whimper off to DVD land, to be sold by the pound, if that.

You probably think your film is special. Well, everyone's baby is special. One thousand independent films are made each year—in the United States alone. Only about forty get any sort of distribution beyond New York and the Mothership (Los Angeles). And those tend to have stars, remember?

Maybe you do have stars in your film. Real bankable stars. Wow, that's cool. You can stop here. This section of the book isn't for you. If you can afford stars, you can afford a large crew of people

Brant Smith is the Producer of Quality of Life. *He worked closely with Director Benjamin Morgan on the story behind the screenplay, and together they produced the film. He is writing this bio in the third person at 3:19am after writing this whole chapter in one night. That pretty sums up both the job and the type of person who does it. Send help.*

If the movie is a surprise hit and a success, Brant will get all of the credit. If the movie is a huge flop, it's all Ben's fault. No wait, it's the other way around. Dammit.

(and a real producer, not a washed-up dot-com refugee like me). If you have genuine, recognizable movie stars (or really anyone famous attached), you are on a whole different level financially than most true indie filmmakers. Tthis book really isn't for you and while you're at it, give me your phone number since you should obviously invest in our next film.

But for the rest of you, the little people with no money and no stars like us, let's face the facts. This is what we learned and what we can offer you:

The entire industry—the producer's reps, the international sales agents, the acquisition execs, the press, the festival programmers and the money people—are 100% focused on avoiding a film like yours at all cost.

There is no oxygen for a film like yours.

So you need to create the oxygen yourself.

Don't waste your time trying to get into the Hollywood or Indiewood club. Don't move to LA and try to "work your way up" (i.e. working crap jobs on crap movies for crap pay, hoping to get promoted to be First Assistant Nobody one day). And please don't go to film school. Save the money and make a movie instead.

That's the bottom line and the core fundamental vision of this crazy independent film movement: you don't need anyone's permission to make your movie, except your own.

For *Quality of Life*, we set a date to start production, over a year in advance. Before the script was done. Before money was raised. Before it was cast or the crew was hired. That date was July 28, 2003. And dammit, we started production on that day.

Our mantra was this: this project is greenlit. Either get on board or get out of the way.

So are you ready to greenlight your project?

It's a big commitment. It will be the toughest thing you ever did. But if you dream about being a filmmaker or dream about making a feature film, you must cross the threshold. If not, no need to read on. Thanks for buying the book; there are lots of pretty pictures to look at.

For the rest of you, you ragtag fleet of starless, moneyless, hopeless filmmakers: fuck it all, let's get to work.

FAILURE IS NOT AN OPTION.

With a film, there are more details and skills required than you can imagine. We were in constant triage mode: deciding what was most important, doing it first and letting less important tasks (no matter how alluring) fall back or off the to-do list.

Through it all, our perspective on *Quality of Life* was simple: failure is not an option.

We just simply refused to take "no" for an answer. Sometimes that meant being polite or being firm or just plain begging.

Sometimes we found another way to get it done, when all else failed. We frequently hounded the people who could help us and quickly earned a reputation as pushy bastards. It was a small price to pay to create the oxygen for our film.

MAKING A MOVIE IS MOSTLY NOT ABOUT MAKING THE MOVIE

The stuff you read about in most filmmaking books or learn in film school (you know, how to frame a shot, how to edit, how to record sound, etc.) comprises about ten percent (often much less) of the actual work required to make a movie.

For instance, *Quality of Life* was shot in three weeks (and a weekend of pick-up shots). However, the lifetime of the project—from the first early script outlines to today (as of this writing in September 2005) has been well over four years. And it's not over yet, since we're distributing the film ourselves.

The *Quality of Life* timeline includes:

- Two solid years writing the script
- Six months writing the business plan
- Six months fundraising for the production
- Six months of casting, hiring and other pre-production
- One partial week of rehearsals
- Three weeks of production
- About four months of solid post-production (editing, sound-mixing, transferring, etc.)
- Five months fundraising for the festival premiere
- Just over a year on the festival circuit
- Six months rewriting the business plan
- Six months negotiating a distribution deal
- Six months raising funds for the distribution of the film
- Six months clearing the music
- Countless months doing other tasks such as marketing, publicity, and fighting fires all throughout

Yes, this adds up to more than four years. That's the point: it's a lot of work and you have to do a lot of it at the same time on parallel tracks. The production period where film is exposed (or video cameras are running) and actors say things and people run around looking for locations at the last minute—while fun and hectic—is a small little fleck of sand in this much larger oyster of total project activities.

If you're lucky and you work really hard, that oyster (the rest of the stuff) will turn that bit of sand into a pearl. (You knew I was going there with the oyster thing.)

Be prepared to tackle these other aspects of your film project and seek advisors who can help provide guidance for the unfamiliar areas.

You might feel like you're alone and totally ignorant about the process. Don't worry. That's right where you should be. But now you should start fixing that.

THE TEAM

The sooner you expand the team, the better. Even if you start just with a ragtag team of wannabes, like you (and me). Figure out what

roles you need filled and post ads for them. Ask friends for referrals. Get out there and network at filmmaking events and organizations.

Some years ago, I found myself unhappy in my job (ironically at a then-successful dot-com business I started and led). I had ignored my filmmaking dreams for years since college and turned to the sterile corporate world. Films weren't going to just happen though. I needed to take a step. So I ran into a guy I knew from my political organizing days who happened to run the local community TV station. He was a filmmaker, so I told him I wanted to get into it. I remember his words: "You need to work with Ben Morgan. He's going places."

Ben was making the second of his three "student" films—projects shot with community TV equipment and local actors. I volunteered to be his PA for a few days. The crew consisted of Ben on camera, his brother on sound, and me doing whatever. The movie (seventy plus minutes, mind you) won a regional cable award and is actually pretty damn good. Ben liked me (well, I think I was the only person who showed up on time consistently, so the bar was low) and he invited me back to partner with him on his next video project. We've been filmmaking partners ever since.

Neither of us could have made *Quality of Life* alone. He was the creative vision-holder and together we produced it.

You don't necessarily need a formal filmmaking partnership like ours, but you need more than just you.

You might be afraid of giving over control or sharing your baby with others. It's a tough issue that I too struggle with, both as a producer and a director. But filmmaking is team sport and learning to play well with others is the key to success.

ADVISORS

You can't be expected to be the world's best director or producer, right out of the gate. If you were as experienced as the best indie producers in the world, you would already have five indie films under your belt. No one expects you to be an expert. And there's a way to mitigate that: advisors.

Advisors are golden. They help you avoid pitfalls and give you inside info about the industry and who's who. We had some fantastic advisors, some of whom were connected via other advisors.

Seek out people who have done what you want to do and/or people who know a certain area that is new to you. We found advisors in all the following areas and more:

- Post-production
- Investment and fundraising
- Distribution/film festivals
- Theaters
- Self-distribution
- Producing
- Business
- Marketing/publicity

Most advisors will give you advice for free, particularly if they like you. Hint: be genuine and ethical . . . That's surely going to stand out if you're hitting up Hollywood folks.

104

Speaking of Hollywood, get advisors who know that world. While we strongly encourage people to greenlight their own projects and take their destiny in their own hands, it helps to know the industry and have insiders with experience to help direct you. This is particularly true if you want to get picked up by a distributor (most small indie distributors are basically just arms of the Hollywood machine).

If you want to self-distribute, getting industry advisors is not as important, but experienced indie film people may help you in ways you can't foresee (for example: understanding the film festival circuit will help you reach your audience since getting into better fests helps sales, both to distributors and viewers).

Basically, you can ask just about anyone out for lunch, coffee, a drink or just a short phone call. Some people (ourselves included) often will give advice and thoughts over email, since that's best for busy schedules. In fact, portions of this chapter were taken from emails I sent in response to questions from other filmmakers. Whatever the case, at least ask.

Some people who start businesses set up advisory boards, comprised of experts in relevant areas. Generally, the members get small percentages of the company (0.25 percent to 1 percent at the most active (boardmember) levels). Be prepared to give a little of the action to your advisors and incent them to help you get a big bump. We didn't do this formally and I really wish we had. If nothing else, they would help keep us working toward our goals when we wandered off the path.

STORY IS KING

We thought we could write the script in one year. As we were approaching the deadline, we realized it wasn't ready. So we gave it another year.

This was the only major milestone we moved out, because it wasn't ready.

We didn't move the production date that was set a year in advance. And we haven't moved the opening date for our theatrical run, which was set months ago. Both of these dates required money we did not have when we set them, and in both cases we didn't have enough money as they came upon us. We knew that if these dates weren't written in stone, they could keep moving back forever, and sometimes seeing the end of the runway has a way of helping the bird get off the ground.

But writing is different.

The story is everything. Forget about the actors. The production costs. The festivals. The parties. The fawning groupies. The unpaid legal bills and unresolved paternity suits. It all starts with the story.

It's like this: there are three things that can make your movie happen. Generally speaking, the spark of life only comes from one (or more) of these:

❍ Big star(s)
❍ Big money
❍ Great script

As we already outlined, if you're reading this, you don't have stars or money.

So you better as hell have a damn good script. Not just my-mom-likes-it good, but strangers-cry-when-they-read-it good. The single best way to get your indie film made is to become the best screenwriter out there.

I'm not suggesting you become a screenwriter and abandon your dreams of being a director and/or producer. Rather, in order to fuel the film, you need to bring the great script so you can be the great director/producer.

Another option would be to buy a great script from someone else. But that's Hollywood thinking, and I don't know anything about that. Sounds risky. Good luck. Of course, our producer's rep was the guy that bought the *Full Monty* script and helped turn it into a movie, so it's possible to find the right script and make it into a successful film. But he's a Hollywood guy and was working at a major Hollywood studio, so there you go. That doesn't sound like you, though.

If you're not the creative vision-holder (i.e. not the writer/director), respect the person's vision, but also push him/her to produce stronger work. I also am a writer/director-in-training, so in learning about story structure for my own projects, I was able to help Ben craft the story structure of *Quality of Life* and push him further. The script was stronger for that.

By the way, even documentary films have stories. Story quality sets a great documentary film apart from the bad ones. The es-sential three-act story structure doesn't change, just your production and editing approach.

Ultimately, what you get with a strong script is something that other people want to be part of. That's what happened to us. Kev Robertson—Director of Photography—read the script and loved it. He really "got it." And once he had bought in, he brought a small crew of regulars with him (guys that he convinced to work way under their usual scale, using his reputation and leverage to get the deals from them so we could afford them).

Our strong script was also used to raise money from friends and family (we showed it to prospective investors, whoe we ap-proached with a solid business plan). We didn't raise a lot, but enough to make the movie (barest of bones).

As you start to build a team around the script, plus maybe get a little money, and perhaps a few advisors . . .

Suddenly you look around and you're a real movie project.

Oh shit.

MONEY

Money sucks. I hate dealing with money. Or at least, I hate deal-ing with it when I have no money. I'm sure even rich people complain about their money; where to put it all? Such a pain for them too.

Well, as you now have a script and you might have a small team

(perhaps ambitious interns from the local college or dreamers like yourself from the local filmmakers' organization), it's time to raise some money to get this project off the ground.

One of the prime commandments of indie filmmaking is to do things differently and creatively. Fundraising is scary, but it can be creative.

First, you need to decide if you're a non-profit or a for-profit organization.

If you're non-profit, you might be able to get grants. You know how many grants there are for narrative filmmakers? About six. No just kidding. Really almost three. And about twelve thousand filmmakers who want them all. Didn't seem worth it to us, since you can't seek investors if you're a nonprofit, just donors. And we knew we needed the kind of money that only investors can provide.

I'm sure that plenty of filmmakers get non-profit status, get some funding and make great movies. Some even seem to do it as a commercial entity with nonprofit sponsorship, whatever that means. That wasn't us. Because of my background running small businesses, I only felt comfortable in the for-profit world. So I stuck to what I knew and knew we needed to raise money by promising a return, and we couldn't do that as a non-profit.

We choose to become an LLC, which is all the rage among small businesses like ours (not just films). You get liability protection (somewhat similar to a standard corporation), but not the double taxation. I don't know why this is legal (seems to be like another way to screw the commons, but I'm cynical about such things), but we used it nonetheless.

One thing to keep in mind when you draw up your investment and LLC documents: have a sunset clause wherein all rights go back to the filmmaker (you or jointly held with other filmmaker(s) on the project) after a certain period (five years after distribution revenues start coming in?). That way, you're not dealing with paying people a few dollars a year thirty years from now. We didn't put a sunset clause in and it's something that has been eating at me. Then I saw that another filmmaker had done it in their biz plan and I thought, shit, we should have done that too.

Incidentally, though we are a for-profit company, we still acted like a non-profit. We had a contribution program, where people who couldn't afford to invest thousands of dollars were asked to contribute to the film in small amounts, just as if we were a non-profit—except it wasn't tax-deductible to the contributors (we didn't call them donors for this reason). We raised about $6,000 this way. That was about 20% of our shooting budget (yes, we shot the film for $30,000, plus about $5,000 that was used to edit the rough cut). We told people we'd put their names in the credits if they contributed. If you contributed over a certain amount, you could even put a message in the credits (and two families did).

We called this "selling screen credit," like selling ad space in the back of the school yearbook. Everyone loves supporting the home team and not everyone can afford an investment.

Also, look to your subject matter for possible funding strategies. Our film was set in the graffiti subculture of San Francisco's

Quality of Life Film presents:

Putting the Pieces Together

A PARTY TO BENEFIT QUALITY OF LIFE

A LOCAL INDEPENDENT FEATURE FILM PROJECT FILIMING IN SAN FRANCISCO THIS SUMMER.
Quality of Life tells the fictional story of a graffiti artist coming of age in the Mission District of San Francisco.

Imagine a world where the Mona Lisa is shredded to bits, hours after it was created, the ceiling of the Sistine Chapel is buffed and painted white to send a message of intolerance to other Renaissance Artists, and Pablo Picasso is locked in a cell for creating "the worst form of pollution we have ever seen." Welcome to the world of a modern day graffiti writer.

FRIDAY, JUNE 27th

8 – 10PM PUBLIC RECEPTION,
ART SHOW, AND SILENT AUCTION
10PM – 2AM HIP-HOP DJs AND DANCING
Punch Gallery
155 10th Street
$10-30 sliding scale at the door

FEATURING SHOW AND SILENT AUCTION
FOR ARTWORK FROM THE FOLLOWING ARTISTS :

Sam Flores	Sophie Kamin	Kieran Swan
Kelly Tunstall	Hollie Smith	Andy Schoultz
Rogelio Martinez	Dave Schubert	RENOS
ESPO	Big Foot	DIET
Demetrie Tyler	Israel Forbes	CYME 742
Nathan Smith	Bryan Dawson	ROLEX

MUSIC BY: **Ren the Vinyl Archeologist (True Skool)**

DJ Bre'ad (Exact Science) **DJ Metasense (Meta4)**

The screenplay for Quality of Life was co-written by an artist active in this movement and has generated major support from the artists participating in this event and beyond.

Mission District. We held two separate art shows featuring graffiti writers and others influenced by street art, mostly from the Mission. We split the proceeds with the artists, to help support them. We netted another $6,000 from that, plus we impressed a number of people who later became investors themselves.

So we raised over a third of our shooting budget from ways other than investment, all done creatively.

The projects I write and direct are all science fiction films (unlike Ben, who writes and directs films all about at-risk youth). So last year for my birthday, I hosted a sci-fi themed party to help fund a sci-fi short I'm working on. I posted it on numerous online event calendars and invited all my friends. There were some DJs (friends of mine), some yummy vegan cake, a silent auction (art, services and other items donated by friends), and a bar (well, a case of wine and a case of beer). I projected old sci-fi movies on the wall.

It was a fantastic birthday. My friends all came, plus some strangers due to the online calendars. Between the door fee, the bar and the silent auction, I ended up with well over $700 toward my short film after all costs. It's not Spielberg money, but it's a start.

As for investors: you need a hardcore business plan. Get a business plan book or template and work from that. We got a softcopy version of an advisor's successful indie film biz plan and did a wholesale copy and paste (our film's name for theirs) throughout the whole thing. Then started ripping it apart, section by section, rewriting it to focus on our target audience and business specifics.

A year later, a new advisor gave us his film's business plan. It was much stronger and more hardcore. So we basically started from scratch and rewrote ours to match that format.

After that, we constantly got compliments on the business plan, since it was fat and looked impressive. And, more importantly, we were seen as a business team that had our shit together and that others should look toward as an example. Soon, we became advisors to others trying to do the same thing.

One other tool that's important in raising funds from investors: a presentation. Usually using PowerPoint, these investor presentations should just focus on the core strengths of the film, talk about the audience and the potential return. In eight to fifteen slides, you should be able to tell the core story from your business plan, perhaps with shots from your scouting photos or even casting calls, to give the clear impression of onward progress.

Our best presentation was done as we were trying to raise money for distribution. We filled half of each slide with a photo still from the movie. The whole presentation basically said: "This film is DONE. Come on in!"

Lastly, about finding investors.

You should pitch anyone you know and anyone you don't know who you think might have money—or who knows people who do. It's good practice, even if they pass.

But in reality, you're going to raise your money from friends and family, unless you're a very, very savvy salesperson.

And that's a good thing. Because all our money came from friends and family, when I was ready to quit and bail halfway through production, all that kept me in was that I couldn't walk away from this responsibility. I had convinced so many friends and family to believe in me and believe in the project. I had basically promised them I would be the custodian of their money.

I'm not proud to admit that it wasn't the dream, it wasn't the art, it wasn't the project and it wasn't my solidarity with Ben that kept me in during that darkest hour. It was the idea of my friends and family losing their money and letting them down. And that thin reed got me through the storm to the other side.

BUDGETING

Budgeting is easy. Just ask your advisors. Find out what things cost by calling vendors and post-production studios and transfer houses. Call SAG.

Our budget was $1,000,000 after we did the research.

We only could raise about $30,000, as it turned out (another $5,000 came in during production, allowing us to fund a rough cut edit of the film).

Most of the heads of the departments and key staff (producers, director, DP, writers, AD, PM, etc.) got equity deferments, which means they had the right to turn their deferments into equity in the production company as if they were investing cash. That was unusual, but highly attractive, since investors get paid back before standard deferments in standard film deals.

A few tradespeople were paid cash, since that was the only way to get them and productions values would have suffered. They were paid VERY low rates since they worked so much with the DP, who fully supported the project. He was able to get us amazing day rates (I can't even say what they were, they were so low).

The DP brought his own Super16 camera and prime lenses, which we rented from him as part of the deal with him (it was a separate equity deal — no cash). The sound guy brought his own cart and we paid extra cash for that per day. Then we rented a grip van from Arthur Freyers. We ended up using the grip van as a prop (the main characters are house painters, so they needed a rig for the story). You need to be creative on these things!

We got our locations for free (when you're this small, you're a "community project" and people are happy to invite you in to shoot). We got donations for wardrobe and even food sometimes (rarely).

Food is important. Even if you can't pay your crew, you better damn well feed them. If you have $500 and you're not sure if you should pay them or feed them, better to feed them well and not pay them than pay them and not feed them well.

Quality of Life seemed really blessed. A lot of people and businesses stepped up to support us, often providing free or severely discounted products and services.

What's the secret of getting something free (or hugely discounted) for your movie?

Just ask for it.

Ben calls this the Birthday Cake Theory, and he does a good job explaining it in the beginning of this section. The basic idea is that everything is more expensive on a big production and that merely by having money, everything costs more. A birthday cake has the same basic ingredients as a wedding cake, but they charge you through the nose for the wedding cake since it's such an expensive event already. So we made it clear we were a birthday and not a wedding, in terms of funding and "vibe." Birthdays, after all, are a lot less formal and more improvisational than a wedding. That matched our style (and budget) well.

Honestly, we couldn't have made *Quality of Life* without the donations and deep discounts we got at nearly every step. As it turns out, most people really want to be part of something cool like a small indie film. They want to see you succeed.

If you're having trouble getting support, it helps to remind people and businesses that others are stepping up and that "the community is supporting this project." Such context helps them rationalize their otherwise crazy behavior of giving you free stuff.

These two rules alone account for about fifty percent of guerrilla producing: "ask for it for free" and "don't take no for an answer."

You can see how these work well together, when combined. Add in "be creative" and you have just about all the rules you need to produce an indie film (of course, the fourth necessary rule is "be ethical," since the world has enough assholes).

Overall, what this all means is that your limited budget is a strength, not a weakness. With it, you get volunteer support and no/low cost services and materials.

Also, having no money makes you more creative. You can't just throw money at a problem. You solve things in other ways, and find ways to turn lemons into lemonade. For instance, a week before production, our lead actor landed a paying TV role and dropped out (we were paying him nothing upfront and the TV role was real cash). Quickly, we cast screenwriter Brian Burnam—a former graffiti writer who had never acted previously (it was his first screenplay too)—and the movie suddenly had a genuine graffiti writer (retired) as one of the lead actors. Brian brought such strength and authenticity to the role; the other actor didn't have any of that (though he was a good actor). That authenticity is what the movie is all about and having no money made it possible.

This is truly the Graffiti Model for filmmaking. Take something with no apparent value, plan well, execute cheaply and quickly, and from that comes art.

PRE-PRODUCTION

Who are we kidding? We didn't have time for real pre-production.

We were too busy casting (Ben's job), trying to raise money (my job), and hiring the crew (together). Plus I had a day job. ("Luckily" Ben was laid off two months before production began.)

Nothing was finalized more than a day or so in advance. In fact,

110

the night before our first day of production, we still didn't have our first location locked (I went out and secured it just as the sun was setting). Throughout the production, there were two teams: the production team with the cast and camera, and a pre-production team, scurrying around a day (or less) ahead of the production team, barely locking locations, securing props and generally pulling things together at the last minute. You could call it "just in time" filmmaking. It nearly drove me crazy, but we got the job done.

How we pulled it off with no formal pre-production and yet ended up with such a strong film:

1. A great DP and crew, who could work well under these unpredictable conditions.
2. Much of Ben's limited pre-production time was spent on casting (the most important part of directing).
3. A subject matter well-suited for a gritty, improvisational filmmaking style.
4. Ben's the fastest director in the west: most shots got one or two takes. Rarely three takes. Never four. We moved quickly.
5. Above all, a great team doing the pre-production work, while shooting was going on. Big shout-outs to Meika, Dan, and Jason. In fact, I'm not even sure our Location Manager Jason really exists in the real world. He basically appeared within the first few days of production and disappeared after production ended. I've never seen or heard of him since. A seriously strong team, with a whole army of assistants and PAs backing them up.

That's the recipe for success.

CASTING IS KEY

We hired Belinda Gardea, an amazing casting director based in LA. I highly recommend getting a casting director who knows what he or she doing. This is a crucial role often overlooked by small indie films.

Casting is ninety percent of directing, so Ben spent a ton of time on this. We cast out of LA because the acting scene is so much stronger there than here (sadly). We recommend you call up casting directors from your favorite recent indie films and see if they have an assistant who is looking to get some experience as a casting director. That's what we did and it worked great.

DAY JOBS

It's tough to produce a feature film while you are trying to pay your bills. Despite the glitter of Sundance gold, it's a rough life. Balancing it all can be challenging. If you can afford to work full-time on your film, go for it.

But if you can't quit your day job? No worries! If you're doing a kick-ass job producing, you'll probably get fired anyway . . . I did.

Let's move on.

FESTIVALS

Even though we dis "Indiewood" and I lambasted the festival circuit at the start of this chapter, the fests serve a vital role in making your film successful.

Remember the three ingredients that make your film attractive to various stakeholders:

- Stars
- Money
- A strong script

Once you have made it, the money is basically gone (as if you had much to begin with) and the script is shot. This narrows to only two possible factors that will determine your success in the traditional Indiewood world:

- Stars
- A great, award-winning film

Assuming you're still the same person who had no stars in your film, you better start getting into some major festivals and winning awards. Festivals validate the film and provide a way for Indiewood executives to market your film, both here and overseas.

But not all festivals are created equal.

Be careful of which festivals you choose, since if you open at a C-rate festival, the A-list fests will likely pass you over since they want world/regional/national premieres. We made it to the short list at Tribeca (would have been a great fest for us), but they weren't happy we were doing our North American premiere at Cinequest in San Jose. They said it wasn't a deal killer, but it definitely hurt us and we didn't get in.

Look at it this way: the three most important things that distributors look for are: stars, stars, and stars.

If you don't have a star, the film better be damn good (think of yourself as a viewer . . . if there are no stars, and the film sucks, why would you bother?). The way that films without stars are marketed is via reviews and festival appearances (and awards).

Thus, what the festival circuit "does best" for a film is make it more marketable—IF you get into the right, high-profile festivals.

At the high-profile fests, you get access to more industry folks, more buyers, more press and so on. But even if you don't connect with any of them (which was our experience basically at Berlin), you still have the laurel wreath ("Official Selection - Berlin 2004," etc.), which lasts forever.

Smaller regional fests can hurt you, as I mentioned (they make you look like you're desperate and not very good, if they are the only fests you've been in), but if you're going direct to DVD (a likely scenario for most small indies), then playing lots of small fests can create awareness for the film, on the festivals' dime(s). But of course, dreaming big, you never plan on going direct to DVD, so it's a tough call.

The festival issue is not a simple one. It's like making sure you aren't seen at the wrong club with the wrong person, but you still have to show up to some club or no one will notice you at all.

A producer's rep should help you get into the right fests and make the most of the fests you get into by getting the buyers there. More on that later.

112

You can also use the festival run as your testing ground for marketing plans and for connecting with your audience for the film. That's what we did, with some good success (sold out screenings, etc.).

Here's an off-the-top list for you:

A-list fests (you probably know these already):
- Sundance
- Toronto
- Cannes
- Berlin
- Venice

The top B-list fests (random assortment, the best are at the top):
- Seattle
- Telluride
- Tribeca
- Rotterdam
- London
- Stockholm
- LA Film Fest
- South-by-Southwest
- Las Vegas
- New York International
- New Directors
- San Francisco International
- Mill Valley (somewhat)
- Cinequest (somewhat)

C-list fests:
- Nearly all regional and local fests (i.e. "The Greater Suburbia International Film and Wine Festival on the Green" etc.)

You can bet that the B-list changes pretty often (and sometimes, every few decades, the A-list too), so this is good for 2005, but probably not for 2015. (I'm sure the death of filmmaking will be predicted about ten times between now and then. Yawn.)

Regional and city-level fests (basically lower B-list fests and below) are pretty disorganized, with some exceptions (Seattle was great!). I have none that I would actively recommend against on singular merit (or lack thereof), but I would recommend against going into any B-list fest (or lower B-list fest) until you know you aren't getting into any A-list fest and/or upper B-list fest. The A-list fests want premierse. So I would only recommend against a fest in context of the overall fest strategy.

You might be able to impress your family with all the B and C-list festival wreaths on your poster, but savvy film people know their festivals and can smell crap, so be careful.

Festivals we played at and why:
- Berlin (World Premiere): A-list festival, where we won a jury award (Special Mention).
- Cinequest (North American Premiere): B-list festival (timing was bad for other North American A-list fests (Sundance and Toronto) and we didn't want to wait another six months to play there).
- Seattle: fantastic B-list festival, great reputation and organization.

The 16th Stockholm International Film Festival
November 17–27, 2005

- Stockholm: biggest festival in northern Europe, best for Scandinavia.
- Gijon, Spain: strong youth festival.
- Cinema Paradise (Hawaii): upcoming festival with reputation for edgy films like ours.
- Film Arts Festival (San Francisco): shut out by the behemoth San Francisco International Festival in our hometown (don't get me started), we decided that the timing was right to have our local premiere here, since so many of us are part of the local filmmaker organization (Film Arts Foundation) that puts it on.
- Stockholm Jr.: youth oriented festival, put on by the Stockholm festival. We won the award for Best Youth Film . . . our second award, so we can say we've won awards (plural).
- Rhythm of the Line Graffiti Film Festival, Berlin: a graffiti film festival in Berlin? We had no choice!

In addition to these, we played a couple other small festivals, mostly to try to get some extra visibility. Doing festivals takes time and energy and ultimately, we were focused on getting the film a distribution deal and into theaters.

Some publicity lessons we learned on the festival circuit:
- Wish we had a better *Variety* reviewer in Berlin (he sucked). Identify the reviewers who will "get" your film based on their other positive reviews of similar films. We didn't do that and got slammed.

- Save up your juice for the theatrical run as much as possible. Some people disagree on this, saying that you want as much publicity as possible, whenever possible. The reality is that many publications will only do a story once. Festivals don't pay you back, the theatrical (or really the DVD) does.

- Don't assume the festival will do your publicity for you. Take control and do it yourself. It may ruffle their feathers at the festival publicity office, but contacting press yourself is the key, in concert to what they're doing. This is particularly true of B-list fests (which have less coverage to begin with). Find a local hook and try to work that angle somehow.

WHAT DOES A PRODUCER'S REP DO?

Good question.

Basically, we studied this one a lot. We weren't convinced we needed a rep. Why should we pay up to fifteen percent of our gross earnings to someone for basically just making a few introductions?

The truth of the matter is that producer's reps serve an important gate-keeping function for the indie film distributors. Basically, they act as unofficial acquisition execs, who watch all the films (remember those 1000 films made each year?) and then pick the best to offer to the distributors. Granted, the distributors are also trying to watch as many films as possible (they don't want to get left behind), but there's just too much "product" out there.

To cut to the chase: without Bob Aaronson, our producer's rep, we probably would have a much worse distribution deal and/or no deal at all. We wouldn't have gotten the film in front

114

of all the main indie distributors' acquisition execs, which is also important for our careers (for future projects). Even though most passed on the project, at least we're now on their radar professionally. And we'll be back with the next project, to be sure.

It was through this process of setting up distributor screenings and putting us in front of the right people that we got four offers for our film. The deal we signed was directly due to one of the two distributor screenings that Bob organized.

How do you find producer's reps? Personally, I suspect they are a semi-dying breed, since it's a tough job (would you want to spend your life watching new films (the majority of which are from the bad side of the 1000 new films a year) and trying to convince acquisition execs to open their wallets? ugh.) You should read up on *Variety* and the various festival reports. They are often cited. Also, you can get referrals from reps who pass on your project (the A-list reps might recommend B-list reps who might recommend C-list reps, etc.). Or ask one of your advisors.

What qualities make a project a good/bad candidate for working with a producer's rep?

Remember, they want to rep projects that have a great chance of selling, since they make most of their money from commission. Thus, they look for what distributors look for: stars, stars, and stars. If not that, then big fests and big fest awards (sound familiar?). If not that, (i.e. if it's before your festival premiere), then a damn amazing film with clear box office appeal (i.e., a clear marketing approach).

Ninety-five percent of the reps we talked to passed on *Quality of Life*. We only had three that were interested, Bob and two others, who came recommended from yet another rep.

Well by now, you're more than hip-deep in Indiewood. In fact, you're pretty much up to your earlobes. If you're interested in a producer's rep, then be prepared to be sold off as quickly as possible, so the rep can move on to the next project. For many reps, films are about quantity, not quality. Since so much of what they make is based on commission, they need to spread their risk around.

Remember, this is the world where you are nothing, since you have no stars. Maybe you have an A-list festival award (like us). Even so, we basically got a glorified home video deal and decided to do theatrical ourselves as part of it. Not exactly Miramax glory.

DISTRIBUTORS

Do not send out your film on tape or DVD to distribution execs! Force them to come to a screening at a festival or outside a fest where they have to sit with all their competitors. We had two buyers' (aka distributors) screenings (NY and LA of course). Our deal came from the NY screening.

Do not give your film out on tape or DVD, even though they will ask for it. Your rep will help with this situation, if you get one. If you don't, then you have to do the leg-work (phone-work, really) of getting distributors to see the film at a buyers' screening or a festival. Keep in mind that most distributor

DUG ONE. TMF at Sycamore and Mission.

types only go to A-list festivals. But then again, the Miramax person saw our film at Seattle, so go figure. Of course, she passed, but we weren't exactly Miramax material (John Travolta couldn't handle the handstyles).

SELF-DISTRIBUTION

We're still writing the chapter on this one. In three weeks we open in one theater in San Francisco. We're renting the theater (called "four-walling") for two or three weeks, because we believe that's actually a better deal for us than if we got a traditional theatrical deal where we might get as little as 35 percent of the box office. With four-walling, we get 100 percent of the box office (but we have to pay for the rental upfront of course). Since we expect (and hope) to do well in our hometown, it seemed like a smart risk.

One thing to keep in mind: know your target audience well and sell them DVDs from your website. Make sure you can do so, even if you get a video deal with someone else, even if you need to buy the DVDs from the distributor (ideally at cost). You should think of your website as the center of your film's universe, so people go there to buy DVDs, find out about the film, and perhaps buy merchandise. In this way, you build an ongoing connection with your fan base, which can provide an ongoing core audience for your future films. The more you connect with your audience directly, the less you need Hollywood, Indiewood or old Ed Wood's second cousin.

The big picture vision for indie filmmakers like you and me is that we can now make the film ourselves (thanks to digital tools, primarily) and distribute it ourselves (thanks to the internet, primarily), owning 100 percent of the rights and earning 100 percent of the revenues. Totally outside of any Hollywood or Indiewood gatekeepers.

Good luck and feel free to invite us to the premiere.

If you want to get in touch with us or see additional behind-the-scenes goodies, we've created a special part of our website for you:

www.qualityoflife-themovie.com/ptpt

116

THE FILMIC THROW-UP
SOLUTIONS FOR THE ULTRA-LOW BUDGET DP

BY KEV ROBERTSON, DP/CAMERA OP.

THE *QUALITY OF LIFE* LOOK

The look for *Quality of Life* came from graffiti. Very early in our talks about how the film should look, Ben gave me a pile of graffiti books, magazines and videos and hooked me up to go on a San Francisco underground graff tour with a local "writer." I have always had a passing interest in graffiti, so I was delighted to have this opportunity to see and learn more about graffiti firsthand. San Francisco has a rich graffiti subculture so there was plenty to see. As I learned on my tour, there are three basic approaches to doing graffiti: (1) a "tag," which is a very quick moniker; (2) a "throw up," which is a more elaborate image, preplanned but executed quickly; and (3) a "piece," which is far more elaborate and design-heavy and takes time to execute. I took photos of all the varied forms of graffiti as my "tour guide" executed tags and a throw up-along the way.

The examples of graffiti I was most drawn to are a certain type of throw-up that depends on placement—that is, the work looks perfect in its environment and has a bold, messy beauty. It is often aggressive and calm, tasteful and garish, somber and funny . . . all in the same image. Such throw ups perfectly illustrate the ambiguity of graffiti—beautiful art or urban blight? The more I looked, the more these types of throw-ups popped out at me like an exciting gift. This work seems to bring harmony to the city, balancing against the omnipresent barrage of slick sales propaganda on every billboard.

As Ben and I talked more about the script and the shooting approach, the Graffiti Model became our mantra. Like the graffiti writers executing a throw up, we would work small and very fast. I was fascinated with the idea of shooting a film that had the same type of ambiguity of beauty versus blight, tinged with an element of danger, like the graffiti I had seen on the walls.

THE FILMIC THROW-UP

We often worked at night in "live" locations with the hovering risk that our shoot would be closed down. The film was executed in a semi-documentary style. While the documentary approach to the look was partly dictated by budgetary constraints, it also was completely in keeping with our visual intent for the film to look like a filmic throw-up. On a hyper low-budget film like this, turning weakness into strength becomes crucial. Our big weakness

Kev Robertson grew up in a fishing town in the frozen north of Scotland. He started out with the BBC in London as an assistant cameraman and moved up to cameraman in the documentary features division. His spare time was spent shooting art films and music videos. While still in London, Robertson had the good fortune to meet and work with two legendary British DPs—David Watkin and Roger Deakins. This experience galvanized a developing passion for narrative film and prompted a move to California. Kev's distinct photographic style quickly gained attention and he became a highly sought-after DP shooting award-winning films, music videos and commercials.

Prior to the brutal eighteen-day Quality of Life *guerilla shoot, Robertson's work included* Americanos, *an official selection at Cannes. This critically acclaimed film went on to win awards at seven international festivals. Robertson is also an accomplished music video DP. His elite group of clients (including Warner Brothers and Jive Records) return to him regularly to film high-profile music videos for artists such as Grammy nominee Jay-J, Jason Newsted of Metallica, and multi-platinum hip-hop star E-40. His second feature film,* Black August, *about the prison activist and writer George Jackson (author of* Soledad Brother) *stars Gary Dourdan of the TV show* CSI. *Robertson's most recent film,* The Flight That Fought Back, *is a drama/documentary chronicling the events on board flight 93 during the 9/11 attacks. The film, narrated by Keifer Sutherland, premieres theatrically across the country September 2005. It will also air on Discovery. His next film is with Oscar-winning director Peggy Rajski and will start principal photography February 2006.* www.gucciboy.com

was having so little money. Our big strength became not having a big crew to move around (logistics is such a huge part of making a film) and being free to work spontaneously as opportunity presented itself.

I took about 200 photographs on my graff tours. Ben and I edited this down to one image that would then be the visual hook for the film. It was the reference point we used in approaching the film's overall look. I deconstructed that image to find the elements that make it work. In this instance the image (a picture of Brian at the tunnel) has a formal composition but not quite. The image has depth but is also quite minimal—it has a soft, almost romantic focus, but is also stark and hard. In short, the image is beautifully "wrong." It evokes the ambiguity of the throw-ups I was drawn to and has the feel we wanted for the film.

STEPPING AWAY FROM ACCEPTED FILM GRAMMAR

While developing the look for the film, it struck me that the preconceived notions in feature film visual grammar of "beautiful" framing and "perfect" focus could be twisted to achieve the *Quality of Life* look. Stepping away from accepted film grammar on my first feature film was perhaps the first risk.

I decided to shoot the whole film with the lens wide open at T 1.3, which makes the depth of field (focus) quite shallow. This introduces inherent focus "problems." If an actor does not hit his mark or moves his head in an unexpected direction having depth of field will accommodate this and keep him in focus. In motion picture photography the DP is usually obliged to have the main actor in any given scene lit and in focus. But there were many

areas in this story that I could see would benefit from shots being dark and/or out of focus. I felt very strongly about being true to the Graffiti Model and there is not much good graffiti without risk. So this risk with focus was important for our film. It also pushed us quite firmly into an area of ambiguity (like the throw ups: "good" art/"ugly" mess). It would become an intrinsic element of the film's look.

A good example of this approach is the liquor store scene where Vain and Heir have a blow-out argument on the sidewalk (brown-bagging it, with real beer). I was shooting a master shot, hand-held (at two stops under wide open) on a 50mm lens (depth of field is about two inches). This scene is unblocked. There is no way to hold critical focus (on this long lens) as the actor moves. I did not attempt to pull focus on the lens, rather I simply set the lens at six feet and felt out the scene, making very small movements forward or backward, allowing the actor to hit focus as it felt right for the emotional intent of the delivery. We could have shot the scene one more time on a wide lens (9.5mm) and used that as the master. We decided against that in favor of this more intimate (technically "messy") approach. I think it works because it feels like a violent argument with a good friend, getting fuzzy then sharp again.

Framing is another main element that helps build the look of a film. It has a far deeper set of conventions than focus, which is an optical phenomenon. These rules and styles go way back in culture before photography to when we first moved away from cave drawings (graffiti?) to putting a frame around a picture. So composition was another opportunity to tweak the "norm." The approach here was to let the emotions of a scene influence the framing

118

more than design or good taste. Allowing the shot to not be beautiful or perfect, to just plain wrong, as the story called for.

I awoke with a start one night about halfway through the film thinking, "What the hell am I doing shooting the entire film wide open? And in this off-kilter way?!" But that is exactly when you do not want to waiver. Don't let the doubts take over; stay the course, stay with the look. It was true and was working (or I thought it was). I had to trust my instinct, as we did not see a frame of film until it was processed after the eighteen-day shoot. I think taking this approach paid off; the look worked, and it was definitely ours—beautifully wrong.

TWO WORLDS

Once the overall idea (the film as a throw-up) was in place, a daytime and nighttime look evolved, too. In the process of looking at graffiti and the graff culture, it became clearer to me why writers do what they do. Apart from the obvious, what twenty year old doesn't want to stay up all night partying and getting up to no good? This is a great creative outlet with a huge audience. From the public, they get reactions ranging from shock and outrage to admiration and imitation (wrap-around ads on buses, for example, are a direct lift from the top-to-bottom graffiti technique used on trains). There is also great respect given to these young men and women by their peers. One important part of this lifestyle is that it takes a rock-and-roll type approach. Painting gets done late at night so staying out all night is normal even on evenings with perhaps minimal painting. Holding down a decent day job is hard, so a lot of writers opt for low grade, easy-to-flake-on type jobs, which are consequently somewhat boring. Their daytime

world stands in stark contrast to their nighttime world. I wanted to give the film this feeling too. So the daytime scenes in the film are cool flat and more static. The nighttime scenes are more golden color and have a lot more camera movement.

The nighttime graffiti scenes are the most colorful and grainy, with a cartoon sprayed-on look. This was achieved as much as possible by finding locations that we could push in either direction (cool/warm) with minimal lighting. Then on the HD Digital Intermediate, I pushed that as far as we could. (In retrospect, we could have gone further. When the HD blows up to 35mm it looses saturation. We had no time to do more than one crack at it, as we were working at a breakneck pace for the Berlin Festival, where had been invited to premiere just a mater of weeks after our wrap.)

UNORTHODOX CONVENTIONS

I had just read *The Art of War* by Sun Tzu (translated by Thomas Cleary). The chapter on "Emptiness and Fullness" was a big influence on my working method.

"To be able to use the unorthodox as orthodox and use the orthodox as unorthodox, changing in a whirl, making yourself unfathomable to opponents, is being formless."

This idea of formlessness and going between the orthodox or "right" (film industry) way of doing things and unorthodox or "wrong" way of doing things and mixing them up was a good method for *QoL*. It fit with the Graffiti Model and helped give the film its look, which is somewhat ironic, as I wanted the film not to

look like a film. This method also had a certain built-in integrity. In simple pragmatic terms, we were so small and under the radar that adopting a more traditional movie model would simply not have worked very well. The trick is to let the script inform these choices and not to take an approach that just looks cool or is contrary for the sake of it.

Early in the film, when Pops calls Mikey on the phone to wake him up, Mikey is very out of focus for the first sequence of shots. He eventually leans forward into perfect focus as he wakes. We shot this in a controlled "set" so bringing the actor into focus earlier was tempting (he is out of focus longer than one would expect) but that would have been inconsistent with our approach. I think this is lovely for a couple of reasons. It fits with that blurry waking-up feeling we all have in the morning and it introduces the audience to the out-of-focus look early on. The street fight scene during the opening credits is a real brawl and perhaps the only true documentary scene in the film (excepting a few pick-up shots). That helps introduce the documentary feel of the film early on as well.

You can get away with a pretty "out there" look as long as it fits the story emotionally and you set it up early in the movie and stick with it.

THE VISUAL FLOW

Managing the visual flow was the most difficult job in making this film. Setting a look and sticking with that look for ninety minutes is challenging. When an audience is in the theatre and the room becomes dark, the world you bring them into has to have some coherent structure in order for them to fully engage in the film. The best films are those in which the story jumps off the screen and there is no awareness of filmmaking technique. Keeping with the look is about self-discipline, teamwork, and good planning. The balancing act with *QoL* was that sometimes we would have a relatively controlled and planned out set-up, but often we would be flying by the seat of our pants. Scenes where we had some control (i.e. Interior Apartment) I filmed a bit rough and grabbed-looking, and scenes where we had very little control (i.e. Exterior Mission Street on a Saturday night at 2am, bars emptying "extras" onto our set) I tried to make more polished. I hoped this would help arrive at a singular look for the film.

FILM OR VIDEO?

Although *Quality of Life* is set in the graffiti culture, there are not that many scenes of actual graffiti painting in the film. Therefore, the texture of shots themselves would have to help carry off the "filmic throw-up" (beauty or blight?) feeling.

We shot on super 16mm. There had been some discussion of shooting on mini DV but we decided that 16 would work best for this film. There are good arguments for shooting DV. The main one is cost. Shooting on mini DV would have given the freedom to shoot many more takes (we shot 6:1) and would have made us even more lightweight and fast. For certain projects, DV is great. There is a lot more to be said about the comparative merits of video and film than we can cover here. For our purposes, creating the *Quality of Life* look relied heavily on the visceral texture that is unique to film. It tends to render beauty more beautiful and ugliness more ugly/grainy. Video tends to look somewhat

120

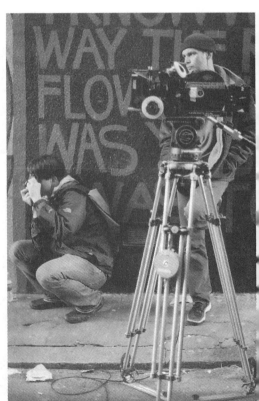

generic and flat without special lighting and treatment. The lack of range inherent in a video image would have been horribly restrictive. Traversing the line between beauty and blight was the key for our film's look.

The contrast range of video would have been problematic. What DV sees from deep black (7.5 IRE) to pure white (100IRE) is much smaller than on film. Once an image, film or video, reaches pure white (no detail) and pure black (no detail), the parts that become interesting and useful are the mid-tones, and on film you have more. There are ways of dealing with this high contrast issue, the main one being fill lighting and perhaps filtration (low cons or ultra cons). For *QoL*, lighting to expand this limited rage was not an option. We simply could not afford to light every scene this way. And, more importantly, we would be filming on the streets at night in a very fluid (doc.) style. Setting lights would have been impractical and would have drawn attention to us. We wanted to catch the feeling of the Mission District of San Francisco at night and would have lost that feel by lighting the streets. Also, because of the laws surrounding graffiti, our talent risked going to jail every time we took out a can of paint. Let alone drinking in the street, jaywalking, climbing buildings, and filming in live train tunnels . . . setting one of our homemade 12v battery lights was pushing it!

CONCLUSION

Quality of Life was a great experience. It was hard work and at times grueling. I learned a lot about what it takes to shoot a feature film and feel fortunate to have had a great crew. For any DP embarking on his or her first feature film, be bold, be humble, and have a sturdy pair of boots.

Equipment: Shot on super 16 color neg (Kodak 7245 & 7218) using Zeiss super speed prime lenses 9.5 16 & 50mm; no filtration; Telecine to HD on a spirit Datacine HD to 35mm print (Kodak premier) by Chris Martin; Small grip and lighting van (largest unit 1x 1,200 HMI par).

Existing light supplemented; exterior night "stolen" scenes lit with MR16 custom rig to 12v marine battery on hand cart.

Brian, Lane, and Kev. Tomata scene.

WALL OF SOUND
CAPTURING THE AURAL MURAL

BY BRIAN COPENHAGEN, PRODUCTION SOUND MIXER

INTRODUCTION

I have a distinct recollection of the first production meeting I attended for *Quality of Life*. In a borrowed conference room at Howard and 2nd Street, our discussion ranged from introductions to covering a bullet-list of topics essential to the rapidly approaching Day One. As the issues facing production were unveiled, I began to understand that this was going to be a roller-coaster of a shoot: less than a week out, the lead actor had flaked; shoots were planned at locations which hadn't even been contacted; questions regarding post-production were met with nearly blank stares.

I walked away with several thoughts echoing through my head: mixed feelings of enthusiasm and apprehension, opportunity and risk. But most of all, it left me with the impression that working on this film was going to be quite unlike standardized filmmaking. I recognized the familiar landscape of film production, but I could see that our enthusiastic director was not too far off the mark in saying it was going to be the ascent of Mt. Everest when it came time to shoot. As I absorbed both the conceptualized vision of Ben and the visual approach that the DP wanted to take, I could see my role developing as not just the sound mixer, but also as a member of the team who could provide a practical approach to the mechanics of the production. It was an opportunity to become part of the core at the heart of production, to be a contributor to the film in its entirety.

But my first job was to tackle the production sound. Based on my previous experience, I knew the way it should be done: we needed a sound mixer (myself), an experienced boom operator, well-organized crew and equipment movement, and a clear schedule of when, where, and what we were going to shoot. These were aspects of production that were fundamental to narrative filmmaking.

What I discovered, however, was that Ben had already laid the foundations for a novel approach to the shooting style we would employ. We would shoot the film in the same way that a graffiti artist would write: run-n-gun bombing. Once I was introduced to the Graffiti Model philosophy that Ben had masterminded and to which the DP, Kev Robertson, had wholeheartedly subscribed, I began to understand how we could pull off *Quality of Life*. For Kev, it meant he would draw on his years of documentary experience to

Since picking up the cello at eight years old, Brian has courted music and sound, finally engaging the world of film sound in 1995 after having recorded his own bands for the previous 5 years. Undertaking film projects of students at Loyola Marymount and San Francisco State Universities, he found a niche in production sound mixing. Brian taught location sound for two years at the Academy of Art University. Since being the Production Sound Mixer for Quality of Life, *Brian has worked in production sound on such projects as* Bee Season, *with Richard Gere and Juliette Binoche, and the film version of the Broadway musical* Rent, *with Rosario Dawson and Jesse L. Martin.* **www.soundfacility.com**

accomplish the daunting task of shooting a feature in three weeks. I didn't mind considering the artistic approach, but the documentary genre tends to have lower standards for what is considered acceptable sound quality. It was a crucial turning point when I realized that capturing the production sound for *Quality of Life* was going to require an overhaul of the tried-and-true methods used to acquire "feature-quality" sound.

As I began to develop my methodology, I realized some of the traps into which a low-budget, guerrilla production like *QoL* could easily fall. I had seen these common mistakes all too often: putting the boom into inexperienced hands, leaving the sound guy out of the communication loop, thinking the sound department needs little or no time to prep, poor shooting techniques, lack of media organization, and, of course, figuring that you can always fix it in post. I was determined to make sure we didn't fall easy prey to these bad clichés. I realized two other factors were going to play important roles in fashioning my approach to *QoL*: time and space. Both were scarce. Our bold schedule had us jumping to three or four different locations on some days (often having never seen them before), and shooting complex scenes in very little time. Space was very limited as well, both for moving gear and often our locations. So the task developed into becoming efficient and portable while maintaining top-notch quality. After some reflection, I came up with a solution that would mostly avoid these obvious pitfalls, while at the same time accommodating some of the specific limitations of shooting *QoL*.

ONE MAN BAND

One of the first challenges was to figure out how to single-handedly achieve the feature-quality sound that normally takes two experienced sound guys. Lingering in my head was the image of me trying to explain which way to point the microphone to an unpaid PA who's been elected boom operator-of-the-day. I'd certainly done it before, but the lightning pace left little time for diligent instruction. I couldn't leave the precious (and too often neglected) role of boom operating to unproven hands.

If you think it's crazy to consider the boom handling so important, take a second and compare it to camera operation. The camera is capturing your images; if the operation of the camera were left to inexpert hands, you'd be a little queasy, no? You're not likely to entrust that job to just anyone. Now think about what exactly is happening with the boom. It's the first place that something can go wrong in acquiring the sound. If the mic isn't cued to the right actor at the right time, the dialogue is compromised. A good boom operator can absorb the dialogue for a whole scene and cue to actors quickly and precisely, while anticipating subtle nuances that can affect how the actors might change their line delivery. It's a formidable task that I wanted to handle myself.

The method worked out well. I boomed most of the film myself with a small portable mixer over-the-shoulder and the DAT recorder on a cart at the end of a thirty-foot snake cable. The cart also gave me the portability of wheels and a place to put everything down between takes. It was easy enough to get someone to push the big red button on the DAT at the beginning and end of a take, and I could listen to what was going to DAT from the mixer. The one occasion where I saw it necessary to use a second boom, Darrell Lee stepped up (literally, to the top of a ten-step ladder). After one take, he said, "How the f*** can you do this all day?"

123

TIGHT SPACES

There were several occasions where the luxury of working from the cart wasn't possible, and those usually involved the difficult task of shooting in cars. A larger production would have an insert-car, the Hollywood term for a truck towing a trailer with the picture car, actors, camera, lights, and several crew members. The picture car is never actually driven by the actors, and the director watches from video monitors on a platform on the back of the truck. For *Quality of Life*, however, executing the car scenes was the quintessence of guerrilla production.

The first and most straightforward was a lengthy dialogue scene between Pops and Mikey (Heir) while Pops drives the painting van. With the camera mounted on the hood and mics mounted inside the cab, we set off cruising the Mission district. Ben, Kev, and I rode in the dark cargo area, huddled around a tiny video monitor, each of us with headphones and Kev with his thumb on a remote on/off switch for the camera.

The second car scene got a little tighter, a dialogue scene with Heir, Vain, and the driver in a taxicab. Throw in a DP, a director, and it left little room for the sound man. Ever the good sport, I suggested I run my cables to the trunk and record from back there. Obviously, it wasn't the safest thing to do, but I was bolstered with the confidence that the first AC, Tom, would be in a vehicle immediately behind us, curtailing the possibility of a catastrophic rear-ender.

Finally, a car scene wherein Vain carjacks a taxi, was possibly our boldest endeavor for the film. Vain was to come running down 17th Street and run into the intersection at Mission St., where we had our picture taxi and driver waiting first at the stoplight. The only way to pull off this scene was to scatter the obvious signs of a film shoot to different areas. Kev was safely out of the way, shooting with a long lens from across the street and down the block, attracting very little attention to himself. Just a guy with a movie camera shooting . . . who knew what? Unfortunately, there's no such thing as a long lens mic, so I had to record this scene a couple different ways, truly hoping that post-production could put the pieces together from the different techniques.

A couple different issues made the scene difficult for sound. A boom was impossible, as the shot was too wide. Wireless lavalier mics could have been possible, but the fact that the actor started by running full speed down the street meant too much clothes noise and scuffling sounds for a clean soundtrack. Also, the distance between the transmitters on the actors and the receivers where I was made radio interference a problem. The first take, in which I positioned myself just outside the left frame across the street from the camera, had a few usable elements. The second take, I hid in the shot behind a garbage can within ten feet of the taxi. Better, more usable elements, but I needed to be right on top of the action. So, one more time, I found myself crouching in a tight space in the backseat of the taxi. No problems with radio interference, clean dialogue, a nice take. And it was a good thing I was in the taxi, because in that take, the actor, Brian, and I were followed by a guy in a van who thought he'd just witnessed a real carjacking and was calling 911! After I popped my head up with headphones on, and we did some charades to let the guy know we were shooting a movie, he finally understood and took off. We all had a moment of adrenalized giddiness and bailed quick.

124

"WHAT'RE WE DOING?"

The absolute most essential element of making a film is communication. This is an aspect of filmmaking that, even on the biggest budget films, has the greatest potential to slow things down. From that very first production meeting, I made every effort to impress upon the production team that we had to keep up communication if we were really going to shoot as aggressively as we were planning. And it was important to know what was important to communicate. Beyond just getting everyone to the same place at the same time, the mechanics of production are based on constant communication.

Every shot requires planning. Getting the camera rolling is an effort of coordination involving nearly every department on a film. If any of those departments are not "on the same page," the inevitable result is the deceleration of the whole production. When time gets tight, stress levels increase, and people start searching for ways to get things done more quickly. I could write a script of the crew dialogue when the pace gets frenzied:

Director: "Do we really need to wire them? Can't we just boom it?"

DP: "Don't worry about focus marks . . . you'll nail it."

Director: "I think we can just shoot, can't we? We don't need a rehearsal . . . "

AD: "Let's shoot the rehearsal."

Then, three takes later, someone suggests rehearsing it once.

And, like magic, all the elements finally come together in the takes that follow. The performances lock in, the focus is sharp, and the sound is great. There are plenty of other things that can go wrong, so make every effort to plan your shot and communicate it to everyone.

Quality of Life had its fair share of frenzied shooting. In some cases we were pinched for time; in others, we didn't have the luxury of planning exactly WHAT was going to happen, so we could only plan HOW we were going to shoot it. In those instances, we found our stride walking the fence between narrative and documentary styles.

POST FIRST

One of the most important and most often overlooked elements to production is to consider post-production as early as possible. So many decisions in production should be based on what's going to happen in the various stages of post: film-to-video transfer (telecine), editing systems, syncing methods, frame rates, sample rates, aspect ratios, whether you're going back to film, the list goes on. The low-budget, guerrilla approach tends to lean toward linear decision-making, dealing with issues as they arise, with little time and usually no money for anticipating curveballs. *QoL*, even with all its bravado and good intentions, was going to be just as susceptible to the unexpected as any other film.

One of the major issues that arose in post-production was the syncing of picture and sound. I recognized the early symptoms of this eventual predicament cropping up during production, as marking takes with the slate became a piece of the puzzle that

struggled to fit into our modus operandi. The effect of no sync point between the film and sound meant that someone, somewhere down the line of post-production was going to have to read lips and try to find the point at which the picture and sound should fit together.

The reasons varied for this hole in production technique: lack of time, lack of coordination, lack of effort. In some cases, Kev's documentary experience bailed us out when we got ahead of ourselves. I can recall more than one occasion in which we finished a take with this conversation (with camera and sound still rolling):

Kev: "Great, now just clap your hands in front of your face."

Actor: "Huh?"

Kev: "Just clap in front of your face!"

CLAP!

And like that we had our sync point.

However, I realized that our fly-by-night methods of sync meant that I should make some extra efforts to organize what went onto DAT tape. After all, what was just as important as having a sync point was being able to find it later.

MEDIA ORGANIZATION

In order to make the job easier for whoever was to be responsible for synchronizing the film and sound, I decided early on to

pay twice the attention to my side of the reporting. Vocal slating ("scene thirty-four, take two") on tape and the use of sound reports is common practice, and, for me, it's one of the bizarre pleasures of doing sound: talking to a recording, with no idea who is eventually going to hear it. It allows a certain freedom in its anonymity.

But on *QoL*, the details which I began to include both on tape and in the reports bordered on obsessive. I found myself talking to the recording for often more than a minute, trying in some fashion to help that faceless post worker with such information as, "Well, that was Scene thirty-four, Take two, but there was no visual slate that ever said that, so what we saw was a close up of Pops driving the painting van; and there was no audible sync slate, so you're going to have to use that little hand clap at the end of the scene for the sync point . . .um . . . good luck."

I spent down-time listening back to the DAT and making sure every take was accounted for on the sound report. And, whenever possible, I noted the timecode where the take started.

I'm pretty sure all this diligence was helpful to someone. When I visited the post-production sound studio, I saw my reports diligently copied and within arm's reach. I was certainly glad to hear that Andy Wiskes, the sound designer and post-mixer, reported that there was no ADR in the film, which means my production sound was the sole source of dialogue. There were some syncing issues that had to be worked through, but Andy had all the elements he needed.

It proved the point that no matter how guerrilla you want to go,

126

there are some basic filmmaking techniques that one should make every effort to employ because everything you do in production will have snowballing effects into post-production.

CONCLUSION

Reflecting on the *Quality of Life* shoot, I'm happy to say that the pleasures outweigh the rigors in my memory of this production. Many of those pleasures were found in the experiences we shared building ourselves into a tight film unit. We grew to trust each other's knowledge and instincts while remaining open to listening to ideas from everyone. By the final day (a 20-hour haul!), I could say we were capable of doing just about anything in the unique style we had developed.

We had managed to overcome the obstacles, both those foreseen and those which blindsided us. For the production sound, I had developed new techniques to accommodate my one-man approach and to work quickly and effectively in the numerous and disparate locations we faced. Most of all, I was happy to have been able to contribute to the film as a filmmaker, instead of just as the "sound guy."

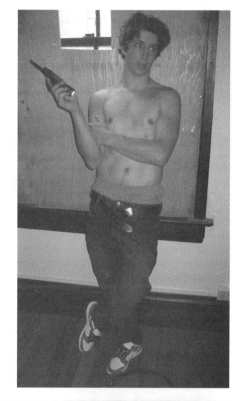

127

GET IN, EDIT, GET OUT
THE GRAFFITI MODEL FOR FILM EDITING

BY SHARON FRANKLIN / FILM EDITOR

SIGNING ON WITH *QOL*

Back in August of 2003, I got a call from a director inquiring about my availability to edit his feature film. I had just come off editing a low-budget feature where the director had camped out on my couch for weeks, frustrating my work process (I see editing as a form of meditation and prefer to work alone), and I was frankly a bit leery about jumping into yet another indie project. I explained that if I were to cut the film, he would only be allowed in the editing suite when I invited him. I got off the phone convinced that I would never hear from him again. However, somehow director Ben Morgan was not dissuaded, and much to my surprise offered me the job.

Kev Robertson, the director of photography for *Quality of Life* and I had previously worked together on Greek director Christos Dimas' short film *Amerikanos*, an impressionistic film that allowed Kev the opportunity to experiment with different film stocks and shooting styles. Kev liked how I worked with his footage, finding beauty in imperfections. With the shooting style of *Quality of Life*, it was necessary to find an editor who would embrace its gritty aesthetic and feel comfortable using shots that dipped in and out of focus, so Kev and colorist Chris Martin had recommended me for the project.

I liked the subject matter of the film. Living in San Francisco's Mission District on mural-lined Balmy Alley, I was surrounded by color. I enjoyed the surprise of glimpsing an obscure sentence scrawled on wall ("You rock my world;" "Help! I need paper") or the ubiquitous "Andre the Giant" stickers and the "Monkey Knife Fight" stencils that appeared on sidewalks all over the Mission District that summer. While not always overtly beautiful, graffiti was part of the fabric that made up my neighborhood.

I also liked the fact that the script had a positive message without feeling overly moralistic. I appreciate films that are more ambivalent and force you to think for yourself.

DIGITAL REVOLUTION

I have been editing with Final Cut Pro since 1998 when Apple hired me as an on-site editor to test their software. While I was a die-hard Avid editor at the time, I was thrilled that I could finally afford to buy my own editing system. Apple had effectively leveled the playing field, allowing more and more people to "own

128

Sharon Franklin came to terms with her obsession with film editing in 1996. Relocating from Washington State to San Francisco, she set about establishing herself as an editor with both artistic and technical expertise. Her first feature, The Cistern, *brought her to Athens, Greece. Shot on Super 16 with an all-Greek cast, the project presented Sharon with the unique challenge of editing a film in a language she did not speak.*

Since then, Sharon has edited two more features, as well as numerous short films and documentaries. After completing Quality of Life, *Sharon continued her migration south, arriving in Los Angeles in 2004. She has since worked on a variety of projects, including Mario Van Peebles's* Poetic License.

the tools of post-production." The digital revolution had begun. And with the dot.com boom that followed, work opportunities were endless, though I soon grew tired of corporate work.

Flash forward to 2003. The dot.com bust had (thankfully) happened. I took stock of the situation and decided to focus on independent film. I gave up my office space and moved my editing suite into my home in the Mission District. I had a G5 edit system set up in my bedroom and a G4 powerbook-based edit system set up in the hallway for my assistant. Footage was captured from a Sony DSR-40 to a series of EZ Quest Cobra FireWire drives with duplicate media at both stations.

The Super-16 footage was transferred to Digi-beta, and from that DVCAMs were made with keycode, picture and audio timecode burn-in. I chose to edit at 29.97 rather than remove pull-down and cut at 23.98. This is not how I would edit a project like that now, but at the time it seemed like the correct approach. Fortunately, the sound was synched in telecine so we didn't have to deal with this ourselves.

The facility that did the transfers did not have the capability of generating flex files but were kind enough to provide Cinema Tools Database files instead. From these, we generated batch lists and captured each roll of film in its entirety. The assistant then broke the rolls into individual takes and subclipped them. Bins were created for each scene. I like to have all the clips for each scene placed into a sequence so that I can easily scroll through all the takes. In the case of dialogue scenes with long takes, I have the assistant create an additional sequence with takes of each individual line grouped together in the timeline.

This makes it easy for me to quickly assess which is the best performance for each line.

I had two assistants working on the project. My regular assistant, Jose Arriaga, was out of the country when the project began so Raymond Bessemer filled in until Jose returned. Jose, also a Mission resident, was already familiar with my editing process on narrative films from our previous work together on *Night of Henna* and *Vanilla*.

THE EDIT

I actually was in Europe on a job as the assistant work began, and by the time I returned to begin editing, I only had three weeks to finish the rough cut in time for our festival deadlines. Fortunately, with our low budget, there was a very low shooting ratio of 6:1. While this meant there was sometimes only one take of a given set-up, it certainly did speed up the process of making selects!

With the deadline looming, I knew I would have to be very efficient at editing. I set a goal of cutting eight to twelve scenes per day and stuck with it, completing the rough assembly in about fourteen days. This meant staying very disciplined and not allowing myself to get caught up in perfecting each cut. I would assemble my selects, whittle them down as quickly as I could, and as soon as the scene flowed coherently, I moved on to the next scene. This approach was very similar to the Graffiti Model employed in production: get in, hit it, and get out.

The advantage of working with this approach is that you can

quickly assemble a film and assess whether or not the performances you have selected are working as a whole. One take initially may seem the strongest, but seen in context once the film is assembled, that performance may not ring true for that character. For this reason, it's better to get the film all laid out before going in and fine-tuning individual scenes. After three weeks, we had a reasonably strong rough cut which we submitted to film festivals, and it was this cut that got us accepted to the Berlin International Film Festival.

One of the most surprising things about the editing process was how hands-off Ben was. I don't even think he had met me in person when I began work (he was already back home in Oregon by the time I returned from Europe), and yet he trusted me completely with his baby. I don't think many directors could have done this with an editor they had never worked with before, and I respect him for this tremendously. Ironically enough, considering the condition I had set in the initial phone interview, it got to a point where I was actually begging him to spend more time in the edit suite. (Be careful what you ask for!)

Ben is the type of director who understands that to get the best results, he must first hire the right people for the job and then give them the creative space to do their work. He was respectful of my creative process and was very easy to collaborate with. That is not to say that we didn't occasionally have differences of opinion, but we were able to communicate well and work out solutions that only made the film stronger.

Kev's approach to shooting this film involved a loose, almost documentary style. Many scenes were shot hand-held with little additional light and shallow depth-of-field, so shots went in and out of focus. I knew this was to be part of the graffiti aesthetic of the film and did not shy away from using these shots. I also allowed myself to be loose in the editing, not waiting for a shot to settle before cutting to the next shot. This created a more dynamic, at times frenetic, energy to the film that worked well with the subject matter.

In the scenes of Curtis's decline, this approach was especially effective. In the suicide scene, Kev employed lots of close-ups and swish-pans between characters. As the confrontation intensified, I used this movement to create a feeling of disorientation not unlike what Curtis himself was experiencing during his final breakdown. All this chaos also meant that I didn't have to pay as much attention to geographical continuity. Which side was that person standing on in the previous shot? It simply didn't matter. Kev also shot one take at 6fps, creating a fast-motion effect. I jump-cut to this take in moments where Curtis was swinging around or slamming into a wall in order to increase the sense of violence in his movements.

When editing a film like this with a low shooting-ratio, it often takes some creativity to find a solution to a problem. In the scene in the abandoned warehouse where Curtis and Mikey discuss their plans for the evening, the scene dragged, but I had only one usable take and nothing obvious to cut away to. Looking through the warehouse footage, though, I discovered a shot of a pigeon

730

flying through the exposed rafters. Ah ha! I took the moment when Mikey pops open his beer to motivate the cut to the pigeon flying, implying that the sound of the beer can opening had startled the pigeon.

One of the most challenging scenes to edit was the argument outside the liquor store. During the shoot, the actor playing Curtis (Brian Burnam) practiced the "method" form of acting and got a little bit too into character. Fueled by a generous quantity of malt liquor, he ended up all over the place and unable to deliver his lines correctly. This is a critical scene where Curtis and Mikey's friendship ends and they go their separate ways. There were certain points that needed to be hit for this scene to work, and Brian kept missing.

With the lines scrambled in every take, in order to assemble the scene I had to first break the takes apart and group the lines in order according to the script. I played through the resulting sequence and began eliminating takes that were useless while placing markers at the "magic moments" of the takes that worked. From there, I experimented with different ways of stitching these "magic moments" together. Some had to be abandoned, while others worked. Some lines from the script ended up being lost because I could not find a way to make them work with the fragmented material I had.

Somehow I was able to cut this scene together well enough for the rough cut, but Ben always knew pickups would be necessary to make this scene work. Once these new takes were available I incorporated them into the cut. As luck would have it, even then the scene had problems (the stick-up kid wasn't visible enough to establish him as a character) necessitating another evening of pickups. The finished scene in the film utilizes takes from three different shoots spread over a three-month period. Yet somehow the scene works.

One of my favorite scenes I edited was what I jokingly call the "bus chase scene." This is the scene in which Curtis races recklessly through the streets in a stolen cab while Mikey is stuck trying to get to the same location by bus. Originally, these were intended to be separate scenes, but I liked the contrast between Curtis flying around corners while Curtis waits anxiously for the bus to reach his destination. Even though they are moving at different speeds, their energy is similar, so I thought it would be fun to cut it in the style of a chase scene. I added "stolen" shots of emergency vehicles in order to up the tension, and concluded the scene with Mikey's bus getting stopped in traffic by a fire truck while Curtis gets away, the siren's wail carrying us into the next scene.

In cities, traffic is a part of life, and when you're shooting a low-budget, graffiti-style film you don't have the luxury of closing down streets, so you just have to accept the fact that cars will pass through your shot at times. Often, I intentionally cut right as a car was still in the frame, and this became part of my editing aesthetic for the film. In fact, Andy Wiskes, the sound designer, took a cue from this approach and used the sound of cars passing by to smooth audio transitions between scenes. This fit in well with the Graffiti Model approach to making this film: taking a potential weakness and making it into a strength.

FROM COMPUTER SCREEN TO 35MM PRINT

The prospect of having our film premiere at the Berlin International Film Festival was very exciting. But with this success came a daunting challenge: how would we be able to deliver a 35mm print in time to screen at the festival in eight weeks? After doing some research, it became clear that even in the best of circumstances it would have been extremely difficult to cut the negative and blow it up to 35mm in that time period. And we were far from being in ideal circumstances, with our very limited budget and technical challenges. I had discovered early on that the keycode window burn wasn't entirely accurate, but with our tight schedule I had been forced to plow ahead—no time to wait for retransfers!

So it became clear that our only option was to go the digital intermediate route. We would do a digi-beta online and transfer that to 35mm. It wasn't ideal but it would do. When the facility that had done our transfers caught wind of this, they offered to retransfer all our footage to HD for free if we did the on-line conform at their facility at a vastly reduced rate. We naturally jumped at this opportunity.

Going the digital intermediate route gave us much more flexibility in creating a look than we would have had, had we gone the more traditional route of cutting negative and color-timing the film. Following Kev's conceptual aesthetic for the film, Chris Martin, our colourist, desaturated the daylight scenes while pumping color into the night scenes. Chris pushed the contrast in the darker scenes, creating a grainy look that most filmmakers would have steered away from, but was appropriate considering our graffiti aesthetic.

Unfortunately, when it came to the on-line conform, the adage "you can get something cheap, fast or good — choose two" held true. Alas, in our case, though, we only got one of those three options: "cheap." We needed the online to happen quickly in order to give Alpha Cine enough time to do the tape-to-film transfer, but because we weren't paying commercial rates, we found our project constantly bumped for higher-paying clients as our deadline approached. And when the facility finally did the HD conform at the last possible moment, it was done so quickly that we weren't given enough time to Q.C. the reels properly before the HD masters were sent off to Alpha Cine.

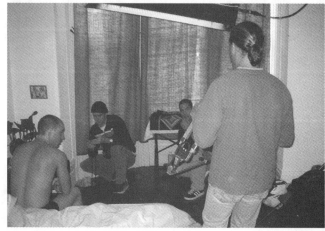

When I captured the DVCAM down-converts of the HD masters, I was horrified to discover that shots had slipped by as many as twelve frames in the on-line. It was heartbreaking as an editor to see all my hard work mangled, but there was no time to go back and fix their mistakes. The worst part was that I had to spend a week resynching the entire film to their scrambled edit, a job further complicated by the poor quality of the down-convert. On wideshots, it was difficult to see whether or not a shot was in synch or not. This is why when you see the finished film there are still shots out of synch.

The folks at Alpha Cine, by contrast, were a pleasure to work with. They were enthusiastic about our film and went out of their way to make sure everything was as correct as could be, given the circumstances. They alerted us to mistakes they found in the on-line and helped us find solutions. The lesson from all this is that when you have a low budget film like ours, it is critical that you work with facilities that truly enjoy working with independent filmmakers and will go the extra mile for you to make sure your vision is realized.

BERLIN & BEYOND

Berlin was the perfect festival to host our world premiere. Berlin is a city rich with graffiti culture. Here is a city once divided by a wall — a wall now nearly gone except for a few colorful, graffiti-covered portions that remain. Winning an award in our category was an honor, especially considering the disparity between our budget and that of the competition, but the true measure of our film's success was the graff community demonstrating their approval by filling our screenings.

Quality of Life is a film I am proud to have been a part of. Seeing the results of all our hard work show on the big screen to an enthusiastic audience is a gratifying experience. You see how all the contributions of the team come together to create something greater than any one individual alone could achieve. Film is inherently a collaborative process and the lower the budget the more you take a part in making that vision whole.

733

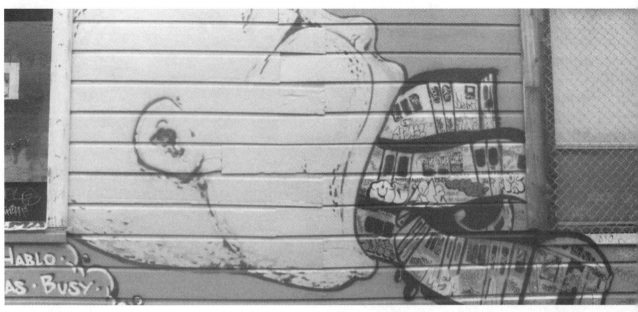

SCREENPLAY

EXT SUBWAY TRAIN TRACKS - LATE NIGHT

BEGIN OPENING TITLE SEQUENCE

TWO ANONYMOUS YOUNG MEN quickly squeeze through a hole in a chain link fence and pace down the dark barren tracks. They drop their bags on the ground, shuffle through them, and begin outlining simple PIECES on the wall with spray paint.

The two young painters work fast but effectively, filling in the pieces, adding borders, and highlights, etc. Their pieces say "HEIR" and "VAIN." As the pieces are revealed, so are the identities of the two writers.

MICHAEL ROSE (22), aka "HEIR", is a bundle of energy. Had he spent enough time in school, he would have definitely been labelled ADHD and pumped full of medication. But he has found an outlet for his creative juices, which has proven far more effective than any prescription amphetamine.

CURTIS SMITH (22), aka "VAIN", is stocky and ripped, one of the few benefits of a lifetime of institutionalization. He and Heir function as a single unit, with little verbal communication. Their precise and fluid can control reveals years of practice and dedication.

Like a paranoid deer at a watering hole, Heir perks up and listens. Vain stops painting and listens too. The SOUND OF A CHAIN LINK FENCE is heard in the distance. When it stops, FOOTSTEPS can be heard. Heir and Vain frantically bag up their stuff. The FOOTSTEPS get closer and closer. Heir and Vain tuck into the bushes. Now they can hear VOICES. Heir and Vain look at each other. Neither makes a move.

Finally two young BOYS, KID (15) and TAD (16), appear. They are not taking the same covert approach as Heir and Vain.

Heir and Vain stay put in the bushes, hoping the kids pass them unnoticed.

> **KID**
> *(loud)* Dude, she was so fine.

> **TAD**
> For real?

> **KID**
> *(hand gestures some large breastesses)*
> Yeah. Arthritis. In both hands.

They laugh out loud.

> **VAIN**
> *(stern whisper)* What the fuck?

Director's note. We obviously moved this scene closer to the end of Act One. I knew I was going to do this during production. It was an incredibly difficult scene to shoot (in a dark tunnel on "live" tracks) and never really carried the impact needed to open a film.

Director's note. Bet you didn't get this one in the movie. Hard to see. But my friend Douglas and I used to always say this and the shit is funny. At least I think so . . .

142

June 24, 2003. Last day in La Grande. So depressed. Don't know how I'm going to survive without my family. We got to spend the weekend together in Cannon Beach. Needed that. So much to do. Truly scary. I have got to find a way to get back here. Mandatory. There is no way I can go almost two months without seeing my family. No way. Need to set up some visits. Both ways. Gotsta. Not looking forward to the long, depressing trip down either. But this is all part of my destiny. And success is measured by the sacrifices you make. **June 25, 2003.** On the road today. Not looking forward to the fifteen hour drive or the sinking feeling of being away from my family. Decided to make a trip back in two weeks. Just can't be away for six plus weeks straight. Anyway, it's time to look beyond

143

The KIDS startle.

> VAIN
>
> What are you doing?

> KID
>
> Oh shit . . .

Heir shushes the Kid.

> VAIN
>
> What are you doing down here?

> KID
>
> We just came down here to paint.

> VAIN
>
> Yeah, well you fools are gonna burn this spot.

> TAD
>
> *(still too loud)* That's what we planned on doing.

> VAIN
>
> Hey, shut the fuck up.

> KID
>
> C'mon. Let's go.

> TAD
>
> Yeah, forget these guys. Let's go paint.

> VAIN
>
> *(walks towards the kids)* Naw, it's cool. Chill. What do you write?

> TAD
>
> Huh? Uh, I write . . .

Vain rips the duffel bag from Tad's shoulder.

> VAIN
>
> Not tonight you don't.

> TAD
>
> *(sucking teeth)* Give it back, man.

> HEIR
>
> *(stressing)* Keep it down, y'all.

> KID
>
> Give us our paint back.

Vain tosses the duffel to Heir and walks up on Tad and gets in his face. Tad cowers and back-pedals to the wall.

> VAIN
>
> Y'all ain't getting shit back. You got no re-spect. Blowing up spots and shit.

Tad bumps into Vain's half-finished piece and gets wet paint all over his jacket.

> VAIN
>
> Watch where you're going.

Tad stands aside, checks out the piece, and realizes Vain's identity.

> TAD
>
> Oh, damn. I didn't even realize y'all paint.

Don't you live . . .

Realizing his identity has been compromised, Vain gets in Tad's face.

                    VAIN
          Y'all outta here. Now.

The kids start back up the slope. Vain grabs Tad by the shoulder.

                    VAIN
          Not ugh. That way.

Vain points down into the tunnel.

                    TAD
          But . . .

                    VAIN
          No buts. Y'all made a big scene already com-
          ing in that way. You gonna blow us up again?
          I don't think so. *(points to the tunnel)* That
          way. Now.

The kids realize Vain ain't playing and reluctantly comply.

                    VAIN
          (to Heir) Damn. Now those toys know what
          we write.

Heir paces after the kids. Vain looks up at Heir, confused.

                    VAIN
          Where you going?

Heir catches up to the kids.

                    HEIR
          (to Kids) Hey.

The Kids turn around and Heir tosses them their bag.

                    HEIR
          Follow the elevated walkway on your right.
          You'll be at sixteenth street in five minutes.
          There aren't that many trains running right
          now, so it's pretty safe. Hurry up though. Can
          never be sure.

                    TAD
          Why's your boy such an asshole?

                    HEIR
          That's a good question.

Heir heads back and the Kids slump into the tunnel.

EXT TRAIN TRACKS - LATER

*Heir and Vain work on their pieces. Heir steps back and lights up
a smoke.*

                    HEIR
          These colors are booming.

Vain steps back and takes the cig from Heir.

                    VAIN
          Which way you gonna rock your three-D's?

144

Director's note. People ask me this
about Brian all the time. What else
can you say?

too. She pulled her resources (mostly just connections) before she even broke it to us. Ugly. She was hinting at coming back, even said "I love you" by the end of our conversation. Fuck it. I'm bummed. We can't afford this kind of blow to momentum right now. But we don't need that kind of craziness during production either. In other news, our lead actor (let's call him Floss) reported that he needs cash up front. I told him there may not be any cash anywhere. We'll see. Bottom line: we need to keep moving forward. I have the most powerful image etched in my mind: my daughter raced me down the sidewalk as I was leaving town yesterday. She stopped at the corner and looked at the ground. I looked into my mirror and saw her standing there, hunched over, thinking about a

summer without daddy. I can't ever forget that image. Ever. That's what I am fighting for. Every ounce of my energy goes into this movie. I have got to make this worthwhile. I can't leave my family for no reason. And I can't live like we have been living—paycheck to paycheck in the boonies. This is my shot. And I need to do everything I can to make it pay off. **June 27, 2003.** The pace has begun. Worked all day at the gallery putting up the installation for our art auction. Up at 5am, in bed at midnight. Everyone thinks I'm crazy for cramming this event in right before production. But we have no money! We need the cash and we need the momentum. Hopefully this event will be the catalyst we need to get this shit off the ground. Brian has lined up some amazing artists: Andy

CUT TO:

Anonymous Footsteps run down the tracks.

BACK TO:

HEIR
I kind of went bigger than I planned. I don't want to cramp this piece right here. Bring yours down and to the right and I'll bring mine to the left and we'll both have this sort of vanishing point going on. We'll tie in the same background deal and a border to bring the pieces together.

VAIN
You're such a fucking artist.

(Jersey accent) This guy? Always with the art. Always with the color schemes.

HEIR
(Jersey) Fuckin douche bag.

CUT TO:

Footsteps again. Running even faster.

BACK TO:

HEIR
You got any more white?

VAIN
Yeah. Save me some, though.

HEIR
I will. Just wanna do some bling blings and a few highlights.

VAIN
Cool, I was gonna...

Heir and Vain both stop in their tracks. They hear the FOOT-STEPS coming from the tunnel. They look at each other and quickly start packing the bag. Low and behold, Kid and Tad emerge from the tunnel.

VAIN
What the? I'ma kill those kids.

But the boys are not walking. They are in a full panic sprint. And they are not alone. Two FLASHLIGHTS bob frantically in the darkness behind the Kids. Heir and Vain are on it. They book it to the top of the hill and quickly duck through the hole in the fence.

The Kids bolt up the hill. TWO POLICE OFFICERS are on their tail. The kids pass right by the hole and try to climb over the fence, but it's quite a task with the fuzz pulling at their heels.

CUT TO:

Heir and Vain bolt down the street.

EXT SAN FRANCISCO STREETS - LATE NIGHT

Shots of a sleeping city: Empty streets, flashing yellow streetlights, a homeless man arranges his newspaper blankets.

INT ABANDONED WAREHOUSE - LATE NIGHT

The place is obviously a mecca for graffiti artists, as every last wall is decorated with pieces by the city's most up writers. Heir and Vain sit, drinking beer and staring off into the night. The camera slowly DOLLIES IN on the boys and out the window into the darkness.

Director's note. Too sketchy to shoot this. (Sitting in the window would have outed us for sure.)

INT HEIR'S ROOM - THE NEXT MORNING

Heir is crashed out in bed. He looks like he could sleep all day. The PHONE RINGS. Heir grabs it in a blind frenzy.

> **HEIR**
> Hello? What? What time is it? Shit.

Heir frantically rushes to get ready.

> **HEIR**
> Where you at?

> **POPS**
> *(barking through phone)* I'm downtown, you loser. I told you I was going in early. Where the hell are you.

JOEL "POPS" ROSE (40) enters, talking into a cordless phone. Due to excess exposure to the sun, years of hard labor, and the kind of stress that only teen parenthood can yield, Pops has aged well beyond his years.

Heir's groggy ass takes a sec to clue into Pops's practical joke.

> **HEIR**
> Man, it's too early for that.

> **POPS**
> C'mon. Let's go. We're late.

Heir HITS RIGGA in bed. [Rigga is an inside joke, invented by Heir and Vain in grade school. It is a re-enactment of a cartoon version of the rigormortis process. The long, horizontal, and usually private version: three deep breaths, arching the back with each breath, stiffen up like a board, arms and legs come up like a dog, and tip over, frozen stiff.] Pops can't help but laugh at his little jester.

> **POPS**
> Come on, man. We're outta here.

Director's note. Rigga is a classic thing we used to do as kids. But we agreed that it really didn't play for adults. (Heir and Vain were originally scripted as teenagers.)

INT HEIR'S HOUSE - MOMENTS LATER

Heir's GRANDMA (60) is washing dishes in the kitchen. Pops and Heir enter. Grandma hands Heir a plate covered with tin foil.

> **GRANDMA**
> Here, take this with you.

Heir grabs the plate in stride and heads for the door.

> **GRANDMA**
> You're welcome.

Heir turns back and gives Grandma a kiss.

> **HEIR**
> Thanks, Grandma.

Heir and Pops make like a baby and head out.

146

Schoultz, Kelly Tunstall, Sam Flores, Big Foot, RENOS and his boys, Dave Schubert, Snow Monkey, Bryan Dawson. It's going to be off the hook. Hopefully people buy some freaking art, or we're sunk. We're making this movie no matter what. But the level of support we see tonight will be telling. If what we're seeing from the SF art community is any indication, we're going to be just fine. **June 28, 2003.** Fundraiser was a huge success. We made a little money (hoping about $3K after costs and split with artists). It's over. That's what really counts. Well, almost over. I have to go back and clean up. Place got pretty hit up outside. The gallery was supposed to provide security—there was none. Now I've got to clean up the mess. Great. Oh well, there were a lot of things that were not

INT VAIN'S BEDROOM - LATER THAT MORNING

CLOSE UP on DEVIN (8), the son of Vain's live-in girlfriend. He is focusing very intently as he draws something, which we can't see. A faint HONKING can be heard in the background.

EXT VAIN'S APARTMENT - CONTINUOUS

Heir and Pops sit in the rig outside of an old sub-divided, Victorian home. Pops HONKS the horn. Judging by the look on Pops' face, this isn't the first round of honks. Pops takes a sip of coffee and throws a 'what's up?' look in Heir's direction. Heir jumps out of the ride.

> **HEIR**
> I'll be right back.

Heir runs up the steps and through the front door, scrambled egg sandwich in hand.

INT VAIN'S BEDROOM - CONTINUOUS

Devin hears BANGING on the front door. He stops drawing and bolts out of the room. Vain wakes up and looks at the clock.

> **VAIN**
> Oh shit!

Vain pops out of bed and rushes to get dressed.

> CUT TO:

INT VAIN'S APARTMENT - CONTINUOUS

The front door "mysteriously" opens up for Heir, who plays along. He enters like Jamie Lee Curtis heading into another one of Jason's traps. Sure enough, Devin pounces out of nowhere. But Heir quickly responds and swoops Devin up with his free hand. Devin yells.

> **HEIR**
> *(yelling)* You ready to go or what? We're late.

Devin kicks and halfheartedly tries to get free. He's laughing uncontrollably, loving every minute of it.

In the background we can hear water running and a toothbrush tapping the sink.

> **VAIN (O.S.)**
> One sec. Be right there.

Heir still has Devin hooked under one arm. He carries him over to the fridge, sets his sandwich on the counter and with his one free hand proceeds to open the refrigerator. Heir peers in for a second and pulls out a container of OJ. He then reaches up into the cabinet and pulls out a glass, all the while, Devin tucked under his arm.

> **DEVIN**
> I want some.

Heir pulls a second glass down and pours some for both of them. A big glass for himself and a smaller one for Devin. Heir teases Devin, holding the glass just out of his reach.

> **HEIR**
> You want some?

Devin continues laughing as he tries to reach the glass, to no avail. Heir still has got a hold of him. Vain's girlfriend, LISA (24), enters the room. Lisa moves with an air of maturity. There is much depth in her beautiful amber eyes. Heir finally sets Devin down and holds out the glass for him. Devin smiles really big and takes advantage of the opportunity at hand.

> DEVIN
> Thank you.

Devin is up on game and quickly continues past the offering and on to the taller glass of OJ and the sandwich. He takes a man sized bite out of the sandwich, grabs the taller glass of juice and runs off into the living room, laughing all the way.

> HEIR
> Did you see that?

> LISA
> I know. He's a wild man.

> HEIR
> What happened to your feet?

CLOSE UP OF LISA'S FEET. There are two eyeballs and a nose on each foot. Each toenail has been painted a different color, looking like a shoddy set of meth teeth.

> LISA
> That little . . . DEVIN!

Heir snickers and literally chokes on his juice.

Vain enters and takes it all in.

> VAIN
> (to Heir) Ready?

> HEIR
> (still laughing) Yeah.

Curtis grabs Lisa and they hug.

> VAIN
> (pointing to Lisa's feet) Damn, what happened?

Lisa shakes her head and sighs.

> LISA
> I hate Mondays.

> VAIN
> Me too. Bye.

Vain and Lisa kiss and Heir heads out.

> LISA
> Bye, honey. Bye, Mikey.

> HEIR/VAIN
> Bye.

Heir and Vain begin to exit. Devin is in the living room and on guard. Heir notices him and keeps his distance. Devin is ready to pounce but with the sound of Pops HONKING the horn in the background, Heir has to leave defeated. Devin has a big grin on his face. Heir makes a loud ROAR and lunges at Devin. Without flinching Devin grabs a WIFFLE BALL BAT and looks Vain directly in the eye. Vain freezes inches away.

the event itself for chrissakes! Nothing was filmed. That's got to be one of my main priorities this week: hire a DV cameraman. We need to be doing the shit ourselves as well. Damn. Oh well. It's all good. Need to have a serious pow-wow with the writers about tagging our venues. The gallery got hit up bad. Marker tags in the bathroom is one thing. But spray paint tags on historic brick buildings? Come on. Is every movie theater we play going to get wrecked on that level? How can we minimize that? Script mtg today as well. Not really feeling the support here, esp since our former producer pulled her AD friend who was going to help me with the breakdown. Nightmare. June 30, 2003. THAT'S why I didn't cast Brian as the lead. A-ha! He's a stubborn, selfish, egocentric

149

Director's note. The Muni bus thing was a real story out of the *Chronicle*. Not sure where the "parking meter" replacement came from. Brian just came up with it on the spot, I think. It worked.

alcoholic. Oh yeah. I love the guy like a brother, but he is so fucking lost these days. The guy gets shit-faced at the party, goes to Santa Cruz the next day, Marin the next. It's all about having a good time. Meanwhile I'm holding down the fort, cleaning up after the event, scrubbing walls, delivering art, sitting in all day meetings. But whatever. I'm the Director. But then this douchebag has the nerve to yell at me because I didn't have auction results for him?! I hung up on his ass. I can tell already this is going to be an adventure with him. My wreckless little brother is clearly not going to be involved in any of the heavy lifting. And he'll bring me down every chance he gets. I was riding a high from the script meeting. Feeling the progress, the momentum, the synchronicity. And

                                    DEVIN
                              I'll get you.

                                    HEIR
                    No, I'll get you . . . at six o'clock.

Devin stops, confused.

                                    HEIR
                    We're going to see that movie, right?

Devin throws down the bat and celebrates.

                                    DEVIN
                              Yeeeeeaaaah!

                                    VAIN
                    Be good. *(to Lisa)* We'll come by for lunch.

                                LISA (O.S.)
                              OK.

Heir and Vain exit the house and shut the door behind them.

EXT DOWNTOWN CLOTHING STORE - MORNING

Heir works on the scaffolding, painting the trim around a window with a brush. Vain is sitting down smoking a cigarette and reading the newspaper.

                                    VAIN
                    Somebody stole a Muni bus yesterday.

                                    HEIR
                              Word?

                                    VAIN
                    Right off the lot. *(reading)* Authorities have
                    no leads on suspects or the current where-
                    abouts of the bus.

                                    HEIR
                    That's craze.

                                    VAIN
                    That would be dope rolling that shit around
                    the city.

                                    HEIR
                    Right?

Pops walks up, scrapes some paint drips off the window.

                                    POPS
                    (to Vain) Tape this window off.

Pops jams roll of masking tape into Vain's hands and moves on to painting the adjacent wall. Vain begrudgingly gets to work. Vain hits ABBREVIATED RIGGA (hands in King Tut, eyes curled up).

                                    VAIN
                    (to Heir) Damn. Pops is always sweating me.

                                    HEIR
                    (sarcastic) I know. And look how hard you
                    work for him. Ungrateful bastard.

                                    VAIN
                    You too? Damn. This shit's a conspiracy.

EXT DOWNTOWN CLOTHING STORE - LATER

Pops crashes out in the back of his rig and pulls his hat over his eyes. Heir and Vain walk up on him.

> **HEIR**
> You want me to bring you something?

> **POPS**
> I'm good. Be back by one though, huh?

EXT DOWNTOWN/INT SUV - MOMENTS LATER

Heir and Vain walk down the sidewalk. As they step into the street, a MAN on a UNICYCLE plows by.

> **HEIR**
> Hey, you lost a wheel.

> **UNIMAN (O.S.)**
> Never heard that one.

A HOMELESS MAN (40s) suddenly appears behind them.

> **HOMELESS MAN**
> *(yelling at the top of his lungs)* For the love of God! I'm really hungry!

Heir and Vain startle and turn around. They wave the guy off.

> **VAIN**
> Naw, naw, naw . . .

The Homeless Man continues to talk to himself nonsensically as Heir and Vain walk off.

Heir and Vain cross the street and enter the TC CARROLL AD-VERTISING AGENCY.

INT TC CARROLL ADVERTISING AGENCY - CONTINUOUS

Heir and Vain enter. They check out the FRAMED ADS poised on pristine white walls. From a distance, Heir enviously spies on a couple of DESIGNERS working at their desks. Lisa approaches and Vain grabs her by the hips and tries to mack.

> **VAIN**
> What's up baby?

Lisa tries to put on a good front.

> **LISA**
> Stop. I'm working.

> **VAIN**
> Sorry, wouldn't want to embarrass you in front of your preppy little boyfriends. That guy right there looks like a real sweetheart. I bet he really cares . . .

> **LISA**
> *(pushes Vain)* Shut up.

Heir checks out the ad on her desk.

> **HEIR**
> What's this?

750

along comes Mr. Hangover to deflate my high. Man. I can't handle that shit. I've got to keep moving. This is a crucial week. We're four weeks out. Four weeks! I need to: nail down our budget, nail down an apartment (ideally one that doubles as a location and crash pad), nail down casting, and get serious about locations. Going to LA tomorrow for auditions with Belinda. Not real excited about that. But I need to do it. Feeling a little overwhelmed. I need Brian—a sober, level-headed Brian. Someone who gets locations, restaurants, and local businesses on board. I can turn to our assoc prod Kevin Heverin for some of that. But I need to be clear with Brian: If he wants to be a key player on this team, he needs to act like one. **July 1, 2003.** My daughter's birthday

151

today. And I'm at the airport on my way to LA. This is the first one I have ever missed. And hopefully the last. There is no doubt about one thing: my commitment to this project. If that has anything to do with the success of this film (and it does) we're golden. Met with graff photog legend Dave Schubert yesterday. Really like him. Looks dead on Ferris Bueller. That man has seen and captured a lot in his days. He was telling me about the real beat- down that he videotaped that Larry Clark used as inspiration for the scene in KIDS. Dave's down for OoL. I'm psyched to have him on board. I just hope he proves to be more reliable than Brian. Also met with John Doffing yesterday. Another perfect fit (on the biz end). We are def on the same page. Feeling the synchronicity. Still no

LISA

It's going to run on the Munis.

Vain puts his arm around Lisa and checks out the ad.

HEIR

Shit's kinda wack.

LISA

Whatever.

HEIR

No offense.

LISA

Oh, I don't care. I didn't design it.

Heir stares at the ad.

HEIR

These guys have no clue.

VAIN

Yo, come out to lunch with us.

LISA

It's Thai Tuesday . . .

VAIN

That's what I'm talking about.

LISA

Employees only.

VAIN

I see how it is. Fuck it. I didn't want to eat with you anyway.

ROBERT (45), the slick, moving-and-shaking art director of the agency, walks by.

ROBERT

What's up guys?

HEIR/VAIN

Sup.

ROBERT

(to Lisa) We all set?

LISA

Yeah, I got a reservation for six at 12:15.

ROBERT

Great, thanks. *(to Heir & Vain)* See you guys.

Robert heads to his office.

Vain leans in to give Lisa a kiss. Lisa turns and lets him kiss her on the cheek.

VAIN

Oh I see how it is.

Heir grabs Vain and drags him out the door.

EXT HEIR'S HOUSE - EVENING

Pops pulls the rig into the driveway. Pops, who is definitely feel-

ing Miller time, lets out a deep sigh and begins to unload a few things out of the truck. Heir and Vain follow with their normal routine, by putting things away and washing up before entering the house.

INT HEIR'S KITCHEN - EVENING

IMPROV: Heir and Vain sit at the table and shoot the shit. Grandma interrupts and serves the boys dinner. Grandma warns Vain about using foul language at the table and he apologizes. She intervenes on his second infraction.

GRANDMA

Curtis.

VAIN

Sorry, ma'am.

GRANDMA

You know why people swear? Because they don't have anything to say.

VAIN

You're right. I'll try . . .

GRANDMA

I have a little story for you.

Vain and Heir look at each other and make Eye Rigga (eyelids curled up). They brace themselves for another one of Grandma's long-winded stories.

GRANDMA

Two Southern Ladies are sitting on their porch, sipping lemonade. One of the Southern Ladies says (Southern drawl), "See this diamond ring? My husband gave it to me when we had our first child." The other Southern Lady says (Southern drawl), "That's nice." They're sitting there for a while and the first Lady says, "See this fur coat? My husband gave it to me when we had our second child." The other Southern Lady says, "That's nice." They watch the sun set into the horizon. Then the first Lady says, "See that Rolls Royce? My husband gave it to me when we had our third child." The other Southern Lady says, "That's nice." After a while, the first Southern Lady asks, "You've had many children of your own. What has your husband bought for you?" The other Southern Lady says, "Nothing, really. Although he did send me to etiquette school." "Really? And what did they teach you there?" "Oh, lots of stuff. Like instead of saying, 'Fuck You!' You say, 'That's nice.'"

The boys break into laughter.

HEIR

You are classic, Grandma.

VAIN

Hey, what about your language?

GRANDMA

I'm not sitting at the table.

Director's note. I always loved this scene. And Bryna, our Grandma, did a great job. But Act One was just way too long. So it got the axe. You'll see it in the deleted scenes someday.

money. But that doesn't seem to be slowing us down. Need to find some good actors today. Doye. Time is running out. People are shitting. I'm not. It's all good. Need to start thinking about rehearsal space, though. That's high on the priority list. That's ALL I want to think about. Fundraising tends to dominate, unfortunately. But I need to stay focused on the Big three: CASTING, LOCATIONS, REHEARSALS. That's it. Nothing else matters. Unfortunately I don't have the production support to do that. Time to go fight for my seat on the plane. The Southworst Shuffle . . . **July 2, 2003.** Really starting to doubt for the first time. And not just little pieces of or people affiliated with the project. But the whole damn thing. What the hell am I doing? This big ambitious cast and location schedule?! With

153

> VAIN
>
> What?

Pops enters the room holding a paint brush.

> POPS
>
> (to Heir) You forgot to wash the brushes.

> HEIR
>
> We washed them.

> POPS
>
> Well you did a pretty crappy job.

> HEIR
>
> (Southern Drawl) That's nice.

> POPS
>
> No, Fuck You! Now get in there and wash those brushes before they dry out.

Heir stands up and heads to the garage. Grandma and Vain can't help but laugh at Heir's predicament.

> HEIR
>
> Ha-Ha. Real funny.

INT PARKED CAR - LATER

IMPROV: Heir, Vain, and their homeboy, DES (20) chill, smoke a joint, laugh, and shoot the shit. They stop suddenly.

> VAIN
>
> Oh shit.

Vain rushes to put out and stash the roach. Devin approaches the car and leans in the window.

> DEVIN
>
> Man, there wasn't no snakes down there.

> HEIR
>
> Yeah there is.

> DES
>
> You just weren't looking hard enough, little man.

> DEVIN
>
> Man, you guys are chumps. Are we gonna see that movie or what?

> VAIN
>
> Yeah, we're going, Dev. We're going.

The boys all pile out of the car.

We pull back to reveal that they were chilling in an abandoned, wheel-less car.

They all bail out together.

INT MOVIE THEATER - NIGHT

Heir, Vain, Devin, and Des sit and watch a movie. They all seem to be enjoying it on the same level.

INT MOVIE THEATER - NIGHT

A SPARSE CROWD exits the theater and pours onto the street. Heir, Vain, Devin and Des follow shortly.

> **DEVIN**
> What's up? What are we gonna watch next?

> **VAIN**
> Naw, Dev not tonight.

> **DEVIN**
> Come on, one more. For old times sake?

> **HEIR**
> Yeah I'm down Dev. You want to just go back
> and watch that one again?

> **DEVIN**
> Yeah!

> **DES**
> Yeah, we probably have enough time to watch
> it two more times. It's still pretty early.

Heir and Des laugh and begin to walk away. Vain grabs Devin and throws him on his shoulders and they follow Heir and Des.

A STREET POET is posted up outside the theater. The boys stop and listen to him for a minute.

EXT MISSION DISTRICT - MOMENTS LATER

A MAN, DINO (36), sits outside a FALAFEL RESTAURANT, eating and reading THE NATION. Heir sneaks up behind Dino.

> **HEIR**
> *(busts out suddenly right in Dino's ear)* For
> the love of God! I'm really hungry!

Dino waves Heir's hand away and attempts to swallow the remainder of the food in his mouth.

> **DINO**
> Chill, chill. I'll save you some . . .

Dino turns and notices it's Heir and not the Homeless Man he was expecting.

> **DINO**
> *(laughing)* Oh shit. I thought you were that
> guy for sure.

They shake hands/hug.

> **DINO**
> What are you up to, Mikey?

> **HEIR**
> Nothing. Chillin.

> **DINO**
> *(to Vain, Des, and Devin)* What's up fellas?

> **VAIN**
> What's up D?

> **DES**
> What are you doing? *(points to the restaurant)* Paying rent?

Director's note. There's really a guy in the Mission who does this. We hired a fake homeless guy (actor) to hit them up on the way to the agency (page twleve) and he did a pretty good job. But it's just not the same. If you eat outside enough in the Mission, you'll see this guy eventually.

154

fight like brothers. And you should NEVER allow the screenwriter on set. Casting him is def last resort. Floss is invested and wants to do this. But he needs to become a writer. He needs to show me he's willing to learn and to get his hands dirty in the process. He can't just come on set and be himself. No diamond earrings, no bic head, no Lugz. This is a different world. And Floss needs to show me something. This week I fax an offer to the agents. That will be telling (since we are not offering him shit up front). If they waffle, I move on. Not sure where, but I move on. Bottom line: I'm scared. There is WAY too much hanging out there. We need help. We need $$. Should this be a SAG project? Should this be an underground, no budget, no permit, no "actors," guerilla film? I think

Director's note. Have no idea how "Narnia" got changed to "way back." Missed that one. Oops.

somewhere in between. But in between is a bad place to be. Need to be committed . . . Fuck it. Need to just keep marching forward. Nothing is perfect. We are going to make mistakes. Shit is going to fall off. But we're going to make this movie. And, at the end of the day, that's all that counts. I'm going to push Floss this week. If he cracks (balks at the 100 percent deferred contract, fails to show willingness to learn about graff, etc.), he's out. He's on the fence, and why? Because of money? He made like a million dollars on his last picture . . . fucking ten years ago. This could be a great opportunity for him. Could totally rejuvenate his career. And the kid is incredibly talented. Best actor I've ever seen for his age. I hope he gets it. In so many ways, he IS Vain, not Heir, like everyone is saying.

DINO
I know, I know. Whatever. This is my man's joint. *(to Heir and Vain)* Where have you two been hiding out though? I seen all these new spots you been getting but never your face. That spot you guys got off at the water is hot.

VAIN
Oh, you saw that shit right? Yeah, it's summer time for sure.

DINO
Yup, looks like you got the fever, huh?

VAIN
You been painting?

DINO
Yeah, man. Nothing out here, though.

HEIR
You still got that rooftop from Narnia.

DES
That shit's been running forever.

DINO
I gotta show coming up. You guys should come check it out.

HEIR
Heard about that. We'll be there.

Dino stands up, tosses his trash in the garbage can, and walks up on Devin.

DINO
Cool. *(to Devin)* What's up with you guy? Don't like me no more?

DEVIN
Naw. It's over.

DINO
Come on, big guy. We can work this out. I'll change, I promise.

DEVIN
You can change your shirt.

Devin points to a bit of Dino's lunch on his shirt. They all laugh. Dino gives Devin a pound.

DINO
You're crazy Dev. I don't know about you. I think you been hanging out with these guys too much.

DEVIN
I know, they can't even hang.

DINO
(glances at his watch) Oh man. I gotta handle this right now.

DES
Where you off to?

DINO
I'ma hit the Temple before I go back to work.

HEIR
Well namaste, brother.

Dino bows to Heir, shakes hands with/hugs everyone, and bails out.

INT VAIN'S LIVING ROOM - CONTINUOUS

Lisa is chilling on the couch reading a book. Devin is crashed out in her arms. Vain and Heir enter. Vain, who is smoking a cigarette, approaches Lisa and looks over her shoulder at Dev.

VAIN
(whispering) I swear, his daddy must have been a marathon runner. That boy never tires.

Lisa waves the smoke away from Devin. Vain pulls the cig back behind the couch.

VAIN
Sorry.

Vain gives Lisa a kiss.

VAIN
See ya.

LISA
Bye.

Lisa goes back to her book. Vain follows Heir out the door and shuts it quietly.

EXT CASTRO - LATE NIGHT

Heir and Vain exit the tunnels through the same hole in the fence they escaped from before and walk down the street.

VAIN
That was cool Dino seen our spot, huh?

HEIR
Wait til he sees this spot. This one will definitely give Dino the fever.

VAIN
Yeah. I don't know why he quit. His shit was off the hook.

HEIR
You swear you're gonna be active when you're his age.

VAIN
I'm in it to win it, fool. I don't know about your punk ass. I'm going to write my name in blood as I die.

HEIR
Shit. I'm a King. I'ma live. I'll be catching tags on your casket.

VAIN
Do it. That shit would be dope.

A group of yuppies walk by them, giggling their asses off.

156

Director's note. This scene simply fell through the cracks. Just not enough time. The night we shot the Auto/cab stuff was so cramped, this scene just got shined. Oh well.

Maybe I need to hear that argument out. Damn! Now I'm starting to question myself. This is crazy. I'm so confused. Need to find some **$$**. That will calm the fires a little. **July 3, 2003.** Still in this shit-hole called Los Angeles. I have worked so hard to stay away from this town. But there is no escaping it, really. Esp when you're looking for talent. Hit a point where every second counts. Six weeks of full-time work in three weeks with only one full-time guy (me). Craziness. Sold a share yesterday. Kev Robertson (DP) and I tag-teamed Brant's uncles. Of course they were already sold before we got there since they were committed to supporting Brant. But it felt great nonetheless. Need about four more of those. Having enough $$ would be nice. But there's so much more—

mainly talent and locations. Oh yeah, and food. Need a driver, too. We really need like twice as much $$ and time. I've had a gut feeling to quit or postpone several times. Love to go home and just throw in the towel and leave the stress behind. This journal is proving to be a great place to dump all my anxiety. Sure in the fuck can't let anyone else see me sweat or the whole thing goes to hell. **July 4, 2003.** Spent half my day (eight hours) breaking down the gallery. So many things about this production are going sour. The Director should NOT spend that much time dealing with bullshit. It's not a power-trip thing. It's about making a good movie. And I need to be focusing on creative, not bullshit. The next wave of nightmares starts with SAG. Should we be a SAG project? Or should

> **HEIR**
> Oh my goodness. I love San Francisco. It's so diverse.

Vain stops and enters a liquor store.

> **VAIN**
> Want something?

> **HEIR**
> No, I'm straight.

Heir chills outside and reflects on the night's accomplishments for a minute. Random, late-night city action unfolds in front of him. Vain exits the store shortly thereafter with a tall can in hand and a new pack of smokes. He hands Heir a cig.

> **HEIR**
> Thanks.

They turn around and start walking, only to practically trip over a HOMELESS MAN who is pushing his shopping cart full of belongings in their direction.

> **VAIN**
> Oh, sorry man.

> **MAN**
> Sorry guys.

> **HEIR**
> It's alright. How you doing tonight?

> **MAN**
> I'm alright, thanks.

> **HEIR**
> *(holds out the cigarette)* You smoke?

> **MAN**
> *(accepts the smoke)* Yeah. Appreciate it.

Without losing their pace, they continue down the street. Vain cracks the beer and takes a swill. Heir gets another smoke and fires it up.

> **HEIR**
> What you want to get into? You still down tonight? Got some spots?

> **VAIN**
> Um, yeah. I got some spots. Hmmn . . . lets see . . . that shit's kinda far though . . .

> **HEIR**
> What are you thinking of?

> **VAIN**
> Well there's this jam I wanted to hit for a while now, but it's still a little early though. But we could rock some fill-ins up in this truck yard I scoped earlier.

> **HEIR**
> I'm down.

> **VAIN**
> Cool it's right up he-

                        AUTO (O.S.)
            Yo, yo. What's the deal?

*Their conversation is interrupted by a Cab Driver, AUTO (28), in
the other lane talking to them.*

                            HEIR
            Ha-ha. Aghh shit, what's up?

                            AUTO
            Punching the clock. You?

                            VAIN
            What's up, man. You on a call right now or
            what?

                            AUTO
            On a call? Have you ever seen me on a call?

                            HEIR
            That's hot. You trying to swoop us or what?

                            AUTO
            What evs. Get in.

                        HEIR/VAIN
            Tight.

They jump on the opportunity and load up.

INT CAB - CONTINUOUS

Heir and Vain pile in and Auto pulls out.

                            AUTO
            What the fuck are you guys doing up here in
            the Castro anyways?

                            VAIN
            Oh shit. Check it out, go left.

                            AUTO
            No shit?

                            HEIR
            Yeah, yeah go left.

*The cab turns a corner and Heir gestures for him to slow down.
BOOM! There are their freshly painted PIECES and they're hot!*

                            AUTO
            That shit is slamming.

                            HEIR
            (leans in) Thanks. But, check it out. The real
            question is, what are you doing up here?

                            AUTO
            (laughing) Shiiiit.

                            HEIR
            What's your girl gotta say about you trolling
            the Castro all night?

                            AUTO
            Ha ha. Fuck you. It's cool man. She digs it. As
            long as I let her watch, you know.

Director's note. We actually did
shoot the Auto scene. But we really
rushed it. It actually came off, but, as
with Grandma's joke, it contributed
to a way-too-long Act One. So it had
to go. Another deleted scene we
hope to share with you someday.

Director's note. Auto is based on a
real character, a cabbie friend of
Brian's who swoops up homies out
of the blue on the regular.

158

we be a small, quirky indie with nobodies? I'm trusting my gut here and that has never steered me wrong. However, I'm still scared. We have no locations, no money, and lots to do. And I don't want SAG up my ass on top of all that. We need to resolve this yesterday. SAG or no SAG, we have a movie to make. **July 5, 2003.** Got exactly what I needed last night—a good meal with lots of garlic and a good night's sleep. Although I was up in the middle of the night fretting. Oh yeah, and I ended up getting up at 4am and writing some e-mails. *Bomb the System* got a great review in *Filmmaker Mag.* Damn. So many things have gone sour with this film. Really makes me wonder if I'm on the right path. Seems so forced. Nothing's coming easy. No synchronicity. And now some

other bastard comes out of nowhere with a graff movie before me??? I have been thinking about this movie for twenty fucking years. This guy is like twenty three years old! Fuck all . . . But, once again, this is a freight train. I can't stop it, nor can anyone else. This is Sunday. I can slow down a little bit. Still have work to do. I'll be the only one on the team working today. Gives me a chance to get ahead. Was considering taking time off myself, maybe go for a surf. We'll see. Need to crank on my list. So much to do it's frightening. The list keeps growing. I'm down for this. I know it's what I need to do right now. But I'll never do this again without a budget. It's not the money as much as it is the personnel. There is enough work for twenty people right now. We have a small handful.

                    VAIN
    Shit, Auto. You're one crazy m.f.

                    AUTO
    Yeah yeah. You wanna see one that's crazy
    huh?

Auto reaches out and hands Heir a coned joint so large that it yells 'BOOYAKA' and shatters eardrums.

                    VAIN
    Deaaaamn, sonny. What the hell?

                    AUTO
    That's right.

                    HEIR
    (handing the joint to Vain in the back seat)
    Yo. Ugh. Why you gotta roll them shits so
    big man?

                    AUTO
    Check it out. It really wasn't my idea. That
    weed is so tough it practically put me in a
    choke hold and made me do it like that.

Heir tosses out his cigarette and hands Vain the lighter.

                    HEIR
    Ganja fi blaze. If my lungs are destined to be
    frail, at least it was for a good cause.

The voice of a female dispatcher interrupts.

                DISPATCHER (O.S.)
    Josh. I've got thirteen fifty-two Masonic at
    Market. Confirm?

                    AUTO
    Story of my life. *(into radio)* Thirteen fifty-two
    Masonic at Market, thank you. *(to the boys)* Is
    this close enough fellas?

                    VAIN
    Don't sweat it. This is fine. *(hands the joint
    back)* Here.

                    AUTO
    I ain't sweating it. That's all you.

                    VAIN
    Oh. Right on, Auto.

Heir and Vain exit the cab. Heir leans in the window and shakes Auto's hand.

                    HEIR
    Going to see your bear?

                    AUTO
    Shit.

                    VAIN
    Yeah. Go tell your daddy I said 'what's up.'

                    AUTO
    You said it. Ha-ha . . .

                                        CUT TO:

Auto speeds off.

> **HEIR**
> That's messed up.

> **VAIN**
> *(gesturing towards a rooftop)* Check it out.

> **HEIR**
> Get out. That is a good spot.

> **VAIN**
> Right? You want to know where we climb up at?

> **HEIR**
> Yeah. Where do you climb up . . . *(beat)* at?

> **VAIN**
> It's kind of early, though. *(whispering)* But check it.

Vain points silently to a window which leads to a drainpipe, which leads to a small landing, which eventually leads to another drainpipe.

> **HEIR**
> Yeah, yeah. That works. But you're right, it is still a little early.

> **VAIN**
> Yeah, but whatever. It's chill once we're up, right? Let's just get up there.

Vain is interrupted by a SQUAD CAR making its way towards them. They immediately play it off like they are giving each other directions. They've done this routine a thousand times and jump right in together.

> **HEIR**
> *(pointing down the street)* Yeah, I think it's like two blocks that way. Pork chop patrol, ummm, bad cop no doughnut, eat a dick, keep driving you fat bastard.

The Cop passes them and they make tracks. The cop turns the corner and, without speaking, Heir and Vain immediately turn 180 degrees.

> **VAIN**
> Come on man. Let's just be up that shit right now.

> **HEIR**
> Hmmmnn. Where's those trucks from here?

> **VAIN**
> No, no. We gotta get this shit tonight.

Vain is scoping the scene. He's got that determined look in his eye.

> **HEIR**
> Where's the trucks though?

> **VAIN**
> Not too far. But lets do this.

Director's note. And we're back to the post-tunnels scene. "You think those toys got popped?" "Who? Your friends?"

Director's note. This joke fell through the cracks, too. I always liked the idea of clowning someone for saying "at" after everything. But, as with most scenes we shot, it was a struggle just to get the damn thing in the can, let alone make sure we were sticking to the script.

760

And, aside from our kickass casting director (Belinda Gardea), I'm the only full-timer. Still don't have the money. Right now we have enough to make the movie with basically me and Kev on the set (and Brant and Meika running around town killing themselves). We need to be able to hire a crew. Some positions will have to be paid. No way around that. Namely our gaffer and sound man. Ideally we can pay our actors as well. Would rather avoid the total deferment nightmare. That shit can come back to haunt you (esp if SAG is involved). I have not been exercising, up until yesterday. Just way too busy. But that shit will do me in. I started busting out some random push-ups. Need to get a little bit of that in every day. Push-ups, sit-ups, walk, run, hoop, whatever. Cannot get

Director's note. These two got axed as well. I liked them both (and Brian based them on real life experiences), but it was just too much coordination for an already complex night exterior.

lethargic. Can't get sick either . . . So many things going on at once. Kev's trying to work discount/free film stock; Belinda is wrapping up LA casting; need to lock down an editor so we can transition directly into post (if we can afford it); locations—haven't secured even one; money, money, money; food—gotsta feed people (and feed them well); crew—need one of those; hotel—The Professor's working the discount angle; Buddhist temple and mandalas; Brian—in or out?; clothes and in-kind . . . Lot on the plate, but at least it's on the plate. Althogh we have no money, we have an incredibly strong core team. Brant is holding down the big picture, despite holding down a day job at the same time. Meika is awesome. Her positive attitude is infectious. Her people skills are going to go

> **HEIR**
> We should come back in a bit, you know?

> **VAIN**
> No, no. Let's do this. Come on man.

> **HEIR**
> You think it's chill?

> **VAIN**
> This shit will run. Nobody's ever hit it either.

> **HEIR**
> Yeah, this spot is the joint. Alright, man lets do this.

They cross the street and make their approach. The whole scene on the ground is dark. They scope it from a little closer, check the street. It's clear, time to move. They take three steps towards the drain and BING! They're lit up like a football field. Cops? Nope. Motion sensors? Yup. It startles them and they both freeze and try to play dumb.

> **HEIR**
> Fuck. Who invented those things?

> **VAIN**
> It's cool, it's cool, lets go!

Just as they step towards the drainpipe again, a door swings open really fast and loud, and a GUY and GIRL exit, causing a big commotion. They notice Heir and Vain, but, once again, they quickly play it off, searching the ground for something lost.

> **HEIR**
> Oh god. Where is it?

> **VAIN**
> Look. I didn't drop it.

> **HEIR**
> I can't find it.

Vain bends over and pretends to pick something up.

> **VAIN**
> Oh. There it is.

> **HEIR**
> You found it. Here, let me see it.

They begin to walk away.

> **VAIN**
> No man. You'll lose it again.

> **HEIR**
> It was my idea to bring it anyway. Give it up.

> **VAIN**
> No.

Heir looks back. They're in the clear now.

> **HEIR**
> So, where's them trucks, my man?

> **VAIN**
> Alright, alright.

EXT TRUCK YARD - LATER

Heir and Vain scope the scene.

> **VAIN**
> Not these ones. But there's like four on the
> other side that run.

> **HEIR**
> Yeah, yeah. I saw these. I got something on
> the back of one of them.

> **VAIN**
> No shit?

> **HEIR**
> Yeah, but I didn't catch it in this yard. I found
> it on the street a month or two ago.

*The two of them slip in the yard with no delay. This is much more
low-pro than the rooftop.*

> **VAIN**
> Those are a buff, but I think there's some more
> over there that run.

> **HEIR**
> There's my truck right there.

> **VAIN**
> Oh shit. Yeah, I've seen that one.

> **HEIR**
> *(talking to himself)* Sleepy little trucks. Hiding
> out in the cuts, huh?

*The two of them discuss the plan for the truck's new image
(who's going over who, etc.) and begin working.*

MONTAGE.

*Heir and Vain do their thing in the middle of the yard. They are
surrounded by trucks and safely out of sight of passing cars.
They duck from a few headlights and each finish their trucks.
Heir immediately starts to work on a second truck.*

*Vain makes his way to the outskirts of the yard and finds a clean
truck. Almost immediately after starting his outline, Vain is lit up.
This time it's serious. He looks towards the street and a COP
CAR who has creeped on them with his headlights off, is onto
them. He's already on his radio, dispatching back up. But Heir
and Vain aren't interested in waiting around to meet his friends.*

> **VAIN**
> *(yelling to Heir)* Fuck! Be out!

It's a mad dash, and Vain and Heir are off.

*The COP proceeds to put the car in gear and attempts to cut
them off at the pass. Heir and Vain find a new route out of the
yard and are out like gazelles on a survival sprint. As they're running, they notice more squad cars approaching.*

> **HEIR**
> Shit! Meet me at the waterfront?

far. Belinda is a freaking animal. So organized, motivated, and hard-working. Kev is like a soul-mate. I don't think I'm going to have to have to say much to him on set. He sees the world through the same lens (no pun intended). I just hope to be able to give him an opportunity to shine, and not just battle his way through hell. It's all going to work out fine. I'm on the right path. Have been for years. All I have to do is keep marching forward. **July 7, 2003.** Three weeks out. Things are starting to come together, but there are SOOOO many holes. I have no apt. We don't have enough $$. No food sched. (No food!) No driver. No actors. But it's all coming together. Everyone's doing his or her job. Brian and I made up yesterday. Good conversation. Worked some shit out. I love the guy. I

VAIN

Ten minutes!

HEIR

Careful!

The two split ways. Vain runs along the tracks for a second but notices a flashlight coming towards him, so makes a quick left and hits a side street. An OFFICER is on his ass.

Heir jumps a fence and runs down an alley only to be cut off at the end by a COP CAR entering it. The Officer revs up and powers towards Heir. Heir attempts to slow down and he looks back down the alley in the direction he came from, but it's way too long for him to outrun the car. So, with the momentum he is already carrying, he continues towards the law. The Officer stops the car and starts to get out. The alley is narrow and, before the Officer can open the door, Heir is jumping onto the hood, booking it across the top, and down the trunk. He makes an immediate left while the cop attempts to shut his door and jam the car in reverse.

Without any headlights in sight, Heir seizes his opportunity to hide out. With an amazing NFL-style game winning touchdown, he dives headfirst into the end zone/bush. Sweating and attempting to catch his breath he lies frozen as the cop car drives by him in hot pursuit of nobody. Heir closes his eyes and breathes a silent sigh a relief. Heir notices another car coming towards him. But he stays put, confident this spot is good, and attempts to wait it out. Suddenly, a CITIZEN blows his cover.

CITIZEN
(pointing at Heir) Right there. He's right there.

Heir springs up, but this time he's in the middle of a street. He heads up the street in the direction of Huffington's car, only to be disappointed by the sight of it returning in his direction. Heir's been had. With cars on either side of him and no alleyways or alternative escapes, he stands sweating and breathing heavily. With spotlights on him, Heir hesitantly raises his hands up in the air.

DISSOLVE TO:

INT POLICE STATION - NIGHT

JUDGE (V.O.)
The court hereby orders one week in County Jail, one hundred hours of community service, and six months probation.

Heir and Vain are printed and photographed.

DISSOLVE TO:

INT HEIR'S ROOM - MORNING

JUDGE (V.O.)
The Court also orders one year suspended time in a California correctional facility for any probation violations.

Pops enters and looks at Heir's empty bed. He takes a moment to digest the situation before exiting.

DISSOLVE TO:

EXT DOWNTOWN CLOTHING STORE - DAY

Pops sets up the scaffolding and works alone.

Director's note. Brian based this chase on real life experiences, but we had to use what we had. So we re-wrote the scene on-the-spot at the truck yards.

163

just hope he recognizes that this is an opportunity, not an obligation. Goddamn. Such a full plate. This is the last week to raise $$. The last two weeks are all about actors and locations. That's the theory at least. **July 8, 2003.** I really have no idea why I'm doing this. I'm swimming upstream on a movie that doesn't seem to want to be made. SAG is up my ass like everyone said they would be. I'm straining my relationships with my friends. Why? I have no idea. I'm like a bee in a fucking raspberry bush, zipping around working my ass off with no fucking clue what I'm doing or why I'm doing it. I do know that it's too late to stop now. In some ways, that bums me out a little bit. Now that we have name actors (sort of), we could totally shop this thing around and raise

DISSOLVE TO:

INT COURTROOM - DAY

> Wearing orange jumpsuits, cuffs, and shackles, Heir and Vain stand before the Judge.

                    JUDGE
This isn't a game, gentlemen. If you continue to destroy other people's property, you will do hard time.

The Judge RAPS THE GAVEL.

INT JAIL HOLDING CELL - DAY

A CRACKHEAD is on all fours gorging himself on peanut butter and jelly sandwiches. Heir and Vain stew in the cell.

                    FADE TO BLACK.

EXT VAIN'S HOUSE - MORNING

Pops and Heir pull up. Pops honks twice and they wait. Pops attempts to take a sip off his coffee, but it's still a bit too hot to drink. Neither of them say a word to each other. Pops turns his head and looks towards the house. He honks again and shakes his head in disbelief.

                    HEIR
I'll get him.

Before Heir can grab the handle and open the door, Pops throws the car in drive, but forgets to place his foot on the break. He chirps out and his coffee sloshes out of the cup and into his lap.

                    POPS
Fuck!

                    HEIR
What?

                    POPS
This is bullshit.

Pops throws his cup out the window, puts his foot on the gas, and accelerates down the street.

                    HEIR
Relax. I said I'd get him.

                    POPS
I am relaxed and no you won't. I've had it, Mikey. I've fucking had it.

Heir looks back and sees Vain emerging from the house.

                    HEIR
You've had it? He's right there.

                    POPS
Fuck him. He's fired. This is bullshit. Miss a week of work and can't even wake up on time?

                    HEIR
What? He's right there, man.

                    POPS
I'm sick and tired of waiting for that guy. I'm

Director's note. Another real-life situation based on some nut-case Brian encountered in jail. We actually did shoot a little crackhead set-up with Brant, the producer. Dragged him around the parking lot, etc. But it was distracting, so Brant's big cameo hit the floor. (Sorry, buddy.)

764

Director's note. A lot of swear words in this scene. Yet somehow, Luis Saguar (Pops) was able to add like ten more!

some real money. Belinda said the script was creating quite a stir in LA. And we're only sending to agents. But we do not want to go there. It is a graffiti movie after all. Why should it be above ground? Truthfully, all we need is about $10-15K more. Just a few people to make our day. But, whatever. We're making this f'ing movie. Making progress every day. Money is trickling in. It's coming together. Just need to re-claim my faith. **July 9, 2003.** I can't believe I intentionally put myself into this position. It's impossible to see the forest through the trees. Amber's out. Bummer. She's a talented young actress and would have been the perfect Lisa. So hard to find someone who is real and has struggle in his or her eyes. Belinda has about ten huge stacks of headshots of beau-

not gonna let him fuck our shit up anymore.

                                                    CUT TO:

EXT VAIN'S APARTMENT - CONTINUOUS

Vain stands outside and watches them in disbelief as they drive off.

EXT SF JOB SITE - LATER THAT DAY

Heir pulls two buckets of paint from the rig and sets them down on the sidewalk. Pops grabs something from the cab of the truck. Pops and Heir spot Vain headed towards them.

                         POPS
            (to Heir) Handle this.

Pops enters the building with his clipboard in hand.

Vain strolls up.

                         VAIN
            How come you guys left?

                         HEIR
            Pops was honking and you didn't come out . . .

                         VAIN
            I came out.

                         HEIR
            I know. Pops was just . . .

                         VAIN
            It's cool. Should I get started on this wall?

                         HEIR
            I don't know. Pops is kind of tripping right now.
            Maybe you should . . .

Vain ignores Heir and takes off his jacket and prepares to get to work on the wall.

                         HEIR
            Pops said you're fired.

Vain stops and looks at Heir and realizes he's not playing.

                         VAIN
            Word?

                         HEIR
            I think he's just a little heated right now.

Vain stops and slowly lets it soak in for a second before grabbing his jacket and putting it back on.

                         HEIR
            Sorry, man.

                         VAIN
            It's cool. I'm over it.

They bump fists. Vain walks off

                         HEIR
            I'll call you later.

Vain doesn't turn around but nods in acknowledgement.

Director's note. We edited it so Vain says nothing after he gets fired. (Used reaction shots.) Played a lot stronger that way.

tiful bombshells, but none of them can act (or the ones who can just aren't Lisa). This would have been a great role for Amber. We worked really well together, too. Oh well. I don't blame her. We must seem like a shaky operation if we can't even offer her a freaking per diem. Money is starting to roll in. Hopefully we'll have enough to do it right (i.e. food, crew, accommodations). Need at least $10K more. Onward. July **10, 2003.** For some reason, yesterday seemed more hopeful. Maybe it was because I worked at home all day and made good progress. Maybe it's because we sold another share. That was a trip. Just as we were starting the pitch, the guy says, "I'm not in a position to invest." I just about stood up and walked out. I've got better things to do. But Brant hung in there.

EXT SF JOB SITE - DAY

Pops and Heir are working on the scaffolding. Heir is obviously pissed off, but he isn't saying anything about it. He takes out his aggression painting the wall instead.

EXT SF JOB SITE - LATER

Heir is loading the equipment into the rig. He isn't showing much respect for the gear or the rig. Passive aggression is reigning supreme.

Pops stares at Heir as he walks away from the rig. He shakes his head and rearranges the back of his truck.

INT POPS'S RIG - DAY

Heir and Pops pull away from the job site after a long day's work. They share uncomfortable silence for a minute, before Pops breaks in and points out a hot chick walking down the street.

>   POPS
> Damn. Shake it, girl.

Silence.

>   POPS
> What's wrong with you, man?

Nothing.

>   POPS
> Look, I know Curtis is your boy and all. But I just
> can't have him around anymore. He's a low life.

>   HEIR
> He's a low life because he paints graffiti, right?

>   POPS
> Did I say that?

>   HEIR
> Am I low life?

>   POPS
> What? The kid doesn't have his shit together,
> man. It's that simple.

>   HEIR
> I don't have my shit together.

>   POPS
> What?

>   HEIR
> I don't. And I got way more than him. I got a
> dad, a grandma, a roof over my head. I've got
> all this so-called support, right? All this love,
> huh? And where am I?

Pops doesn't answer.

>   HEIR
> Look, we paint graffiti. That's what we do.
> It's . . .

>   POPS
> That's what you do, huh?

766

I followed his lead, figured it can't hurt to practice the pitch. Then finally the guy says, "I'll do it." He was cool. Wants to be in the movie. No problem. We can find a background role for him. Also talked to Jello Biafra. Would love to cast him. He's such a legend in my mind. It's going to be hard to be objective since I have idolized him since before I had hair on my balls. Anyway, feeling much better today. We're getting close on $$. If we can raise $10K in the next two weeks, we're golden. I've got a few luke-warm leads. Very hard to reach outside the inner circle right now. It will be different when we have a finished film. And even easier next time around when we have a track record. Everything will fall into place. Feeling good. We'll see if it holds through the day. **July 11, 2003.**

Going home today. Need to hang with the fam and recharge the batteries. Making progress. Hired a great sound-man. He's skilled, has a great rep, and understands the story. He's also down for going doc mode, which is key. Everyone has to be feeling the guerilla model. That's mandatory. I also found Vain's apartment. It's a first class dive in the heart of the Mission. Reminds me of my high school days. Not real fond memories, but nostalgic none-theless. Met with SPIE yesterday. Our paths never crossed in the 80s. But CRAYONE hooked me up with him. He'd be a great Dino. I gave him the script. We'll see. It's all coming together. We still need $5-10K to do it right. Need an A.C. lighting package, and more food. Home stretch . . . **July 15, 2003.** Had a good weekend with the fam.

HEIR
Yeah.

POPS
So, you destroy other people's property for fun? For what? Fame? Notoriety? What?

HEIR
Whatever, man. That's my thing. That's how I express myself.

POPS
What's so wrong with pen and paper? A fucking canvas? What makes you think the whole city needs to be exposed to your 'artwork'?

HEIR
This city is littered with bullshit, Pops. Look around you. Billboards, advertisements, fuck-ing skyscrapers. What gives them the right to cram that garbage down our throats?

POPS
That's different. They pay for it.

HEIR
So, just because I don't have money, I don't have the right to be heard?

POPS
Well, why don't you start a business and buy a billboard. Then you can put whatever you want up there.

HEIR
(under his breath) I ain't paying for shit.

POPS
What?

HEIR
You got your own business, right?

POPS
Yeah.

HEIR
You work hard for it, huh?

POPS
Yeah.

HEIR
Worked your whole life for it, right? Now tell me if you can afford one of those billboards.

POPS
So you're gonna keep doing graffiti? Keep going to jail? Until what? Until they throw you away for good? They aren't fucking with you, Mikey. You will do hard time, eventually.

HEIR
I know that. I'm not stupid.

POPS
Then what is all this shit about?

HEIR

Look, you've put in so much work. Yeah you've put food on the table and that's a good thing, man. I love you, Pops. But you're not happy. Mom wasn't happy. It's discouraging. I'm sorry. I really am. But what am I supposed to do? Take over the business? Follow the leader? Live the American fucking dream? I'm not trying to do that. I'm not ready to do that. And you knew I did this. I didn't think you of all people would have a problem with it. But clearly you do.

Heir opens the door at the traffic light and steps out of the ride.

POPS

Where are you going?

HEIR

I gotta go. I'll see you later.

Heir walks down the street. Pops sits and thinks things over.

EXT MARKET STREET - MOMENTS LATER

Heir sits at a bus stop and thinks about his situation. Crazy everyday downtown city life unfolds behind him.

INT HOME SUPPLIES STORE - DAY

Vain and Des enter. Des sets down a boom box in the middle of the store and turns on some jams. Everybody stops and looks up. Vain starts up-rocking and then busts out breaking in the middle of the store. An EMPLOYEE tries to stop him.

EMPLOYEE

Hey. Hey! You can't do that in here.

VAIN

Check this out.

Vain busts out a many continuation. Another employee and the manager try to intervene, to no avail. It's a big scene and everybody is taking notice.

On the other side of the store, Des subtly fills a duffel bag full of aerosol cans and goes completely unnoticed.

The manager and seemingly the rest of the store are on Vain, who has stopped dancing.

VAIN

Y'all tripping. You see something different and you don't know what to do about it. I bet y'all wouldn't trip if I was doing ballet or some shit.

EMPLOYEE

I don't care if you're doing a goddamn rain dance. You can't do it in the middle of the store.

Vain spots Des slipping out the door.

VAIN

Alright then, you fascist pigs. I'll take my culture lesson somewhere else. Peace.

Vain exits. Nobody knows what to make of this episode.

Director's note. Brian doesn't know how to break, so he came up with the Chinese food thing instead (the day of the shoot).

Needed that. Reminded why I'm doing this. Back to work. Busiest day of the month. SAG at eleven. Brant before that. All day script breakdown with an inexperienced AD, which means I'm doing the freaking breakdown myself. (Ah yes, thanks again to our producer friend who ditched us at the altar and took my AD mentor with her.) Production meeting 7-9pm. Full day indeed. Better get used to it. SAG is the biggest thorn right now. I'm a little scared to be honest. Our whole movie is riding on them. Gotta play ball though. They aren't going anywhere, and neither are we. Better get used to working with them. It's all about cold hard cash at this point. If we can pull the Limited Exhibition contract (basically $100/day) we're there. So need to raise $10K this week. Period. Man! And I haven't

Director's note. This is based on one of Brian's real community service expeditions. No lie.

EXT SF INDUSTRIAL AREA - NIGHT

Vain and Des work on a piece. Vain is going off.

EXT PARK - MORNING

A MAN plays fetch with his DOG. A COUPLE power walks. A few random COMMUNITY SERVICE WORKERS do community service: paint over various tags, pick up trash, and handpick clovers from the grass.

Heir is digging a hole in a dirt patch by some trees. The SUPERVISING OFFICER walks up on him.

> **HEIR**
> I think I'm done.

> **OFFICER**
> Lemme see.

Heir sticks his shovel in and reveals that the hole is indeed handle-deep.

> **OFFICER**
> Alright. Get the hose and fill it up with water.

Heir complies. He hooks up the hose, drags it to the hole and fills it up.

EXT PARK - LATER

Heir approaches the officer.

> **HEIR**
> Now what?

> **OFFICER**
> Fill it.

> **HEIR**
> With water?

> **OFFICER**
> With dirt.

> **HEIR**
> What?

> **OFFICER**
> Fill it with dirt. You hard of hearing?

Heir shakes his head and walks off. He returns to the hole and starts filling it with dirt.

INT ABANDONED WAREHOUSE - DAY

Vain is chilling in a window/hole in the wall drinking a brew. Heir enters.

> **VAIN**
> What's up? Where you been?

> **HEIR**
> Community service. They asked about you.

Vain shrugs it off and hits the brew. Heir puts his hand out and Vain hands him the bottle. Heir sits down, takes a load off, and enjoys some nice warm beer.

                              VAIN
So what's up? Let's get that rooftop tonight?

                              HEIR
Shit.

                              VAIN
Serious.

                              HEIR
Naw, man.

                              VAIN
What?

                              HEIR
I'm chilling for a minute.

                              VAIN
What? You gonna let one court case take
your shine?

                              HEIR
I'm not gonna let them put a case together.

Vain shrugs it off.

                              HEIR
You down to check out Dino's show tonight?

                              VAIN
(shrugs) Whatever's clever.

They chill and share silence.

INT VAIN'S APARTMENT - EVENING

*Heir chills in the living room with Devin and watches TV.
Lisa enters.*

                              LISA
Hey, Mikey. How you doing?

                              HEIR
Alright, I guess. What have you been up to?

                              LISA
Same ol' same ol'. The days never end
around here.

                              HEIR
I hear you. Pops has been working my ass off.

                              LISA
That's good, though. Keeps you out of trouble.

                              HEIR
I guess. But painting walls blank all day ain't
all that creative, you know? Gets kind of tired.
How's your job?

                              LISA
OK. They're talking about hiring me full time.

                              HEIR
Cool. That would be a tight place to work.
Draw ads all day for a living. I'd take that job.

Director's note. This seemed like
too much when we rehearsed it. So
we went with the simpler, paired
down version.

Director's note. This dialogue
seemed a little too expository. So
we condensed it into the scene
where Mikey goes into the agency
for his "interview." Hard to broach
this without looking Hollywood,
since it is a pretty predictable, traditional angle. But we felt Mikey just
going for it all at once was the most
realistic way to approach it.

170

plished. But fuck that. Stop worrying about results. It's all about the process! Enjoy it. There will be snags. But failure is a necessary step in success. Accept it. **July 17, 2003.** Still crazy. Still not enough $$. Still not cast. But I'm feeling so good. Went to John Doffing's opening last night. He's a maniac. So stoked on him. I like associating with different kinds of people. I never would have hung out with someone like him or Brant when I was a kid. But they bring a different perspective to the table. And we're all down for the same cause. John pulled together an amazing event last night. Met some cool people. The crew was all there—TopR, RENOS, Sam Flores, Abhor. Just starting to realize what a powerful movement we are part of. We have so much synergy. It's like Marc Levin said

171

Director's note. We peppered Grandma's joke throughout the script. The joke actually works better like this (as an after-shock). But, since we pulled Grandma, we pulled the references as well.

Director's note. Another casualty of the schedule.

> **LISA**
> You'd be good at it. You've got more talent than half of the clowns that work there.

> **HEIR**
> Hook me up.

> **LISA**
> What?

> **HEIR**
> Hook me up with a job there.

> **LISA**
> It's not that easy. Usually they recruit people.

> **HEIR**
> You saying I'm not recruitable?

> **LISA**
> It's not that. Look, Mikey, I want to help you out, but I'm a temp there. I don't really have any pull, you know?

> **HEIR**
> Yeah, it's cool. I understand.

Vain enters. He is sporting brand new white low-top Converse, creased pants, and a white T-shirt. He's pressing the O.G. factor for real. Vain and Heir shake hands/hug.

> **HEIR**
> Damn, slick.

> **LISA**
> *(to Vain)* Can you take the trash out?

> **VAIN**
> Yeah.

> **LISA**
> It smells like a corpse in there.

> **VAIN**
> I said I'd get it. Damn, stop sweating me.

> **LISA**
> That's nice.

Lisa exits to the kitchen.

> **HEIR**
> Her, too?

> **VAIN**
> *(Jersey accent)* Always busting my balls.

EXT SOMA - EVENING

Heir and Vain strut down the street. The city's starting to heat up a bit. Heir and Vain are feeling it. Heir stops and looks up at a big, fresh 'VAIN' tag on a store window. Heir stares at Vain. Vain laughs it off. Heir shakes his head in disbelief.

> **VAIN**
> You hungry?

> **HEIR**
> Starving.

> **VAIN**
> Word to the motherfeeder. Let's grab a slice.
> This is my spot right here.

They enter a pizza joint.

INT PIZZA JOINT - MOMENTS LATER

Heir and Vain grab a couple of slices and dig in. But the pizza is still pretty hot. As Vain attempts to bite into the slice, a huge amount of tomato sauce oozes out from under the cheese and into his mouth. It's so hot that he can no longer keep it in his mouth and towards the floor it falls, but stops short as it lands all over his right foot.

> **VAIN**
> Damn.

> **HEIR**
> Oh, dog. The cons?

> **VAIN**
> This is some bullshit. No wonder the slices
> are four dollars. They use a whole can of this
> shit in every piece.

> **HEIR**
> (laughs) This is your spot, man.

> **VAIN**
> (sucking teeth) Man.

> **HEIR**
> Check it out, though.

Heir removes the cheese from his pizza. Confused, Vain looks on as Heir begins to lower his slice towards Vain's other shoe.

> **VAIN**
> Whoa, whoa, man.

> **HEIR**
> It's cool, I got you. Check it out.

Heir slaps his pizza all over the clean converse and starts laughing hysterically as he attempts to explain his actions.

> **HEIR**
> Yeah, this is our new line of cons, called To-
> mata, yeah, Tomata. You gonna wanna get
> some new ones.

> **VAIN**
> (laughing) You fucked up, dog.

> **HEIR**
> Yeah, check it out. It's new. Not too many
> people are into it yet, but it's catching on.
> Just think, you know, this time next year you
> can tell people, 'last year at this time I was
> rocking Tomatas. I was there when it all
> started and let me tell you, it was a Tomata
> epidemic for real.'

> **VAIN**
> Shiiiiit. You're fucked up, man.

EXT MISSION DISTRICT - MOMENTS LATER

and move on. Stress will destroy this project. Things are going to go wrong. Lots. But there is no time to dwell on it. One step at a time. Things are lining up. It's all going to turn out fine. I just need to remember that I am the leader. People look to me for guidance. I just need to be myself (i.e., an anal-retentive, detail-oriented, control freak). It's time to take control. **July 19, 2003.** Floss is out. Despite the fact that we are one week out and now in a panic to find our lead, I was actually a bit relieved when he told me. Floss is not trustworthy. And he's incredibly selfish. Unlike Lane, he is not a team player. He could have sunk the whole ship. Best damn actor we saw. Period. But, on a personal level, we never clicked. So, he's gone. Got some TV spots (paying ones). Good for him.

Heir and Vain walk down the street, Tomatas and all. They're still laughing and talking shit. Vain's whole fit is tight, so his shoes are really making a statement. A few people notice them. Heir and Vain start making comments to random passersby.

> **VAIN**
> You know, it's new. Not everyone's down with it, but watch . . .

> **HEIR**
> Yeah, this time next year . . .

Continued funny looks from strangers and random comments. The boys are cracking themselves up.

> **VAIN**
> (to Heir) Hold up a sec.

Vain stops in his tracks and stares into a store window. Heir approaches and peers through the window.

> **HEIR**
> Who? That girl?

> **VAIN**
> Chill, chill. Don't look.

> **HEIR**
> What? You know her?

> **VAIN**
> What? Oh, nah, why don't you hook it up?

> **HEIR**
> For real?

> **VAIN**
> Yeah, I got your back.

> **HEIR**
> I don't need . . . hold up. What are you scheming?

> **VAIN**
> What? You scared? Get the digits, punk.

> **HEIR**
> Aw shit. Here we go again.

INT CLOTHING STORE - MOMENTS LATER

Vain plays dumb, looking at a few prices as Heir macks on the girl at the counter. Vain moseys to the front window, looks over his shoulder again to make sure things are still chill, and spies a crispy pair of dunks on the manikin in the window display. A fat smile breaks out across his grill.

CUT TO:

EXT CLOTHING STORE - MOMENTS LATER

Close up of Vain's feet. He's now sporting the new dunks.

> **HEIR**
> You're a sav.

> **VAIN**
> You want me to go to the spot, rocking those?

Heir and Vain walk off down the street, shooting the shit.

> **HEIR**
> That would have been off the meter. People would be like, 'Which magazine do you work for? Hmmm. Very cutting edge. And who is your designer?' But I feel you, man. I wouldn't want to be responsible for all those hipsters losing sleep over your shoes. Shit, that statement we made was enough to crush people's lifelong dreams.

The camera pans back to the store window. The MANIKIN is now sporting the tomatas.

> **VAIN (O.S.)**
> People just aren't ready for our steelo. What would be left for them to do?

> **HEIR (O.S.)**
> Exactly.

EXT SPINNAZ - NIGHT

The LINE to the club outside is well congested. Muffled JAMS THUMP through the walls. A few GROUPS of PEOPLE are scattered down the alley finishing off their brown bags and smoking cigarettes. As Heir and Vain turn the corner the look on their faces tells they are impressed with the turnout.

> **VAIN**
> Ibiza 2003. Mardi Gras.

> **HEIR**
> What the hell? Dino for president. I told you this shit would be booming.

> **VAIN**
> What's up with your boy's followers?

> **HEIR**
> I'm saying. Applewhite lookout. Fuck the comet. We want to stay right here.

The two make their way through the crowded alley. Lots of familiar faces. A few what's up nods and a few pounds later they bump into Auto, who is chilling in line with their homey, JOSH (23).

> **VAIN**
> What's up Auto? *(to Josh)* Look at this guy. When did you get out?

> **HEIR**
> Ha ha. The roustabout.

> **JOSH**
> Just what I suspected. Who else shall I find in the vortex of this chaos? What the fuck?

> **HEIR**
> *(Jersey accent)* You never call. You never write.

> **JOSH**
> I know, I know. But I'm here right now. What's going on here? This your shit?

> **HEIR**
> No, no.

Director's note. We had to cut this off b/c we were staring at the Cons in the window for way too long.

174

Director's note. We clipped ALL of this dialogue b/c the party shoot was totally overwhelming as it was. We had to shoot like ten very difficult pages of script with tons of extras, stunts, etc. in one night. We substituted TopR in the cipher.

falling into place. Now I just need to find some actors. Brian is supposed to be here today. I have mixed feelings about that obviously. But I need to nurture the guy. He's family and he's key to the success of the film. I can't let him take the wheel, as he is apt to try and do. (I've actually seen him grab the steering wheel from people while they're driving.) On the other hand, I want to make him feel important, because he IS! And respected. But he def needs to managed. He could sink this whole thing if we let him. So, finding Heir. As if my life wasn't complicated enough. Damn, where is this kid? What if Floss came back? Would I take him? Probably have to. Would really like to find someone else. Someone who won't bitch about accommodations. Someone who would be PSYCHED to do

this. Not some spoiled rotten little washed up child actor. Whoa, whoa. Can't start bagging on Floss. He's an established actor and we're asking him to slum. That takes a serious leap of faith that he's just not ready for. I'm just bummed. Should have trusted my gut. You can't marry the supermodel. This puts Lane on the fence. I'm afraid. May have to switch roles. Don't know where to go really. Just have to trust the process. It will all work out exactly how it's supposed to work out. We will find Heir. And we will make our movie. Period. **July 20, 2003.** Brian's here. The love/hate relationship begins. He already started the back-seat driving. We had our first yelling match yesterday. I can already tell this is going to be a nightmare. We are just too much alike. Too bull-headed

                    VAIN
This is Dino's gig.

                    JOSH
Craze. You been inside?

                    VAIN
No, we just walked up. Let's check it out.

                    JOSH
Cool.

Before they can take a step they're interrupted by Des.

                    DES
What's up Mikey? V?

                HEIR/VAIN
What's up, Des? Just get here?

                    DES
Yeah.

Des hasn't noticed Josh standing there. Without saying anything to Des, Josh grabs his pack of smokes out of his shirt pocket and throws one into his mouth.

                    JOSH
(to Des) Got a light?

                    DES
Holy shit. Where did you come from?

                    JOSH
You know. Got a light?

                    DES
Yeah, you want me to smoke it for you too?

                    JOSH
No, that's cool. But could you get it going real good for me though?

He takes it out of his mouth and points to the tip of the cig, about a 1/4 inch down.

                    JOSH
Right about there should do.

                    DES
Being locked up didn't teach you shit, huh?

Des whips out his lighter and holds the flame up to Josh's cigarette. As Josh begins to inhale, Des intentionally burns half of the cigarette leaving half of it black. They all laugh.

                    DES
But it's still good to see you. *(puts his arm around him)* Well? What's new motherfucker?

                    HEIR
Let's grab a beer? You guys coming in?

                    JOSH
Go ahead. Lemme finish this and we'll catch up

                    VAIN
Cool, we'll be at the bar.

Heir and Vain make their way through the crowd towards the front door, but it's way too packed for that. So, they approach the side door instead. This door is almost as crowded with people, only they are exiting rather than entering. The door man, BIG DAVE (35), is a bit preoccupied with a few FEMALES, so they attempt to enter, but it seems they have underestimated his peripherals as his arm is extended, halting their progress towards the party.

> BIG DAVE
>
> Whoa, fellas. What's going on here? The front door is over there.

> VAIN
>
> Oh, shit. That's the front door?

> BIG DAVE
>
> Ah, yeah. You see, this is the back door, also known as "the exit."

> HEIR
>
> This is the back. That's the front. Got it.

The girls aren't sure what to make of this.

> BIG DAVE
>
> Yeah, you see, the back door is reserved for those who have paid their admission, been inside, and have decided upon "exiting."

> VAIN
>
> I see, exit. As in leave or exit.

> BIG DAVE
>
> Yeah, you're pretty quick. But check it out, on certain occasions it also doubles as an alternative entrance. You know, but this is where it gets tricky. You see, it's for employees, DJs, the owner, lovely ladies. *(moves aside to let the females through)* Ladies? And one other. *(beat)* Oh yeah, friends. It's cool if you guys don't like me but at least pretend you do. I mean, I'm talking to girls right here. *(Dave puts out his hand for a pound)*

> HEIR
>
> What's up Big Dave? How you been?

As Heir throws his hand down to Dave's palm, Big Dave brings him in for a hug. The girls are still watching the scene unfold from the entrance way. Big Dave gives Vain a pound as well.

> BIG DAVE
>
> That's better.

Heir looks at the girls and then back to Dave.

> HEIR
>
> I didn't want to interrupt you when you were telling them about me.

Vain laughs out loud and makes his way past the girls.

> BIG DAVE
>
> Man, you are just so much better at this than I am.

They laugh and Heir jokingly pushes him.

176

and we know each other too well (so we have no qualms about brawling). And he has already started drinking. I don't care if the guy wants to have a good time. But it's time to go into battle. He needs to be on game. And you just can't be there if you're partying every day. But what choice do I have? I have no HEIR! And he's right there!!! Today will be the final test. We'll see if (a) any Heirs turn out or (b) if Brian can act. Last day of auditions. Got to be. Still need: Lisa, Grandma, Devin, and oh yeah . . . Heir!!! This is madness. What am I doing?! No time for that . . . One thing's for sure, Brian needs to get his God damn hands off the wheel. There is no room for two visions. He just took my positive vibe away. I need to get it back **July 21, 2003.** – 7 DAYS LEFT! Things are falling apart

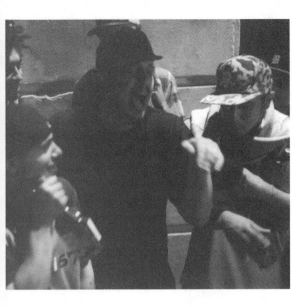

HEIR
Good to see you.

BIG DAVE
You too.

Heir makes way inside, stops with the girls, and looks back at Big Dave.

HEIR
Lovely ladies.

Heir gestures with his hand towards the inside of the club. The girls again laugh and continue towards the bar.

INT SPINNAZ - MOMENTS LATER

The place is live as it ever was. The muffled sound heard from outside is amplified once indoors and there's no doubt that this is the place to be tonight. Heir says what's up to the coat check girl and makes his way deeper into the building and stops with Vain, who is checking out the art work. They stand silently and take it in.

VAIN
Man, this ain't even graffiti.

HEIR
Who said it was?

CUT TO:

There's a female PATRON at the bar.

PATRON
Can I get a Rock Star please?

Heir and Vain sit down at the bar. The BARTENDER (25) notices them and gives them a nod. He slides the girl her DRINK and grabs the fellas a few BEERS, setting them all down at once.

PATRON
How much for this?

BARTENDER
(gestures to Heir) He said he'd get that for you.

PATRON
(to Heir) Well, thank you.

HEIR
(caught off guard) Oh, yeah hmm hmm. No problem

The girl exits. Vain has a good laugh.

BARTENDER
(big smirk) I was wondering if you guys were gonna show. How's it going?

Vain is still laughing.

HEIR
(laughs and throws down a twenty) You mean how am I doing? Or how is my wallet doing?

BARTENDER
It's good for you. You need the practice.

and coming together at the same time. Still no: Lisa, Dino, HEIR, Tad . . . Brian reads for Vain today. Supposed to do it yesterday, but he slammed his pinky in his car door. Of course. It's always something with Brian. But I'll give him another shot. Why? Because I'm desperate. He's my only choice right now. There is no question that he would be great in the role. But if we have domestic disputes on set, it will sink the whole goddamn ship. Important decisions are never easy. This one is no exception. **July 22, 2003.** Not enough hours in the day. Still no Lisa . . . or Dino or Tad. Not so bad, I guess. Could be worse. Oh yeah, no Heir's house. And we shoot there on day one. No shoes either. And we shoot the tomatos scene in the first week. Need a sponsor if we're going to feature the

HEIR

Practice?

VAIN

Yeah, job guy. You gotta brush up on your game. Besides, you guys would look good together.

HEIR

Practice? Practice is flirting with lesbians.

BARTENDER

(laughing) Shit.

HEIR

Yeah, it's like golfing on a driving range. You know, low key and no pressure.

Vain and the Bartender laugh and shake their heads.

BARTENDER

(Jersey) Douche bag.

Dino walks up behind Heir and Vain. The Bartender sees him but Heir and Vain are oblivious.

HEIR

Exactly. You see, I'm a class act douche bag.

VAIN

(Jersey accent) Yeah, he is. And you see, you're a guy's guy. Me and Mikey right here, well, were douche bags' douche bags. One of a kind douche bags.

Dino continues to eavesdrop.

HEIR

(Jersey) Mmm hmmm. We're top notch douche bags.

VAIN

(Jersey) Yup, we're at the height of our game.

Dino bumps Heir from behind to get his attention. Considering the club is so packed, Heir assumes that it was just someone passing by or standing behind him, so he pulls his shoulder away and continues his conversation (if you can call it one).

HEIR

That's right, V. We're there huh?

Dino bumps Heir again. Heir pulls away looking slightly annoyed.

VAIN

The apex.

HEIR

The zenith.

BARTENDER

Sounds like the anti-Christ to me.

VAIN

Yeah, the anti-Christ. Where is Dino posted anyways?

178

shoe. Sometimes I feel like this isn't the movie I wanted to make. That sucks for me and my family. But what about all these people giving up a month of their lives? Oh well. I guess I just need to fight like hell to make it as good as it can be. Can't fight fate. Brian is Vain. I know he'll do great in the role. That was never the question. He adds another dimension of realism that would otherwise be absent from the film. And it's good P/R. His read is pretty good and getting better. He just needs to relax and be himself. Rehearsals in two days and I have no actors. Damn. This sucks. Giving me an ulcer. I want to blame everyone else. But, the bottom line is, I moved 800 miles away from home. I abandoned film fifteen years ago. Blah, blah, blah. We just need to make the movie.

There's no stopping now. Full steam ahead. **July 23, 2003.** Craziness. July twenty-anything is just surreal. We have had July 28 on the calendar for over a year now. The number has taken on mythic proportions in my scattered brain. I can't believe we're this close. I feel solid about our crew. Kev has a very calming effect on me. He is a true genius and completely understands the punk rock element of the film. I know that the film is going to look and sound great. That's comforting. Locations are coming together, slowly but surely. Got two strong Lisas to choose from. Tough choice actually. One is more established than the other, but they both give great reads. Going to have to base partially on chemistry with Brian. Might be able to cast Tajai as Dino. He would be perfect.

> **BARTENDER**
> I don't know. I haven't seen him for a bit.

Dino bumps the two of them at the same time.

> **HEIR**
> Someone needs to hold the fuck still.

Heir turns around and notices who it was all along.

> **HEIR**
> Well speak of the-Oh wait, that's right. I'm the devil.

> **DINO**
> (to Heir) What's up class act? (to Vain) Top notch.

> **VAIN**
> Yeeeaaah. See, Dino knows the deal.

> **HEIR**
> (throws a well deserved pound to Dino) X amount of respect is due.

Vain gives Dino a pound as well and the Bartender hands Dino a beer.

Des, Auto, and Josh appear, laughing. Big Dave's in the background smiling.

> **BIG DAVE**
> (yelling) Do not serve those three.

> **BARTENDER**
> You think I don't know that?

Des, Josh, Auto, and Vain start talking together while Dino and Heir walk into the gallery area to take it in.

> **HEIR**
> This shit is looking real good. I'm psyched for you.

> **DINO**
> Thanks. Your opinion means a lot to me. Nine times out of ten, the authenticity of opinions are questionable at best.

> **HEIR**
> What do you mean?

> **DINO**
> Well, it's like I've got hundreds of acquaintances but really only a few friends. You know what I'm saying? You're one of them, Mikey.

> **HEIR**
> Thanks. I feel the same way. It's like that with me and Curtis. He's my boy, you know what I'm saying?

> **DINO**
> Definitely. You gotta appreciate that.

They tap bottles and start nodding their heads to the beat.

CUT TO:

Three GUYS (20s) wall flower, looking hard. One of them points across the room and singles someone out.

CUT TO:

The DJ is nodding his head and listening to one side of his headphones.

CUT TO:

A few various shots of the party. Laughs, dancing, girls, guys, some artwork. Some B-Boys get down.

CUT TO:

Vain, Auto, and Des are near a corner shooting the shit and laughing at Josh's newly acquired dancing skills.

VAIN

Check it out. Look at Josh's new moves.

AUTO

(laughing) That's some African anteater ritual shit right there.

VAIN

Yeah. That explains the anteater he's freaking, too. Who is that girl?

They laugh. Des walks away from Vain and Auto and approaches Josh, imitating his style the whole way through the crowd. Auto follows and they start a little circle in the middle. Everyone is tripping off them. Vain is still laughing. He swallows the rest of the beer in the bottle and glances at the bottle, as if there should still be some stuck to the sides. Vain begins to make his way towards the bar. Before he takes two steps, he's stopped short by the three Guys who were apparently pointing at him.

VAIN

Excuse me, fellas.

GUY1

Not ugh. *(points the opposite direction)* That way.

The two other Guys stand there without saying a thing and watch the scene unfold. Vain looks to the kid on the left, then the kid on the right. All three of them are about his size. Vain gets a wild look on his face.

VAIN

Oh, you think like that huh?

GUY1

You heard me.

VAIN

Yeah , I heard you. You said "that way." But what you trying to say motherfucker?

GUY1

(confrontational) What?

VAIN

I said if you want me to get you some Q-tips, you're gonna have to get the fuck out of my way.

CUT TO:

180

Always loved the Souls of Mischief. And he totally has Dino's zen personality. Some smaller roles to fill. But it's getting there. Belinda has been amazing. She is one of those people that I know I will work with forever. Just so dedicated and good at what she does. We were blessed to connect with her. The hardest part is being the only full-timer on the project for pre-production. I get stuck with so much bullshit. Hard, even impossible, to focus on the creative vision. But, anyway, the time has come to focus on the positive and ONLY the positive. No time for anything else. Speaking of which . . . Amy and the kids are coming today. It's a catch-22. Yes, I'm beyond excited to see them. But I have so much to do. Screw it. It's nothing but a positive. It's beautiful. I couldn't be happier.

It's all coming together. My dream come true. **July 24, 2003.** Clock's ticking. Lane got in last night. Put him right to work auditioning Mackenzie Firgens. I love this kid. He is so talented and has such a great attitude. I'm going to have a blast working with him. Mackenzie won the role. It was really tight. I loved her in *Groove* and know she will do a great job. Still haven't nailed Dino. Jello is an option, but I was hoping for a black guy. I will NOT cast minorities as stick-up kids, Vain, etc. But I am trying very hard to cast people of color in more important, intellectual roles, a la Robert and Dino. Only a couple of roles to fill. So close. Need Heir's house and we're rolling. (Also need some gear and props for day one—I have a feeling that is going to be a constant dance with no props

---

Josh, Auto, and Des are oblivious to the altercation and continue dancing.

CUT TO:

A few HEADS roll up to pay respect to Dino. Heir is chilling.

HEADS
Shit's looking fresh Dino. Nice. Goddamn.

DINO
Thanks, guys. Glad you came down.

Heir spots what is going down with Vain and gets an "oh shit" look on his face.

BACK TO:

Vain is squared off with Guy1. The argument has reached a peak. Heir interrupts.

HEIR
What's going on V?

VAIN
This son of a bitch is trying to step. I told him to get the fuck out of my way but he won't move.

HEIR
Yo, fellas chill out. What's the beef, man relax.

GUY1
Son of a bitch? What?

HEIR
V, chill, relax man! Not here.

VAIN
I'm relaxed.

He's not at all.

HEIR
Guys, chill out man. This is my boy's spot! What's the problem?

GUY1
He fucking punked my little cousin in the tunnels the other night on some bullshit and I ain't having that.

VAIN
Yeah, I did.

HEIR
Yeah, I know I was there. They were blowing it up. We just sent them the other way.

GUY1
Well he got them popped. And that shit ain't cool.

Guy1 mad dogs Vain.

HEIR
No, it ain't cool but neither is this.

VAIN
Don't screw face me you bitch. Come up in

here with your boys that's shook as hell.

                    HEIR
V, chill.

                    GUY1
Trying to say I'm shook?

                    VAIN
Shook like your mom.

                    HEIR
V, fucking chill out. Not in here man.

                    GUY1
What you got on my mom? You don't know my
mom.

                    HEIR
Fuck this shit. Squash it V.

                    VAIN
I don't know your mom? Who was that nervous whore in church then?

                    GUY1
What?

*Guy1 steps right in Vain's face and before he knows what hit him,
Boom! Vain decks the shit out of Guy1 and it's on. Guy2, who's
closest to Heir, takes a swing. Heir ducks it and immediately connects back at him with a right. The kid goes flailing into the crowd.
BOTTLES and GLASSES fall out of people's hands. DRINKS are
spilled on GIRLS. The crowd is not happy with that and Guy2 is
literally consumed by them. Heir sighs with disappointment, but
no time for that. Guy3 is coming right at him. Quickly thinking, Heir
uses the kid's momentum to his advantage. He dodges right, puts
his left foot out, grabs the kid by the back of his head and drops
him to the floor. Totally in control of the situation, Heir pops him
once quickly. He then gets a glance at his boy Vain who is steadily
mopping the shit out of Guy1. Heir restrains the kid from getting up
and without hitting him any more he sternly states the facts.*

                    HEIR
You guys want to come in here and stir some
shit up, huh? Trying to doubt my boy's wind?
He could go all day with all three of you.
That's what your man wanted? That's what
he's gonna get. Try to tell you guys to chill.
But no one wants to listen.

*Heir is on top of the guy still, literally forcing him to watch Vain
kick the living shit out of his friend. What once looked like a fight
is beginning to look like attempted murder.*

                    HEIR
Stay down.

Heir gets off the kid and heads towards Vain.

*Vain is freaking, in a zone so dark Charles Manson would shit
himself. Heir manages to get through to him and Vain allows
himself to be pulled away.*

*The music has stopped and everyone is holding completely still,
with their jaws dropped. Some "Oh my god!" type chatter. Some
employees, including Big Dave, make their way through the
crowd. The kid that was hurled into the crowd emerges with a
look of disbelief.*

782

master.) Feeling really good. Stoked on my leads, which is crucial. This shit is going to come off. I know it. I just need to keep a cool head and trust my judgment. That's all that matters, at this point. Making a movie!!! **July 25, 2003.** Coming down to the wire. Many holes to fill. But, fortunately, we've got a strong team of people who are all working their asses off to make things happen. That's a relief. We're going to be throwing down the tracks ahead of the train like freaking Wile E. Coyote. But it's all good. I've got to keep a cool head. That's my job as the engineer of this runaway train. To show faith and confidence and remain calm in the face of crises. This is not going to be perfect. Shit will hit the fan. Loads of it. But we're making a movie. Got to keep that moving forward.

Director's note. I like how Big Dave's reaction is scripted. But our Big Dave actor came barging in and broke it up how he would break up a fight (he's a real bouncer by trade). I was so exhausted from shooting the party scene all night (and trying to block the fight scene) that I let it go. The scripted response tied together the first Big Dave scene a lot better (i.e., validated their casual exchange and friendship). But the final version kept with the intensity of the scene and, thus, worked fine.

Director's note. We did shoot the water thing. But it didn't come off. Not the end of the world.

Director's note. We toned this exchange way down because it started to look too much like their later exchange at the liquor store. We wanted to build up to that scene, not repeat it. So we went with a much more subtle, subdued reaction from Mikey.

It's on me . . . deep breaths . . . **July 26, 2003.** TWO DAYS until production and we are MILES from being ready. So many holes to fill, it's ridiculous. But I feel good. It will all come together. We are a great team. And we are dedicated to making this movie happen. There are a million things that are f'ed up, a complete mess. The table is set for disaster. But we're stepping off the ledge anyway. This is it. My one chance. Either I make it or break it. Either way, at least I'm taking the chance. And that's something to be proud of. **July 27, 2003.** One day. It's almost surreal. Everyone is shitting their pants about the pace and workload. I'm seeing the finish line already. I've been running this pace for three years. Three more weeks is nothing. I can see the holes and weaknesses already,

---

BIG DAVE
(to Heir and Vain, calm and respectful) You guys should probably go.

The club OWNER (50s) emerges and he's hopping.

OWNER
That's it, everyone. We're calling it a night.

Heir holds his head low to hide the tears building in his eyes and heads for the door.

BARTENDER
Mike.

Heir turns around and the Bartender tosses him a bottled water. He catches it as well as one last look at Dino's disappointed and shocked face. Heir gives the Bartender as grateful an expression as he can muster.

EXT MISSION DISTRICT - MOMENTS LATER

Heir and Vain make their way quickly down the street. Heir says nothing.

VAIN
Fuck that buster. Trying to come up in our spot and front.

Heir silently paces on.

VAIN
Should have brought his little cousin up correct. Little smart ass. *(beat)* You alright? You get hit?

Heir shakes his head.

VAIN
Slow down, man. We're chill.

Heir doesn't lose his pace.

VAIN
What time is it?

HEIR
I don't know.

VAIN
What's wrong with you? That punk got what he deserved.

HEIR
Yeah, mmm hhmmm.

VAIN
What's your problem? Dude comes up in our spot. Try to say some . . .

HEIR
(interrupts) Our spot? Our spot? You're tripping. You think—

VAIN
What?

HEIR
You think that's our spot? You're slanted man. I told you to chill. Flossing your ego

ain't gonna get you anywhere.

                    VAIN
What the fuck? Those dudes stepped to me?

                    HEIR
Yeah, they did. But check it out. *(stops and looks at Vain)* You should have let them step away from you, man.

                    VAIN
What?

                    HEIR
You stepped to their cousin man. And that ain't our spot! You don't own that shit. Dino don't either, but that was his night and you fucked it up for him.

                    VAIN
Fuck that little kid.

Vain pulls out a SILVER PILOT PEN and lines one of TAD's tags.

                    HEIR
Yeah you're learning a lot.

                    VAIN
Fuck that bitch.

                    HEIR
Yeah, fuck him. Exactly. Why you even want your name associated with his?

                    VAIN
Man, forget this shit. What do you want to do? Let's go get a beer.

                    HEIR
Naw, man. I'm out. I'm going home.

                    VAIN
Come on man lets go to Cats.

                    HEIR
No, no. Scratch that. I'm over it. I'm going home.

Heir gives Vain a pound and begins to cross the street towards his house. Half way across, Heir glances back. Vain is writing a quote next to his tag: "KINGS AND PAWNS." Heir shakes his head in disbelief and continues on his way.

EXT DOWNTOWN CLOTHING STORE - THE NEXT DAY

Heir is sitting on a bucket eating a sandwich and looking somber. Lisa strolls up.

                    LISA
What's up, Mikey?

Heir nods unenthusiastically.

                    LISA
What's the matter?

                    HEIR
Nothing.

184

which is good. We actually don't even have the locations for day one locked down yet (Heir's house). Nor do we have day two. I have a feeling that's going to be symptomatic. But it's all good. Just need to keep the faith. We're going to make a great movie. **July 28, 2003.** DAY ONE Hard to believe we're finally here. Been a long hard road. Time to make it pay off. Had a shit night's sleep. Slept at Vain's apartment. Cars, sirens, busses, vatos having a late-night fiesta next door. Been so long since I lived in the City. Need to get back in the habit of sleeping with the radio on. So amped to shoot today. All eyes are on me. Need to handle day one with poise and levity and clarity of vision. Work with my actors. Communicate with Kev. And make shit happen. Need to stay FOCUSED, which

185

is going to be a fricking challenge with all the distractions of no-budget filmmaking. But I'm going to do fine. Directing is the only thing I am truly a natural at. The only thing I don't have to think about. It's all me. And this is my movie. Here we go. This is what I have been waiting for. ACTION! **July 29, 2003.** DAY TWO What a relief to write "July 29." One day in the can. Smooth first day. Brant pulled Heir's house out of his ass. That was crucial. The crew working well together. Cast is coming alive. Stoked we didn't do anything too emotionally taxing yesterday. Brian's doing great. So is Lane. And Kev and his crew are everything I knew they would be. The first set-up took like three hours, as expected. Getting our sea legs. But we're a well oiled machine now. Today's a big

> **LISA**
> Don't give me that. What's up?

> **HEIR**
> I don't know. I'm just burnt.

> **LISA**
> Why?

Heir points at the blank wall he has been painting all morning.

> **LISA**
> Where's Curtis?

> **HEIR**
> Huh?

> **LISA**
> Where's Curtis?

> **HEIR**
> What, uh, he didn't tell you?

> **LISA**
> Tell me what?

> **HEIR**
> Uh, nothing. Maybe you should talk to him.

> **LISA**
> What? Isn't he working with you anymore?

> **HEIR**
> Well, Pops is kind of downsizing . . .

> **LISA**
> What? That little . . . ugh!

> **HEIR**
> Don't trip. I'm sure he'll find work somewhere.

> CUT TO:

INT DEPARTMENT STORE - CONTINUOUS

> QUICK JUMP CUTS.

Vain: Scopes the store. Racks a leather jacket. Then later returns it for cash. He is all smiles.

> CUT TO:

EXT DOWNTOWN CLOTHING STORE - CONTINUOUS

> **HEIR**
> Don't tell him I told you.

> **LISA**
> I can't believe he didn't say anything.

> **HEIR**
> He probably just . . .

> **LISA**
> I gotta get back to work.

Lisa exits. Heir sits on his ass, dumbfounded.

INT VAIN'S APARTMENT - DAY

Vain is smoking a cigarette and working on a sketch in his black book. It's a big BLOCKBUSTER 'VAIN' with dimensions written out next to it. Devin is sitting next to him doing his own piece. Devin admires Vain's piece.

                    DEVIN
          Where you gonna do that?

                    VAIN
          I got this rooftop. Watch. This is gonna be
          the shit.

Lisa enters and storms into the kitchen.

                    VAIN
          What's up Lisa Lisa?

Lisa inspects a pile of cash sitting next to two brand new GUCCI BAGS on the table. Lisa knows what's up.

                              CUT TO:

Vain is still into his sketch. Lisa appears out of nowhere and knocks the cigarette out of his mouth.

                    LISA
          I told you not to smoke in front of him. God
          dammit! Why can't you ever listen?!

Lisa storms out of the room in tears. Vain is frozen with shock.

                    VAIN
          What the? Lisa. Lisa!

No response.

                              CUT TO:

INT VAIN'S BEDROOM - MOMENTS LATER

Vain walks in on Lisa, who is packing a suitcase in less than thoughtful fashion.

                    VAIN
          What are you doing?

No answer.

                    VAIN
          What's the matter? What . . .

                    LISA
          When were you gonna tell me?

                    VAIN
          What?

                    LISA
          You got fired like two weeks ago. How come
          you didn't tell me?

                              CUT TO:

INT VAIN'S LIVING ROOM - CONTINUOUS

Devin is working on his sketch. In the background Lisa and Vain can be faintly heard arguing. Devin is oblivious.

                              CUT TO:

Director's note. Once again, too much exposition. Decided not to blatantly foreshadow the rooftop so much.

Director's note. Uh, couldn't hook up the Gucci bags. Went with the dvds with the security tags still on them which I was able to secure pretty easily from Virgin music.

786

one with lots of locations—Des's house, Roxie, restaurant, and abandoned car. Of course Kev and I haven't seen any of these locations, but I'd better get used to that. Doc mode, baby. A little sketched about Dev and the set teacher. Hope she doesn't break our balls. Still have some locations, etc. to figure out: rooftop, jail, and cops most notably. Just have to keep the faith. Hopefully having a few full-time producers on board will help keep things on track. One down, seventeen to go. **July 30, 2003.** DAY THREE So far so good. Some minor obstacles. (True to character, Bill Banning spaced out and forgot we needed to roll film while we shot our scene at the Roxie.) But nothing major . . . yet . . . Starting to find my groove. The crew is gelling. Had to demand more on-set support

from the producers. Communication is horrible between set and production office. But that's to be expected. We are certainly reaching outside of our means. Everyone is going to be spread thin. Think I'm going to Pops's house tonight. Need a good night's sleep. Not mandatory, though. Staying here is cool, too. Saves gas, time . . . Brian's doing great. Doing his thing (twenty questions, etc.), but serving the film well. Lane is no surprise. He is a gem. This kid is going to go places. Beyond his obvious natural talent, he's a hard worker and a total team player. Those traits will take him far. Still no cops, no mandala, no rooftop. I've got faith . . . So hard to be objective now. Are performances good? The dialogue? Story? Who knows? Time will tell... **July 31, 2003.** DAY FOUR I'm in my

---

INT VAIN'S BEDROOM - CONTINUOUS

Lisa is trying to force the suitcase closed. She has stopped talking to Vain.

> VAIN
> Why are you tripping so hard?

Lisa ignores Vain and manages to close up the sloppily packed suitcase.

> VAIN
> I lose one job and you split? What's up with that?

Lisa stops and looks Vain in the eyes.

> LISA
> You just don't fucking get it, do you?

> VAIN
> Apparently not.

Lisa shakes her head barges out of the room with the suitcase.

INT VAIN'S LIVING ROOM - CONTINUOUS

CLOSE UP on Devin. He is still into his sketch. Out of nowhere, a hand grabs Devin and he is yanked out of the frame.

EXT VAIN'S APARTMENT - CONTINUOUS

Lisa charges out of the apartment with a suitcase in one hand and Devin in the other.

Vain catches up and stops them.

> VAIN
> What the fuck? Just like that?

> LISA
> Come on, Devin.

Lisa attempts to push past Vain, but neither he nor Devin budge.

> VAIN
> Lisa. You need to chill. We can talk about this. But not now when we're all heated. Just chill. I'm gonna get a job. But it's not that easy . . .

> LISA
> Please. What about your restitution? How are you going to pay that?

> VAIN
> I'm not tripping off that right now.

> LISA
> Obviously.

> VAIN
> That shit ain't a priority right now. They can't get blood from a stone.

> LISA
> Yeah, but they can lock you up, Curtis. Don't you even care? What would that do to Dev? He doesn't need to go through that shit

again. Do you ever think about that?

VAIN
They won't lock me up.

LISA
Bullshit! You think you're invincible? You think you can blow them off and they won't notice? You think you can keep painting and they won't fucking arrest you? *(beat)* Look, I need someone who is going to be here for Devin. And it's obvious that that's not important to you. I'm not going to let anyone break his heart again.

Lisa tugs at Devin, but he pulls away.

DEVIN
I don't want to go, momma.

LISA
Come on.

Lisa drags Devin a couple of feet down the hallway, but he is fighting it all the way. Lisa stops and kneels down next to him.

LISA
Come on, honey. We'll find a nice place to live with a yard and everything.

DEVIN
(falling apart) I don't want to go, momma. I want to stay here with Curtis. He's not gonna break my heart, momma. He's good to me, I swear. He's the best daddy I ever had. I want to stay here.

Devin starts bawling.

DEVIN
I want to stay here.

Lisa is starting to crack, too.

LISA
Come on, sweetie. Let's go.

Devin hunkers down on the floor.

LISA
Come on. *(starts crying)* We could have a yard.

Vain reaches down and puts his hand on Lisa's shoulder. Lisa drops the suitcase, leans in, and cries on Vain's shoulder. Devin scoots over and joins the family hug.

EXT DOWNTOWN SF - LATER

Heir and Pops stop working and break for lunch.

HEIR
You want me to bring you something?

POPS
A tall blonde with ass.

HEIR
How about that guy right there?

Director's note. Nixed this. Liked it better that Pops and Mikey weren't really talking.

element. Producing more than I would like, not to mention doing pre-production shit and various other tasks that distract me from directing and will ultimately hurt the film. But oh well. What's a cracker to do? People are working hard, trying their best. Guess that's what really counts. On schedule, so far. Getting what we need. Brian's performance is a little flat. He's trying too hard. Needs to just be himself. He's in it, working his ass off. But probably not getting the direction and support he needs from me. I'm too f'ing scattered to focus on anything creative. Totally free-balling this shit. Late call today so we can shoot some more night exteriors. Same tomorrow. Going to check e-mails, make calls this morn. This pace is cake. Shit, I've been on this pace for over a year. Coming down

The whole mandala thing was Brant's idea. He pitched the ending to me and I promptly told him that he was out of his fricking mind. Sorry, Brant. That does not happen. Ever. Especially to a memorial piece. Then he told me about mandalas. I was intrigued and looked into it. It made sense that Dino was a Buddhist, and the whole mandala ritual was mind-blowing. I was sold. Old school writers (esp piecers) still have a little trouble swallowing it. But the overwhelming majority of the writers we have talked to are down for it. It's some different level shit, for sure. But it captures the impermanence of graffiti (and life itself!) better than anything we could come up with.

789

the home stretch . . . **August 1, 2003.** DAY FIVE Things heating up a bit. Poor communication between producers and set almost sunk us again. Having a meeting today to try and iron things out. We need to lock down the Mount Everest concept. Everyone needs to be in that mindset from hereon out. We're climbing to the top. And we need an open line to base camp at all times. Brian and I came closer to throwing blows than we ever have. Right off set. And over some eggrolls, no less. Inevitable, I suppose. Now I know what Phil Jackson has to deal with coaching Kobe. We definitely need a couple of days away from each other. But, overall, the ship is moving forward. That's what counts at the end of the day. Capturing images on film. Just have to keep pushing . . . **August 2, 2003.** First

Pops makes a mocking/stupid, buck-tooth laugh face. He then collapses in the back of the truck and pulls his hat over his eyes.

> **POPS**
> Be back in an hour.

Heir bails down the street.

EXT DOWNTOWN SF - DAY

Heir walks down the street. He stops in front of the Buddhist Temple and checks it out.

INT BUDDHIST TEMPLE - MOMENTS LATER

Inside, Heir tentatively looks around. Some MONKS are meditating. He spots Dino, who is working on a SAND MANDALA.

> **HEIR**
> *(way too loud)* Yo, what's up, Dino.

Everybody looks up at Heir, who realizes his mistake.

> **HEIR**
> My bad.

Dino gestures for Heir to come over and he complies. Dino continues working on his mandala as they talk.

> **HEIR**
> *(whispering)* Sup, Dino?

> **DINO**
> What's up, Mikey?

> **HEIR**
> Hey, sorry about the other night.

> **DINO**
> It's cool, man. What happened?

> **HEIR**
> Some stupid shit, er, stuff. I dunno. I tried to squash it. It just exploded right before my eyes. I'm really sorry . . .

Heir puts his hand over his face.

> **DINO**
> Don't sweat it, Mikey.

Dino puts out his hand and they shake/hug.

> **DINO**
> You can't change the past, brother. The future, however . . .

Dino taps his head with his finger and winks at Mikey and goes back to work on his mandala. Heir trips out on the Sand Mandala (a detailed portrait of a Temple with clouds above). It's an amazing piece of work with an array of colors and a fine attention to detail.

> **HEIR**
> What is that?

> **DINO**
> It's a Temple.

HEIR

No, I mean what's this called? This kind of artwork?

DINO

Oh, it's a sand mandala.

HEIR

Trip. How long this one take you?

DINO

I've been working on this one for about a week now, maybe ten hours.

HEIR

Damn.

DINO

Sometimes we put days, even weeks, into these things. Each grain of sand has to find its perfect place.

HEIR

For real? That's crazy. Looks dope though. *(beat)* Your show was tight last night. I was really impressed, man.

DINO

Thanks, Mikey. That means a lot coming from you. You been painting much lately?

HEIR

Nah, not really. I got the itch though, bro.

DINO

And you got suspended time.

HEIR

Yup.

DINO

I feel ya. Can't be taking those same risks anymore.

HEIR

See, you know what I'm talking about.

DINO

Of course. *(beat)* I know I'm an old man, but there's more to life than bombing, Mikey.

HEIR

Yeah, I know.

DINO

Don't get me wrong. I know the rush. There's nothing like it. But sometimes you gotta go with the flow, work with what you got, know what I'm saying?

Dino works on the mandala for a minute as Heir stands by silently. Dino then rises and bows to the mandala, retrieves a broom, and begins to sweep the sand into a pile.

HEIR

Whoa, whoa! What're you doing?

Dino doesn't budge. He's in a rhythm.

790

197

different baggage. Brian has some good ideas. And, when it comes to story and graff culture, he needs to and will be heard. But he does NOT need to be heard about everything (i.e. where the camera goes, how other actors deliver their lines). Two brothers, control freaks both of us. Could lead to disaster. Could lead to success. Tomorrow we shoot the suicide scene. That will be a true test. **August 3, 2003.** DAY SIX Vain killed himself. Brian went off! It was a phenomenal performance. We drank tequila shots and listened to Freedy Johnston ('This Perfect World') in my car over and over for like an hour. I kept the windows rolled up and we just got all hot and uncomfortable and talked about Brian and how I don't want him to be that guy. It was pretty heavy. Can't wait to see how it looks

> **DINO**
> That's the tradition, man. When you finish your mandala, you sweep up the sand and return it to the river.

> **HEIR**
> What river? Why? That's craze.

> **DINO**
> It signifies the impermanence of all that exists, brother.

> **HEIR**
> What? Why do it in the first place?

> **DINO**
> Just doing it is meditative. You enjoy the act of creating. The result is insignificant.

> **HEIR**
> Trip.

> **DINO**
> It's gonna get swept away at some point anyway, right.

Heir shakes his head. Not really feeling it.

> **HEIR**
> You want to grab some lunch?

> **DINO**
> Nah, I gotta get back to work.

> **HEIR**
> Alright then.

Heir and Dino shake hands/hug.

EXT DOWNTOWN SF - DAY

Heir and Pops sweat away on the job. Heir is going off, taking out all of his frustrations on the wall. Pops likes what he sees, but doesn't say a word.

INT HEIR'S ROOM - DAY

Heir pulls a couple of shoe boxes from his closet and begins rummaging through photographs of his work.

INT THAI PLACE - DAY

Lisa, Robert, and a couple of Designers are eating lunch. Robert has an cell phone ear-jack plugged into his cranium and is rambling away.

> **ROBERT**
> Uh-huh. Uh-huh. He said that? Sure let me talk to him.

The rest of the crew are talking, half business, half social. They are looking at the MUNI AD Lisa showed Heir and Vain back at the agency.

Looking dapper in a button-down shirt and a slick hair-do, Heir enters and approaches the group. Heir sets a large PHOTO ALBUM down on the table and sits across from Robert. Lisa gives Heir a crazy look.

ROBERT
Hey. How's it hanging, you old dog?

HEIR
Uh, pretty good. I just came to . . .

Robert gives Heir the palm and continues his conversation on the phone.

ROBERT
Uh-huh. Yeah, we did. We played the Presidio. Great. Eighty-two. Yeah. Well you're a hack, what do you expect? *(laughs)* Yeah. Sure. *(beat)* So what do you got for me?

Heir hands Robert his portfolio/photo album.

HEIR
Uh, this is my portfolio . . .

Robert gives Heir the "one sec" finger and Heir sits back down. Robert motions for the portfolio and Heir eagerly obliges. As he talks, Robert checks out Heir's portfolio with less than enthusiastic efficiency. The portfolio contains PHOTOS of Heir's graffiti as well as assorted FLIERS and SKETCHES he has done over the years.

ROBERT
Uh-huh. No problem. We can use the same designer from the last campaign. Yeah. OK. Let's do lunch. OK. No. Yeah, that'll work. OK, Bob. Work on that backswing. Alright. Tuesday. *(beat)* So what can I do for you?

Silence. Robert is finally talking to Heir, but it's impossible to tell.

ROBERT
You, man. What can I help you with?

HEIR
Oh, sorry. I just wanted you to check out my work.

ROBERT
(checks it out) Cool.

HEIR
I was hoping, I dunno, maybe we could work on something together.

ROBERT
Really.

Heir nods enthusiastically. Robert flips through the portfolio once more.

ROBERT
You in school?

HEIR
No, I graduated . . .

ROBERT
Where did you go to college?

HEIR
Well, actually, I just received my GED.

Robert closes the portfolio and hands it back to Heir.

on film. A lot of people questioned my choice to shoot this scene in week one. But I wanted everyone to FEEL Vain's loss. Mikey and Lisa know he's got that in him. And this was the only way to infect Lane and Mackenzie with this emotion. Things are rolling along. Plenty of hurdles left: no cops, courtroom, or fricking SAND MANDALAS. But all we can do is all we can do. So many things to worry about— ccations, money, editor, film fests, family, job. But there's no time to worry. One scene at a time. **August 4, 2003.** DAY SEVEN Shooting the funeral this morning. Random shots of Heir all morning. So much to do in so little time, it's frightening. But we'll put this thing together somehow. In pre-production, I told everyone we were adopting the Graffiti Model to get this film

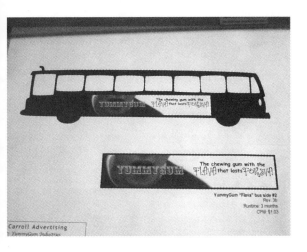

YummyGum "Flava" bus side #2
Rev. 3b
Runtime: 3 months.
CPM: $1.03

Carroll Advertising
YummyGum Industries

193

> **ROBERT**
> Your work is really good, kid. And graffiti is a very marketable medium these days. But, I hope you understand, I can't just hire some kid off the street. Especially during these lean times.

Robert digs into his lunch.

> **HEIR**
> I really think I could bring a different element to your team. Add a different perspective, you know?

Heir picks up the ad from the table that the designers had been discussing.

> **HEIR**
> Take this ad, for example. It's all wrong.

That gets everyone's attention. Now all eyes are on Heir.

> **HEIR**
> No offense. But, see, the new busses ride real low, so if your piece isn't higher than the wheel well, no one will even see it because it's blocked by all these SUVs everywhere. Plus the letters are too small and weak. Anything you put on that bus has to be bigger, more colorful, and more powerful than the bus itself.

Robert keeps munching. Everyone blows Heir off and goes back their discussions. Heir stands up, retrieves his portfolio, and shakes Robert's hand.

> **HEIR**
> Thank you for your time.

> **ROBERT**
> No problem. Good luck.

Heir exits.

CUT TO:

EXT THAI PLACE - MOMENTS LATER

Heir is walking away. Lisa exits the restaurant and runs up behind him.

> **LISA**
> What's was that all about?

> **HEIR**
> What?

> **LISA**
> What are you doing?

> **HEIR**
> I just thought . . .

> **LISA**
> Look, Mikey, I think it's great you're trying to do something, but . . . All these guys went to art school, you know.

HEIR

So? Look, Lisa. We been at the bottom of the food chain our whole lives. How long do you want to take these clowns' lunch orders? I'm ready to make moves. I'm tired of this struggle. Painting walls blank every day. Going to jail for expressing myself at night. But, fuck it. I don't want to jeopardize your job either. I'm sorry. I was just trying to do something. I'll see you later.

Heir bails and leaves Lisa to think it over.

INT TAD'S HOUSE - DAY

Tad is sitting on the couch. His MOTHER (45) sits next to him. His FATHER (48) stands by with his arms folded. OFFICER CHARLES (40) from the vandal squad sits in a chair across from him with a clipboard and gives him the third degree.

TAD

I told you, I don't write no more.

MOTHER

(to Charles) Don't you have some real criminals to catch?

OFFICER HUFFINGTON (30) enters the room.

HUFFINGTON

Found this under his bed.

Huffington displays a duffel bag and slams it on the table. Charles sifts through the bag. It's filled with markers and spray cans. Charles removes a black book with a wack "TAD ONE" tag on the cover.

CHARLES

'TAD' huh?

Charles lays a PICTURE on the table. It's a photo of a "TAD" piece on a wall.

TAD

That's ancient. I already got busted for that.

CHARLES

I beg to differ. *(refers to his clipboard)* You were cited on July twenty-third. This wall was painted on August fourth and this photo was taken on the sixth.

Tad sits back and stews.

CHARLES

See, you aren't playing fair with me, Jimmy. That's not cool. Are you aware of the consequences of your actions?

Charles retrieves a piece of paper from the clipboard and hands it to Father.

CHARLES

For possession of an implement of crime *(displays a marker)* and destruction of county property you can be fined up to fifty thousand dollars and serve a maximum of three years in jail.

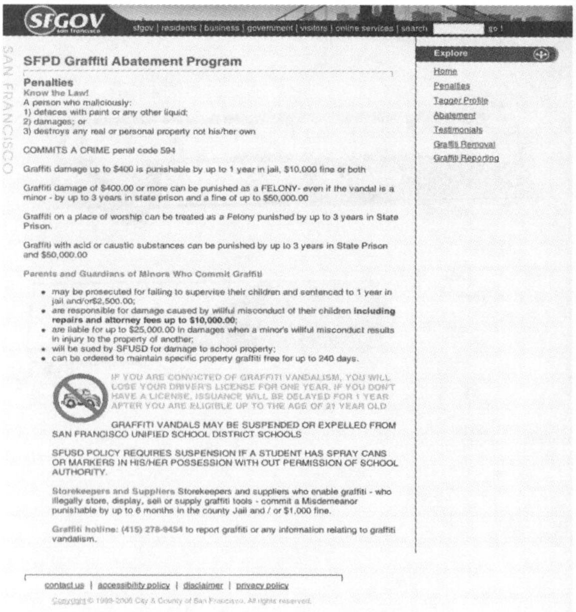

SFGOV

sfgov | residents | business | government | visitors | online services | search go!

SAN FRANCISCO

SFPD Graffiti Abatement Program

Penalties

Know the Law!

A person who maliciously:

1) defaces with paint or any other liquid;

2) damages; or

3) destroys any real or personal property not his/her own

COMMITS A CRIME penal code 594

Graffiti damage up to $400 is punishable by up to 1 year in jail, $10,000 fine or both

Graffiti damage of $400.00 or more can be punished as a FELONY- even if the vandal is a minor - by up to 3 years in state prison and a fine of up to $50,000.00

Graffiti on a place of worship can be treated as a Felony punished by up to 3 years in State Prison.

Graffiti with acid or caustic substances can be punished by up to 3 years in State Prison and $50,000.00

Parents and Guardians of Minors Who Commit Graffiti

- may be prosecuted for failing to supervise their children and sentenced to 1 year in jail and/or$2,500.00;
- are responsible for damage caused by willful misconduct of their children **including repairs and attorney fees up to $10,000.00**;
- are liable for up to $25,000.00 in damages when a minor's willful misconduct results in injury to the property of another;
- will be sued by SFUSD for damage to school property;
- can be ordered to maintain specific property graffiti free for up to 240 days.

IF YOU ARE CONVICTED OF GRAFFITI VANDALISM, YOU WILL LOSE YOUR DRIVER'S LICENSE FOR ONE YEAR. IF YOU DON'T HAVE A LICENSE, ISSUANCE WILL BE DELAYED FOR 1 YEAR AFTER YOU ARE ELIGIBLE UP TO THE AGE OF 21 YEAR OLD

GRAFFITI VANDALS MAY BE SUSPENDED OR EXPELLED FROM SAN FRANCISCO UNIFIED SCHOOL DISTRICT SCHOOLS

SFUSD POLICY REQUIRES SUSPENSION IF A STUDENT HAS SPRAY CANS OR MARKERS IN HIS/HER POSSESSION WITH OUT PERMISSION OF SCHOOL AUTHORITY.

Storekeepers and Suppliers Storekeepers and suppliers who enable graffiti - who illegally store, display, sell or supply graffiti tools - commit a Misdemeanor punishable by up to 6 months in the county Jail and / or $1,000 fine.

Graffiti hotline: (415) 278-9454 to report graffiti or any information relating to graffiti vandalism.

Explore

Home

Penalties

Tagger Profile

Abatement

Testimonials

Graffiti Removal

Graffiti Reporting

contact us | accessibility policy | disclaimer | privacy policy

Copyright © 1999-2006 City & County of San Francisco. All rights reserved.

(finding out no one does these "for hire" since it's such a sacred tradition . . . doh!), cop cars (hoping Dan the UPM can pull this miracle out of his sphincter), rooftop, etc. But, for some odd reason, I have confidence that we will pull this off. Ten more days. That's all I need to worry about. Must admit I'm a little skeptical about the end result. What are we making? Will it really be worthy of a theatrical release as I envisioned? So hard to tell. But I can't think about it. Not even for a minute. Just keep moving forward. One scene at a time. **August 6, 2003.** DAY NINE Getting good stuff on film. Hasn't been easy with the makeshift staff we have pieced together. Everyone is wearing ten hats and the stress is starting to show. But we're getting the job done. Some of the hardest stuff still

unresolved—mandala, gallery, stick-up, carjack, cops. No editor either. That is CRUCIAL. We have got to get a good editor to make sense of this mess. Pretty much everything is upside down right now. Yet, somehow, things keep falling into place. It has always been about momentum. Gotta keep that going. The truth is, at this point, there aren't many options. Just have to finish the movie. Everything will turn out exactly how it was supposed to. **August 7, 2003.** DAY TEN Really starting to wonder about this thing. Is this shit going to come off? It seems so staged, so fake, so lame sometimes. It's a tricky dance. How far can we let go and still have a cohesive story? I'm tripping. But there's not much more I can do. Just need to make the film and hope for the best. I do miss my

---

MOTHER

Fifty thousand dollars?

FATHER

(to Tad) You stupid little prick!

Father goes after Tad. Chaos! Everyone dives in and eventually breaks it up. Father gets one more lick in and slaps Tad upside his head.

CHARLES

Whoa, whoa. Settle down.

Charles backs off and straightens his hair. Everyone else follows his lead and chills out.

CHARLES

It doesn't have to come to this. There is an alternative.

Charles drops a handful of pictures of various graffiti on the table.

CHARLES (CONT'D)

If Jimmy cooperates with our investigation, I can ensure that all charges be dropped against him.

TAD

I ain't no rat.

FATHER

(steps up) My ass!

MOTHER

Calm down, Bill.

FATHER

God dammit, just tell him what you know.

MOTHER

These kids aren't your friends, Jimmy. You don't need to protect them.

Tad picks up a photo of a 'Vain' throw-up. He glances at the pic, then around the room. Tad takes a deep breath and studies the picture.

EXT VAIN'S APARTMENT - DAY

A car pulls up and drops Devin off. Devin walks up to the house and tries to enter, but the door is locked and nobody is answering. Devin comes back to the porch and sits down on the steps. Devin looks around, not really sure what to do.

INT ABANDONED WAREHOUSE - DAY

Vain is sitting in the window drinking a beer. Heir enters and sits down in the window. Vain, who is obviously hammered, hands a twelve pack to Heir. Heir shakes it, revealing that there are only a couple left, before reaching in and grabbing a brew for himself. He cracks it open and takes a long, fulfilling swig. He and Vain stare out the window and share silence.

INT VAIN'S HOUSE- LATER

Devin is chilling watching TV. Heir and Vain enter.

LISA

(to Vain) Where were you?

Vain gives Lisa a perplexed look.

                    LISA
          Devin sat on the porch for two hours waiting
          for you.

                    VAIN
          Oh shit!

Vain sits down next to Devin and puts his arm around him.

                    VAIN
          I'm sorry little man. I forgot.

                    DEVIN
          It's cool.

                    VAIN
          You know I love you, right?

                    DEVIN
          Yeah.

                    VAIN
          Ha-ha. That's my boy.

Vain leans in and gives Devin a smothering hug and kiss on the
head. Vain stands, approaches Lisa, and holds her by the hips.

                    VAIN
          Sorry about that, honey. I was just, I don't
          know what happened.

                    LISA
          Are you drunk?

Vain makes a "little bit" gesture. Lisa sighs and shakes it off.
Vain heads to the fridge, gets a beer, cracks it open and heads to
the couch with Dev.

Lisa hands Heir a manila envelope.

                    HEIR
          What's this?

                    LISA
          Open it.

Heir opens the envelope and finds a customer sketch.

                    HEIR
          What's this?

                    LISA
          Your first job.

Heir gives Lisa a puzzled look.

                    HEIR
          How'd you pull this?

                    LISA
          I have my ways.

He gives Lisa a tentative high five.

                    LISA
          I thought maybe you and drunk boy could
          work on it together.

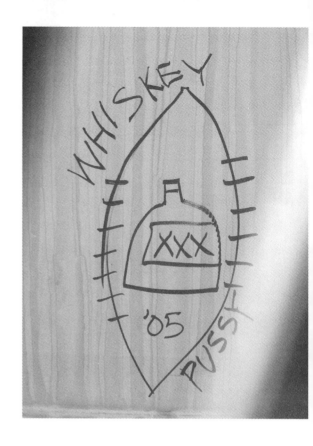

family like hell. My son stopped talking to me. Usually you can't shut the kid up on the phone. But he has shut down. He's pissed. He may not know it, but he's pissed. I miss sleeping and eating like a normal human being. And this shit ain't really fun anymore. It's a total burnout. Get through the day kind of shit. I love directing, I love filmmaking, but with our severe lack of resources, it has seriously lost its charm. We're halfway home. But the hardest stuff still remains. Just gotta stick it out. This is still my ship. Can't abandon now. Need to step up and show the way. I have no choice. **August 8, 2003.** DAY ELEVEN Fatigue setting in a little bit. Got four hours of sleep Wednesday night, then went full-speed all day yesterday until 2am. Still not really getting what I need on

Director's note. We cut this to
maintain the tension (between Vain
and Lisa, as well as Vain and Heir—
i.e. jealousy over Heir getting the
agency job).

set in terms of production support. But we're moving forward, getting good stuff on film. Or so I hope (no dailies). Still have the hardest shit to do. This is fine, in theory. But if we keep back-loading shit we can't pull off . . . we're going to be in real trouble the last couple of days. We'll get what we get. Party scene this weekend. Totally unprepared. But can't get above sea level long enough to line shit up. All I can do is all I can do . . . **August 9, 2003.** DAY OFF What a doozy. Two Fridays in a row have completely flopped. Both times were all Brian. Tried to shoot the big blow-out between Heir and Vain at the liquor store. Brian decided that the scene needed a complete overhaul. He rehearsed the scene with Lane without telling me. Came on set: "Got it all figured out. It goes like

HEIR
Hell yeah. Thanks, Lisa. Check it out, Curt.

Heir displays the ad to Vain. Vain gives a clueless thumbs up.

HEIR
(to Lisa) Thank you. You will not be disappointed. I promise.

LISA
Robert wants it done by next Friday.

HEIR
Alright, cool.

LISA
Make sure you turn it in on time. They like to make you jump through hoops. And if you're late, Robert won't give you another chance.

HEIR
I will. Thanks.

Heir gives Lisa a hug.

INT VAIN'S APARTMENT - LATER THAT EVENING

Vain, Heir, and Lisa watch a movie on TV. Vain is chilling on the couch with his shirt off. Lisa is lying down with him running her fingers along his tatted chest. She stops and caresses a gnarly scar that looks like it just never healed right.

The movie ends and Vain and Lisa kiss.

VAIN
I'ma head to the store.

LISA
Get some milk.

They kiss again.

INT LIQUOR STORE - MINUTES LATER

Heir and Vain talk as they walk down the aisle and grab some beer and a half gallon of milk.

VAIN
Aw yeah. Gonna get this shit right here.

HEIR
You gonna help me out with that ad, or what?

VAIN
Huh?

HEIR
Serious, you could make your rent off one drawing. For real.

Vain is obviously not tracking the conversation

VAIN
(gibberish) Yeah, uh, extra large. Thanks. Pigs Feet.

Heir gives Vain a confused look as Vain heads for the counter.

                              VAIN
          (to Heir) You got this?

Heir walks up to the counter and throws down a bill.

                          CUT TO:

EXT LIQUOR STORE - CONTINUOUS

Heir and Vain emerge from the liquor store. Vain gets straight into a tall can and slyly catches a tag behind his back on a garage door.

An everyday JOE (40s) exits his car with a bag of groceries and spots Vain doing his thing. Joe walks up on the boys.

                              JOE
          What the fuck?

                              VAIN
          (confrontational) What?

                              JOE
          This is my house, you little punk.

                              VAIN
          That's your problem.

Heir starts to walk off and Vain follows.

                              JOE
          You're a genuine asshole.

                              VAIN
          (southern accent) That's nice.

                              JOE
          Can't you see how ugly this shit looks?

Vain stops and turns around.

                              VAIN
          (slurring) Ugly? Shit, welfare's ugly. Government cheese. That's ugly.

Vain turns and walks right into a young MAN and spills beer all over himself.

                              VAIN
          Fuck. Watch where the fuck you're going, man.

Dude steps up. He's pretty fit and obviously not too timid.

                              MAN
          What?

Heir intervenes and pulls Vain away.

                              HEIR
          Sorry, man. It's cool.

                              VAIN
          What? It's my fault? Yeah fuck me huh?

Heir continues to pull him away. There's no physical altercation, thanks to Heir's timely intervention.

                              HEIR
          Let it go man.

Director's note. We decided tagging the liquor store was easier and made more sense dramatically than all this Joe stuff..

Director's note. There's Grandma's joke again. It just gets funnier and funnier.

Director's note. We decided to tie this in with the Stick-up kid. Gave him more motivation to jack him in the alley way later on. Without this confrontation, the stick-up seemed like a blatant mechanism to get Vain the gun. This scene adds a little history.

798

this now." And it was off. Way off. We never got the take. The liquor store owner shut down on us. Our first re-shoot. What a nightmare. Brian does not understand or trust this process at all. And I'm so distracted running around town all day taking care of menial shit that I never have time to spend with him or Lane. But, in the big picture, it was a good thing. Brian will learn that (a) we can't re-write the script anymore and (b) we need to trust each other. I'm going to try and spend more time with him off-set. I hope he makes it through the week. **August 10, 2003.** DAY TWELVE We shoot Dino's art opening tonight. Nervous as hell. Still have to get the art up at John Doffing's. Two missing links: people and stunts. Buddy Joe Hooker, a legendary stuntman and old family friend

was supposed to help out. But I just couldn't put the pieces together. Going to be tricky to shoot thirteen pages of script and pull off a realistic fight scene with no stunt coordinator. But we'll do what we can. Very concerned about extras, too. We have no extras coordinator. We need to have enough people (and the right kind) to make this scene come off. This is the first shoot that I'm really nervous about. But nervous ain't gonna help me. Need to be confident and organized. Home stretch. **August 11, 2003.** DAY THIRTEEN Holy crap! What a night. I still can't believe we pulled that off. Brian rose to the occasion. Rallied like fifty extras and kept them in check all night. We managed to shoot over twelve pages of script. Amazing. It's shoots like that that validate this suicidal journey. As of 9am,

VAIN
(to Man) Fuck you!

Vain pulls free from Heir.

VAIN
(to Heir) Why you being a bitch?

HEIR
What? What did I do?

VAIN
It's cool. Let's see what it's like when I don't have your back.

HEIR
I got your back, fool. You don't need that shit.

VAIN
Let go of me.

HEIR
I'm trying to help you, man.

VAIN
I don't need your fucking help. You need to help yourself, shit.

HEIR
You're out of line.

VAIN
Fuck your line.

HEIR
Curtis, we're above this. What are you doing? Arguing with people on the street?

VAIN
That guy can eat a dick.

HEIR
Yeah screw him. But is it worth it?

VAIN
What happened to your heart, Mikey?

HEIR
What are you talking about? I'm right here. Why are you acting like this?

VAIN
What are you trying to prove?

HEIR
I got nothing to prove. Grow the fuck up. This ain't about egos.

VAIN
OK, so you figured it out. I'm just a kid. I gotta grow up. You win. *(gets in Heir's face)* But you know what? You ain't better than me, Mikey. No matter what you think, you ain't no better than me.

HEIR
You think I'm trying to show you up? Fucking bury the hate.

                    VAIN

　Fuck you man.

                    HEIR

　Clearly.

Heir gives Curtis a disappointed look and slowly turns and walks down the street and out of sight.

INT HEIR'S HOUSE - NIGHT

Heir paints a canvas in his room.

                                        CUT TO:

EXT VAIN'S ROOFTOP - NIGHT

Vain scopes the scene from the ground briefly before quickly scaling the drainpipe to the top. He reaches the roof, grabs on the edge, but quickly pulls his hand back in pain. Vain stretches to see what he cut himself on. The roof edge is covered with broken glass bottles that have been intentionally imbedded in the tar to deter burglars. Seeming to thrive on the challenge, Vain grabs on and hoists himself up.

Once on the roof, Vain gets to work on a piece, bloody hands and all.

Before he finishes the outline, he is lit up by a spotlight. Vain ducks down and creeps to the edge. He slyly peers down at the street and spots a cop car posted up. The officers are on their way. Vain heads for the drain pipe, but, due to the glass bottle situation, he can't turn around to get in position to climb down. Time is running out. Vain frantically surveys his options. There really aren't any. Except...If he got a running start he could jump to the next rooftop. There is no room for error. Another cop car pulls up. One of the COPS calls out to Vain over his P/A. Vain takes a deep breath and gets focused.

                                        CUT TO:

EXT ALLEY WAY -CONTINUOUS

An OFFICER runs through the alley below. Unbeknownst to him, Vain goes soaring from one rooftop to the other three stories above his head.

                                        CUT TO:

EXT NEXT ROOFTOP - CONTINUOUS

Vain comes flying into the rooftop, scrubs hard, and pops to his feet all in on motion. He continues across the rooftop to a fire escape and zips down it.

                                DISSOLVE TO:

INT TC CARROLL ADVERTISING AGENCY -DAY

Heir submits the mock-up to Robert, who is busy on his cell phone. Robert glances at the sketch, gives Heir the thumbs up, and bails to his office, leaving Heir hanging.

                                DISSOLVE TO:

INT VAIN'S BEDROOM - MORNING

Vain is crashed out in bed

Director's note. Mikey worked on the "Yummy Gum" ad instead. Made more sense.

Director's note. This was based on something that happened to a friend of ours. But, in terms of set design, stunts, and make-up, was just too difficult to pull off.

Director's note. Once again, great on paper, but unable to execute on our budget. We knew this when we wrote it, but also knew we would be able to adapt the scene to our resources.

Director's note. We clipped this because we wanted to leave Mikey's future with the agency hanging. Will he ever take a crack at it? Or did the Vain incident destroy any chance Heir had? You decide.

200

we had zero extras (aside from crew). Brian grabbed his cellie and just started hitting fools up. I think the buzz from the film helped a little, but it was pretty much all Brian. To top it off, he got Sam Flores to "design the set" with an amazing installation. This is exactly why we put up with Brian's antics. When he puts his mind to it, he is an incredible creative ally. Stoked on him right now. Tajai came through. He's a natural. I'm a little concerned about the fight scene. We shot it last and everyone was so tired, we really just whipped through it. Should have taken a break and blocked it out better. Fuck it. What's done is done. Still have some of the hardest scenes to do: rooftop, truck yard, tunnels, mandala. It's all about faith and confidence. And momentum. Gotta keep the snowball rolling. **August 12, 2003.** DAY FOURTEEN That was the day! We nailed the carjack. Right on the edge of disaster. Should be great on film. No one was shot or arrested, which is a success in itself. Brian almost got run off the road by some vigilante who thought the Professor was really getting jacked. That was some crazy shit. Going to be a guerilla week for sure. Still have the rooftop, truck yard, and tunnels. And no new money in. Which means one thing: Graffiti Model. We produce this film with the resources we have by any means necessary. Nothing to do but move forward and hope for the best. Shooting the courtroom/jail scenes today. Our part-time, volunteer location manager, Jason, has actually been coming through like a champ. He has hooked up some great

Director's note. We decided to make this much more vulnerable: Devin alone on the couch, and then curled up in bed with mom. (And Curtis out the window immediately, leaving Lisa and Devin in this compromised position.)

Director's note. This was too expository. It made more sense to just jump to Des' house. It was too obvious: of course he wouldn't go to Mikey's house!

INT VAIN'S APARTMENT - CONTINUOUS

Lisa clears Devin's dishes from the table. Devin is reading a comic book. There is a KNOCK at the door. Lisa answers it. It's Charles and Huffington and they've got a search warrant. Lisa puts up a little fight and it heats up a little bit.

INT VAIN'S BEDROOM - CONTINUOUS

Vain pops up in bed and figures out what's going down.

> CUT TO:

INT VAIN'S APARTMENT - CONTINUOUS

Charles and Huffington push past Lisa into the apartment.

> CUT TO:

INT VAIN'S BEDROOM - CONTINUOUS

Charles enters the room and looks around. Nothing. The window is open and the screen popped out.

> CUT TO:

INT VAIN'S APARTMENT - MOMENTS LATER

Lisa sits on the couch clutching Devin by her side. Charles is raiding the apartment. He finds a bindle of coke in Vain's dresser.

> CUT TO:

INT VAIN'S CLOSET - CONTINUOUS

Huffington opens the closet and spots some shoe boxes filled with pictures.

> CUT TO:

INT VAIN'S APARTMENT - CONTINUOUS

Lisa and Devin sit helplessly on the couch as Charles and Huffington confiscate items left and right and place them in a box.

EXT HEIR'S HOUSE - LATER THAT MORNING

Vain approaches Heir's house from a distance. He spots Pops loading up the rig. Vain turns and heads in the opposite direction.

INT DES' HOUSE - DAY

Des opens his front door and finds Vain standing there looking like hell, bed-head and all. Des lets Vain in.

INT VAIN'S APARTMENT/INT DES' HOUSE - NIGHT

Cut back and forth between CLOSE-UPs of phone conversation.

The phone rings. Devin answers it.

> **DEVIN**
> Hello?

> **VAIN**
> What's up, little man. You OK?

> **DEVIN**
> Yeah.

> **VAIN**
> Can I talk to your mom?

> **DEVIN**
> Alright.

> **VAIN**
> Hey, everything's gonna be cool, alright? I promise.

Devin hands the phone to Lisa.

> **LISA**
> Hello.

> **VAIN**
> Hey, baby. You OK?

Lisa is silent.

> **VAIN**
> What did they take?

> **LISA**
> How am I supposed to know?

> **VAIN**
> They probably got all my pictures and shit. They're trying to build a case against me. Motherfuckers. Look, we just need to let this shit chill for a minute. It will all blow over, I promise.

Lisa doesn't say a word.

> **VAIN**
> I'm gonna stay at Des' tonight, but I'll come by tomorrow, OK?

> **LISA**
> *(less than enthusiastic)* Alright.

> **VAIN**
> I love you.

Click. Vain is bumming. He sets down the phone and collapses on the couch.

CUT TO:

INT VAIN'S APARTMENT -CONTINUOUS

Lisa grabs her suitcase from the bed. She and Devin leave the house with their hands full of bags, blankets, etc.

EXT SF JOB SITE - DAY (ONE WEEK LATER)

Heir and Pops work a job. Neither says a word. It's all business.

EXT SF JOB SITE - LATER

At lunch, Pops and Heir both crash out in the rig, Pops in the back, Heir in the cab. They both have hats pulled down over their eyes.

INT VAIN'S APARTMENT - DAY

Vain sneaks into the apartment. It is clear that something is not right. The place is still a wreck from the raid, but it's also looking a lot more vacant.

202

locations. Meika tracked him down somehow. She has a way with people. If you turn her loose, she makes magic happen. We're going to call it a short day today. Crew's burnt. One week home stretch. **August 13, 2003.** DAY FIFTEEN Four more days. And we have a long week ahead of us. Busted some late night pick-ups last night. Feeling the heat. Tired as hell and not prepared to finish. We shoot Officer Charles's scenes today and we have no wardrobe for him. We shoot the rooftop tomorrow and we don't have one. We need a rough cut for Sundance in one month and we don't have an editor or even telecine $$, fer chrissakes. Very scary. But this film has been made by the skin of our teeth since day one. Why should now be any different? Just have to keep the faith and

take it one day, one scene at a time. I know the performances are strong. Pops has been amazing. What a score Luis has been. He wouldn't have done this film if it weren't a true local story. And I know Kev is getting great shit on film. Even though we aren't seeing dailies, I can tell by how he approaches the material that he is on it. I have completely robbed the guy of any real opportunity to shine (since we never get to scout locations, etc.) and yet he still has risen to the occasion and approached every challenge with passion and determination. Seems like everyone is really stepping up. If that's worth anything, we're going to have a great film. **August 14, 2003.** DAY SIXTEEN Home stretch. Shot Officer Charles's scenes. Some of the writers were a little sketched to have a real

INT VAIN'S BEDROOM - DAY

A 'DEAR CURTIS' LETTER from Lisa rests on the bed underneath Vain's cell phone. Heir picks up the letter and starts to read it. He drops to the bed and, as he finishes letter, his blood starts to boil. Vain crumples the letter and hucks it across the room.

Vain starts rifling through shit. He looks in the dresser, but the bindle is gone. The search continues. He eventually finds another bindle in a record cover and indulges himself.

Vain stares at himself in the mirror. He looks like hell. Vain cocks back and throws a right hook into the glass.

Vain puts on a jacket, grabs his cell phone from the bed, and heads for the door.

EXT MISSION DISTRICT - MOMENTS LATER

Vain walks down the street, tweaking. He takes a short cut through an alley, and breaks out his cell phone. He punches in some numbers but stops short and listens to a message.

> **OPERATOR (V.O.)**
> We're sorry, your cellular service is currently inoperative. If you feel you have reached this . . .

Not what Vain wanted to hear. He slams the phone shut. Out of nowhere, a wiry little STICK-UP KID (20) jumps out and jams a gun in Vain's face.

> **STICK-UP KID**
> Don't play dumb bitch. Give up the phone, and your wallet.

Vain gives up the phone immediately, but doesn't reach for his wallet.

> **STICK-UP KID**
> Give up the wallet, punk. And them mother fucking dunks.

> **VAIN**
> *(under his breath)* Fuck this, man.

Vain hands him his wallet.

> **STICK-UP KID**
> Yeah, what's up? *(points to Vain's shoes)* Give it up. Right now.

> **VAIN**
> Oh what? You want my shoes?

> **STICK-UP KID**
> Don't play dumb, motherfucker. Yeah take them shits off!

Vain bends down to untie his shoes.

> **VAIN**
> *(under breath)* Yeah, take my shoes? At least I rack them when they're new. Fuck it, take em. I'ma go get me some crispy ones right now!

> **STICK-UP KID**
> *(looks down the alley to make sure it's still cool)* Shut the fuck and make it happ . . .

Vain sees his chance and seizes it. He springs at the kid and slams his ass up against the wall. They struggle briefly, but Vain could outdo this kid any day of the week. On this particular day, the cocaine and adrenaline pumping through Vain's system make for an especially quick match. Vain slams the kid to the ground and pins his gun hand. BOOM! The gun goes off and startles the Kid and Vain alike. They both freeze momentarily until they realize that the shot went astray.

Vain is still on top and, while the kid is using his upper body to try and get up, Vain connects a couple hard blows that send his head directly back into the concrete. Vain stands up, feeling amped, and slightly relieved. The Kid is dazed; he doesn't move much. Gun in hand, Vain bends over and picks up the cell phone.

VAIN

You want this?

Vain throws the phone at the ground and it shatters just inches from the muggers head. Vain holds the gun over his head with one hand and looks the kid in the eyes.

VAIN

You want my shit? Huh? You want my shit?!

Vain is looking extremely unstable. The stick-up kid never had it in him to look half as crazy as Vain does right now.

STICK-UP KID

No man, no man. I'm sorry.

VAIN

No. Lemme see you take something from me. What? You gonna take a gun from me? Take it motherfucker. Oh what you want the dunks? You want the sneaks? What motherfucker? Don't play dumb.

204

Vain gives one swift kick to the dome. Dude doesn't move. Vain looks around. No one yet. He waists the gun behind him and bails out. He reaches the street and tries to blend in, but it ain't happening. People are staring. Vain's got a bloody nose and is looking real hot right now. People are getting nosy and everyone is looking down the alley, where lays the bloody mugger. Or is he the victim? Either way, Vain's out of his mind on rage and cocaine and not thinking real straight. With his head down, he paces down the street. SIRENS are nearing. Vain ducks into a pay phone.

INT HEIR'S HOUSE/EXT MISSION DISTRICT -
CONTINUOUS

HEIR

(answering phone) Hello.

VAIN

Yo, Mikey. It's me man. I need your help.

HEIR

Curtis? Where you at, man? You still at Des's?

VAIN

You gotta come and get . . .

Vain stops and watches a COP CAR drive by slowly.

HEIR

Curtis? Curtis?!

cop (retired) on the set. Former vandal squad guy no less. But he was down to earth. I trusted him, but we didn't show him our cards just to be safe. Shooting the rooftop tonight. Problem is, we have no rooftop. No piece either (or at least none submitted to me as requested). This is where Brian absolutely flails: long-term planning and teamwork. I can't stay at Vain's house anymore. Brian and I are going to rip each other's heads off. Lane is a total team player. I made an effort to spend some quality time with him. (Seems like the bad son gets all the attention.) We went and hooped at the gym. That was a good call. We both needed the outlet and it was good bonding time. I need to remember to thank him once in a while. I take him for granted . . . three days left. Gotta

VAIN

(frantic) Yeah man. Lisa left me. This fucking kid. I got jumped. I beat dude's ass real bad. I got his gun. I don't wanna get locked up already, Mikey. Fuck. I got evicted. I gotta talk to Lisa.

Vain's eyes are on the cop car: the BRAKE LIGHTS come on.

HEIR

Wha . . .

VAIN

I'll call you later.

Vain hangs up.

HEIR

What? Hello? Curt!

EXT MISSION DISTRICT - CONTINUOUS

Vain books it down the street and around a corner, up to the next block, makes another turn and spots a CAB coming towards him in the other direction. Vain is relieved to see his boy Auto. He runs across the street in a big fuckin' hurry.

As Vain approaches the cab, he realizes that it's not Auto at all. It's some random CABBIE. Vain is visibly disappointed. The Cabbie initially gestures that it's all him, but, as Vain gets a little closer, he starts to realize that there's something wrong with Vain. Not the usual "I'm in a hurry" look, but more of the "I just beat the shit out of this dude and took his gun and I'm higher than a mother" look. Vain looks up at the STREET LIGHT, which is RED. Bloody nose and all, Vain approaches the cab.

VAIN

Thanks, bro. I need to get downtown, Market and Fifth.

CABBIE

Oh, uh. I'm on a call, I mean, I just got a call.

VAIN

Come on, man. Let me get a lift.

The Cabbie has no plans of letting Vain in the car. The LIGHT turns GREEN and the cars in front of the cab slowly begin to move. Vain knows the deal.

VAIN

What the fuck? This is bullshit. *(pulls out the gun)* You're gonna give me a ride bitch. Matter of fact, scoot your ass over.

Vain pulls the cab door open.

CUT TO:

INT CAB - CONTINUOUS

Vain hops in and the Cabbie starts freaking.

VAIN

Get the fuck out.

The Cabbie complies and frantically falls out onto the street. Vain peels out and barely makes it through a yellow light.

INT TC CARROLL ADVERTISING AGENCY - DAY

The phone rings. Lisa heads to the desk to answer it, but Robert stops her.

> **ROBERT**
> Let it go to voicemail. We gotta get this meet-ing started.

Lisa complies.

CUT TO:

INT HEIR'S HOUSE - CONTINUOUS

> **HEIR**
> C'mon. Pick it up. Pick it up! Damn! *(beat)* Hey, Lisa. It's Mike. I really need to talk to you. I'm worried about Curtis. I was hoping to talk to you. Uh, I'm gonna come out there. I need to talk to Robert about the ad any-way. Hopefully you're there. Alright. See you in a bit.

Heir hangs up the phone. He takes one last look at the ad, slides it into the manila envelope, and heads for the door.

EXT TC CARROLL ADVERTISING AGENCY - LATER

The Cab is parked up on the curb.

INT TC CARROLL ADVERTISING AGENCY - CONTINUOUS

Looking like a junkie on a career binge, Vain waits in the lobby. Sounds of laughing and lunch conversation can be heard from the other room. One of the Designers, who is returning from the bathroom, stops and approaches Vain.

> **DESIGNER**
> Can I help you with something?

> **VAIN**
> I need to talk to Lisa.

> **DESIGNER**
> She's not available right now. Is there some-thing I can help you with?

> **VAIN**
> I need to talk to Lisa.

> **DESIGNER**
> Uh, would you like to leave a message?

> **VAIN**
> Look, motherfucker, I said I need to talk to Lisa!

> **DESIGNER**
> If you're going to be disrespectful, I'm go-ing to have to ask you to leave.

> **VAIN**
> Fuck you, you little emo bitch! I ain't going nowhere until I talk to Lisa!

Lisa enters the room.

OFF Not going to be much of a day off. So much prep to do for tomorrow. We have a few days of difficult shoots to cram into one day. It's impossible really. But I have to believe. If I don't, no one will. I also need to create a formula that I can use to convince people that this is achievable. This means a detailed shot breakdown, includ-ing specific time allowances. And I need to nail the first few to keep morale alive. That is today's assignment. That and nailing our final handful of locations. Going to be quite a feat, to say the least. We are climbing Mt. Everest. The air is getting thinner. But we did not come this far only to turn around at the base of the peak. Au-gust 17, 2003. DAY EIGHTEEN. LAST DAY OF PRODUCTION!! The final day. Made the miracle of nine light

> LISA
>
> What are you doing, Curtis?

> VAIN
>
> We need to talk, alone.

> LISA
>
> There's nothing to talk about, especially not here. You need to leave.

> VAIN
>
> I'm not trying to change your mind, Lisa. We just need to talk.

Robert enters and intervenes. Shit gets chaotic and everybody starts talking over each other. Way too many cooks in this kitchen.

> ROBERT
>
> Look, pal, you're going to have to leave before I call the authorities.

> VAIN
>
> This don't concern you, mark.

> LISA
>
> Curtis, just go.

> ROBERT
>
> Oh I beg to differ . . .

> DESIGNER
>
> Should I call the cops?

> ROBERT
>
> Are you going to go peacefully?

> VAIN
>
> Lisa, I just need to talk to you.

> LISA
>
> It's too late, Curtis.

> ROBERT
>
> Call the cops. Alright, buddy. party's over.

Robert attempts to put Vain in an arm-lock, but Vain slips free and pulls out the GUN. Panic! Everyone takes cover.

Vain calms down and looks past the frenetic agency crew at Lisa.

CUT TO:

INT BUS - DAY

Heir rides the bus and stares out the window. A private screening of the city flies by his window.

CUT TO:

INT TC CARROLL ADVERTISING AGENCY - DAY

A Designer is huddled under a desk on the phone.

> DESIGNER
>
> *(whispering)* Yes, he's got a gun . . .

CUT TO:

EXT DOWNTOWN - CONTINUOUS

Heir exits the bus. *A SQUAD CAR flies down the street, SIRENS BLARING. Heir jogs, then runs down the street.*

CUT TO:

INT TC CARROLL ADVERTISING AGENCY - CONTINUOUS

POLICE SIRENS can be heard outside.

Vain looks to the door, then back at the mess he has created.

CUT TO:

EXT TC CARROLL ADVERTISING AGENCY - CONTINUOUS

A COP CAR is posted up outside the agency. One OFFICER has his gun drawn and is covering his partner, who is cautiously approaching the agency.

Heir shows up and assesses the scene. It does not look good. He bolts toward the agency.

OFFICER
Hey! Hold it right there!

Heir stops and puts his hands up.

HEIR
I gotta go in there, it's an emergency.

OFFICER
Get out of the way! Now!

CUT TO:

INT TC CARROLL ADVERTISING AGENCY - CONTINUOUS

Vain slowly turns the gun to his head.

CUT TO:

EXT TC CARROLL ADVERTISING AGENCY - CONTINUOUS

HEIR
You don't understand . . .

OFFICER
I am ordering you to retreat immediately or . . .

Heir pauses momentarily, then darts through the agency door.

The camera cranes up to a group of pigeons sitting on a ledge.

HEIR (O.S.)
Curtis, no!

BOOM! The pigeons scatter from the storefront.

FADE TO BLACK.

EXT CEMETERY - DAY

Vain's funeral. Dino is giving a sermon, which can be heard in the background. It's a quiet, somber, and low-key event. Heir, Pops, Grandma, Lisa, Devin, Dino, and a few of the crew stand

preparation, communication, and organization. It's a miracle we finished. But we did. Not sure what we have. But we finished. That's worth something, I suppose. Had to work eighteen hours last night to finish. Nightmare. But we got it done. Shot the rooftop, cop cars, truck yards, tunnels, and T-Dome. It was pretty exhilarating, actually. Way too rushed. Guaranteed some of it will have to be re-shot. I'll be happy to get the fuck out of Dodge. It's funny, all of my friends who grew up in the burbs and then moved to the city later in life seem to love it. I can't stand it. When I was growing up here, I felt so trapped by the claustrophobic housing and surrounding muni wire cages. I'm just completely over it. I love coming back to visit. I feel right at home in the grime. But, after tasting *in the rain and pay their respects to an unmarked grave as Dino gives his sermon.*

Charles and Huffington watch from a distance and take pictures. Des flips them the bird as they snap his pic.

DINO (V.O.)
Curtis Smith was a bundle of energy, a raging hurricane destined to change the landscape of this barren cage we call a city. Determined to let the world know he existed, Vain attacked the canvases of concrete and steel with passion and diligence. That could have been any of us in that casket. Vain is American youth: you and you and you. Do not let him die in vain.

EXT CEMETERY - LATER

DINO (V.O.)
Approach every day like it's your last. Make your mark. Let your voice be heard. Do it for Curtis. Do it for Vain. But, most of all, do it for yourself. As Curtis continues his travels through the universe, his spirit lives on in the hearts and souls of all who had the privilege of knowing this brilliant young artist. May he rest in peace.

Everyone chills, cries, hugs, and mourns the loss of their homeboy.

INT HEIR'S HOUSE - DAY

Heir and Pops walk in the door. Grandma walks up and holds Heir close. He fights back the tears.

INT HEIR'S ROOM - DAY

Heir goes through some old photos. He stops at one of him and Vain when they were in elementary school and thinks back to better times.

CUT TO:

Grandma is sweeping outside Heir's window.

Slo-mo close-up of dust disappearing into the air.

EXT RESIDENTIAL NEIGHBORHOOD - EVENING

Heir walks down the street. He's holding a piece of a paper and apparently looking for an address.

INT LISA'S NEW PLACE - EVENING

Lisa opens the door and finds Heir standing there. They share a long, emotional hug.

INT LISA'S LIVING ROOM - EVENING

Heir sits next to Devin on the couch.

HEIR
How you doing, man?

Devin shrugs.

HEIR
I brought something for you.

Director's note. The Vandal Squad Officers were much more prominent in earlier versions of the script. This is a remnant of these more graffiti-centric drafts. We wanted to focus on the mourning, not the graffiti. So we clipped the Officers from the funeral.

Director's note. Didn't seem appropriate to have this sermon here. Silence worked a lot better.

Director's note. I decided that nixing all physical affection/consolation from family during and after the funeral made the scene where Pops' hugs Mikey (just before he leaves to paint the memorial piece) much more powerful. So this thing with Grandma went out the window.

Director's note. The sweeping was a nice tie-in to the mandala. But we got enough at the funeral (i.e. ashes in the wind). Also had the guy sweeping the street in front of his Mission Market. Only so much sweeping you can take.

209

the slow, peaceful life that all my friends seem to have run away from, I can never go back to the city. I'm proud of my pussiness. And I'm psyched to be headed back to bumblefuck. Not feeling like we shot enough b-roll kind of stuff on this shoot. I really wanted to give Kev an opportunity to document the world we were living in. But it wasn't to be. Just not enough support and way too ambitious a sched for the budget we had. Editing is going to be a nightmare. Not even sure HOW we're going to edit at this point. No money. No time. I'll go to LA if I have to. Sundance is looking unlikely. Got to keep that faith, for now. That's what got us this far. All depression and regret aside, I need to stop and pat myself on the back. I had a goal (make a movie) and I accomplished that. We brought

Heir busts out the picture of him and Vain.

> HEIR
> We were like your age there.

Devin checks out the photo.

> HEIR
> You've seen a lot of crazy stuff in your day,
> Devin. Way more than you should have. You
> need to learn from this.

They share silence for a minute.

> HEIR (CONT'D)
> I'ma be here for you. OK?

Devin nods. Heir grabs Devin and holds him close.

INT ABANDONED WAREHOUSE - NIGHT

Heir sits in the window and stares into the night.

The camera pulls back and leaves Heir sitting alone in the window.

INT HEIR'S ROOM - NIGHT

Heir packs his backpack full of spray paint.

INT HEIR'S HOUSE - NIGHT

Wearing a heavily stuffed backpack and dressed in jeans and a black hooded sweatshirt etc. Heir heads for the door.

> POPS
> Hey.

Heir stops and turns towards Pops. They stare at each other momentarily before Pops pulls Heir in for a long overdue hug.

EXT MISSION DISTRICT - LATE NIGHT

Heir prowls the neighborhood. He comes to a three storey building and scopes the scene. It's the rooftop where Vain was chased from. Heir backs up to a drainpipe. The coast is clear. He zips up the pipe like Spider Man to the rescue. Just as he gets to the top, he spots a COP CAR. Heir quickly grabs the roof edge, but pulls his hand back in pain. Heir has no choice at this point. He promptly grabs on and pulls himself up.

CUT TO:

EXT ROOFTOP - CONTINUOUS

Heir lands on the roof and hits the deck. He checks the street. The cop car slows down, then creeps away. Heir checks his hands, which are oozing blood all over the place. Heir takes off his t-shirt, rips it up, and tapes some makeshift bandages on his hands.

EXT ROOFTOP - LATER

Heir surveys the wall briefly before hitting it up. Vain's unfinished piece has already been buffed. Although he is interrupted several times by the constant presence of cars, birds, and cops passing by, Heir never slows down. He is in a zone, not entirely in control of his creation. Tears stream down his face as the piece comes to life. Shaded in blue, the piece is a huge memorial dedication to Vain. It is unlike anything Heir has ever done. Although there is a WILD STYLE 'VAIN' in the center, this is a

together a group of talented, passionate people and pulled it off. That's pretty amazing. Hopefully, once I have slept a little, hung with family, and fought through the post-partum depression, I can reflect on this journey and be thankful for the opportunity. I definitely need to be thankful for all of the people who put their asses on the line to help me realize a vision. Can't ignore that . . . but, for now, I just need to forget about it for a few days and relax. We made it to the top of Mt. Everest. Stop and enjoy the view. **August 20, 2003.** Drove back to Oregon today. My wife and kids met me at the Inn at 7th Mountain for a little R&R. Just what the doctor ordered. Great to see the fam. Batteries are re-charging quickly. Always such a downer leaving production, even if it was a

huge production, with **LANDSCAPES OF THE CITY**, a **RENDITION OF VAIN'S FUNERAL**, and a **PORTRAIT OF VAIN**, floating above it all. And, for the first time in his life, the piece does not contain Heir's name or signature.

EXT SF - PRE-DAWN

MONTAGE

The sun rises. The fog begins to lift. Empty streets. A garbage truck makes its rounds. A homeless man dreams of a king-sized bed with fluffy white pillows.

EXT ROOFTOP - PRE-DAWN

Heir checks his piece. He is beaming with pride and satisfaction.

Heir reaches into his backpack, breaks out a **ROLLER** and a **BUCKET OF PAINT**, and proceeds to paint over the piece beige.

EXT ROOFTOP - DAWN

The camera pans across the wall. It is completely blank.

Heir makes his way back over the ledge and disappears.

FADE OUT.

complete nightmare shoot. At one point on the drive home, I had "Weather" by Built to Spill on repeat for like three hours straight. That song really has a grip on me. I called Brian and sobbed like a baby. As much as we butted heads on this project, I still love the guy like a brother. I bawled and told him I do not want him to become that guy (Vain). When we wrapped, everyone else bailed and went back to their lives, while he's stuck in SF with no security whatsoever. I hope he gets out soon. His fast lane is way too fast. I'm going to try and forget about the movie completely for the next few days. Need to catch my breath before I jump back in the pit. I have a feeling that I'm going to be the only one driving the train for a while.

R. Martinz

R. Martin

Acknowledgments

We need to thank hundreds of people for their amazing support along the way in making this movie. There are too many people to name and surely some people will be forgotten (we tried to add everyone we could remember in the end credits of the film itself). But there are a few people we'd like to thank now who really came through.

We couldn't have made the movie or this book without you:

Amy, Summer, Shane, and Braeden, Pappins, Lonnie & Jacquie, Evelyn & Joel Morgan, Samo, Nicole, Manman, Jack Pinkham, Jen Stewart, Jim and Elva Smith, Jeff and Maureen Stewart, Lou Kent, Cathy McQueeney and Dean Claeys, Sol Lipman, Steve Capasso, Tom Mullowney, Aron Coleite, Clay Butler, Jeff Dunn, Peter Broderick, Greg Harrison, Debbie Brubaker, Brian Benson, Andy Wiskes, Maryanne Redpath, Ron & Louise Rosequist, Sue & Ron Rouda, Wayne Whelan, Number9, StartSoma, John Doffing, Austin Williams, The Bogerts, The Cimons, Chris Jennings, Richard Minogue & Kathy Pfister-Minogue, John Angelo and Dick May, Marc and Lisa Tamo, Julia and Don Harrison, B Waldraw, Jeff Fleeman, John Andreas, Bob Bryan, Neon, Montana paint, Jase, Flowin Immo, Esher, Overkill, Sam Flores, Andy Schoultz, Bryan Dawson, Abhor, Kelly Tunstall, Steve Perlman, Steve Popper, Jannat Gargi, Alpha Cine Labs, Kodak, Chen Design Associates, and The Mission District of San Francisco.

Thanks to all the cast, crew, investors, contributors and friends who believed in us and helped us along the way. Filmmaking is a team sport and we'd go on the field again with you any day.

And a final special thanks to all the independent filmmakers and artists and musicians who showed the way and made the quality of this life a little better for the rest of us.

Photography

Leslie Bauer
Valerie Bischoff
Felipe Buitrago
Brian Burnam
Stefan Fitzgerald
Patrick Griffin
Kevin Heverin
Camille Johnson
Amy Morgan
Ben Morgan
Linda Nguyen
Anthony Peterson
Kev Robertson
Meika Rouda
Dave Schubert
Stefan Simikich
Tom Simonian

Illustrations on pp. 206-207 by Rogelio Martinez

Design

Chen Design Associates
San Francisco
www.chendesign.com

About the Author

After being rejected by UCLA and inspired by filmmaker Robert Rodriguez (*El Mariachi, Spy Kids, Sin City*), Benjamin Morgan "enrolled" in his own personal, independent film school. Refusing to spend tens of thousands of dollars on a formal film school education, Morgan instead spent under $5,000 (raised from friends, family, and local businesses) to produce three narrative video features, with the intention of shooting for theatrical release on film number four. These "student films" won him critical acclaim and a reputation for creating entertaining, incredibly realistic films with little or no resources.

All of his movies revolve around the lives of at-risk youth. The stories are drawn from his own real-life experiences as a former troubled teen and his thirteen years of professionally working directly with at-risk youth in the juvenile justice and children's mental health systems.

The success of his do-it-yourself film school subsequently spawned the birth of Live and Learn Productions, a video production company for at-risk youth. Live and Learn Productions put Morgan's vision into the hands of local teens, empowering them with hands-on experience with video equipment and decision-making responsibility. Live and Learn has produced Public Service Announcements on gangs and drugs, documentaries on successful teen programs, and a teen talk show on Community Television.

Quality of Life is Morgan's feature film debut.

Thanks to massive state budget cuts late in the pre-production of the film, Morgan was laid off from his job overseeing a diversion program for juveniles arrested for misdemeanors. Since production has completed, he has been re-hired part-time — with no

benefits — supporting a family on this and his wife's part-time job and their credit cards while the film is being sent to film festivals.

Back in his own teen years, Morgan was a founding member of Fantastic Fource, one of the most dominant Breakdancing crews in the San Francisco Bay Area from 1984-1986. Fantastic Fource won mainstream competitions held in the Bay Area during that period and was widely respected on the streets as the crew to beat (See the website for some old school video). Please do not ask Ben to prove this, as he will surely hurt himself.

WWW.QUALITYOFLIFE-THEMOVIE.COM

We've put together a special website with some additional resources, links, and additional
behind-the-scenes info that couldn't fit into the book:

www.qualityoflife-themovie.com/ptpt

Also available online
The movie trailer
Quality of Life DVD (available summer 2006)
Putting the Pieces Together DVD: Behind-the-scenes footage and interviews (available fall 2006)
T-shirts, posters, soundtrack and other stuff

team@qualityoflife-themovie.com